D1433839

THE

The Holocaust and its Contexts

Series Editor: **Claus-Christian W. Szejnmann, Loughborough** University, UK.

Series Editorial Board: **Wolfgang Benz, Robert G. Moeller** and **Mirjam Wenzel**

More than sixty years on, the Holocaust remains a subject of intense debate with ever-widening ramifications. This series aims to demonstrate the continuing relevance of the Holocaust and related issues in contemporary society, politics and culture; studying the Holocaust and its history broadens our understanding not only of the events themselves but also of their present-day significance. The series acknowledges and responds to the continuing gaps in our knowledge about the events that constituted the Holocaust, the various forms in which the Holocaust has been remembered, interpreted and discussed, and the increasing importance of the Holocaust today to many individuals and communities.

Titles include:

Caroline Sharples and Olaf Jensen (*editors*)
BRITAIN AND THE HOLOCAUST
Remembering and Representing War and Genocide

The Holocaust and its Contexts Series
Series Standing Order ISBN 978–0–230–22386–8 Hardback
978–0–230–22387–5 Paperback
(*outside North America only*)

You can receive future titles in this series as they are published by placing a standing order. Please contact your bookseller or, in case of difficulty, write to us at the address below with your name and address, the title of the series and the ISBN quoted above.

Customer Services Department, Macmillan Distribution Ltd, Houndmills, Basingstoke, Hampshire RG21 6XS, England

Britain and the Holocaust

Remembering and Representing War and Genocide

Edited by

Caroline Sharples

Lecturer in Modern European History, School of Historical Studies, University of Leicester, UK

and

Olaf Jensen

Lecturer in Holocaust Studies, School of Historical Studies, University of Leicester, UK

First published 2013 by
PALGRAVE MACMILLAN

Palgrave Macmillan in the UK is an imprint of Macmillan Publishers Limited,
registered in England, company number 785998, of Houndmills, Basingstoke,
Hampshire RG21 6XS.

Palgrave Macmillan in the US is a division of St Martin's Press LLC,
175 Fifth Avenue, New York, NY 10010.

Palgrave Macmillan is the global academic imprint of the above companies
and has companies and representatives throughout the world.

Palgrave® and Macmillan® are registered trademarks in the United States,
the United Kingdom, Europe and other countries.

ISBN 978–1–137–35076–3

This book is printed on paper suitable for recycling and made from fully
managed and sustained forest sources. Logging, pulping and manufacturing
processes are expected to conform to the environmental regulations of the
country of origin.

A catalogue record for this book is available from the British Library.

A catalog record for this book is available from the Library of Congress.

Contents

Illustrations

Figures

Plates

Preface and Acknowledgements

This volume is largely based on papers given at the conference 'Britain and the Holocaust – Remembering and Representing War & Genocide: The Impact of WWII & the Holocaust on Today's Britain' held by the Stanley Burton Centre for Holocaust and Genocide Studies in cooperation with the Wiener Library, London, in May 2009. The call for papers for the conference asked scholars to engage in recent research from all disciplines and fields on Britain's reactions to the Second World War and the Holocaust during and after the 'Third Reich', focusing mainly on questions of memory and representation and their implications for today's Britain. Given this rather specific focus, this volume does not attempt to give a historical overview of Britain and the Holocaust or claim to get close to answering all the questions in relation to the memory and representation of the Holocaust in Britain, let alone above and beyond this frame. However, the editors are of the opinion that the essays presented here explore the complexities of British memory culture in more depth and, by presenting a wide range of approaches, reflect and inspire a critical interdisciplinary discourse.

The editors thank the keynote speaker, Professor Dan Stone, Royal Holloway London, who delivered the Aubrey Newman Lecture on 5 May 2009, along with the participants in the conference and the contributors to this book for their interest and their cooperation. We also gratefully acknowledge the cooperation provided by the Wiener Library, London, and its Director Ben Barkow, in setting up the conference. Thanks also go to Professor Norman Housley, Head of School of Historical Studies, and Professor Douglas Tallack, Pro-Vice Chancellor and Head of the College of Arts, Humanities and Law, Professor Aubrey Newman, Thomas McKay, Sarah Whitmore and Lynne Wakefield.

The editors and publishers also thank Frank Meisler, the Imperial War Museum, the Mass Observation Archive, the BBC Written Archive and the Immediate Media Co. for permission to reproduce copyright material. Every effort has been made to trace rights holders, but if any have been inadvertently overlooked, the publishers would be pleased to make the necessary arrangements.

Finally, the editors are grateful to Clare Mence, Commissioning Editor, Scholarly Division – History at Palgrave Macmillan for enthusiastically taking this book project on for the book series 'The Holocaust and its Contexts'.

Olaf Jensen and Caroline Sharples
Leicester, March 2013

Contributors

Antoine Capet is Head of British Studies at the University of Rouen. He has edited a number of collections on Britain's diplomatic and military policy in the twentieth century, the latest being *Britain, France and the Entente Cordiale since 1904* (2006) and was general editor of the *Revue française de civilisation britannique* from 2003 to 2006. He is editor of the 'Britain since 1914' section of the Royal Historical Society Bibliography and sits on the International Board of *Twentieth Century British History*.

Tim Cole is Professor of Social History at the University of Bristol. He is the author of *Images of the Holocaust/Selling the Holocaust* (1999), *Holocaust City* (2003) and *Traces of the Holocaust* (2011) and a co-editor of *Militarized Landscapes* (2010) and *Geographies of the Holocaust* (2013). He is currently writing a book on Holocaust landscapes.

Mark Donnelly is Senior Lecturer in History at St Mary's University College. He is the author of *Britain in the Second World War* (1999), *Sixties Britain: Culture, Society and Politics* (2005), and *Doing History* (co-authored with Claire Norton, 2011). His latest book is *Liberating Histories: Truth, Power, Ethics* (co-authored with Claire Norton, forthcoming).

Olaf Jensen is Lecturer in Holocaust Studies at the University of Leicester and Director of the Stanley Burton Centre for Holocaust Studies. His research has focused on National Socialism and the Holocaust, particularly on the impact of memory on contemporary German society, and on how the past is transmitted from one generation to the next. He is the author of *Geschichte machen. Strukturmerkmale des intergenerationellen Sprechens über die NS-Vergangenheit in deutschen Familien* (2004) and *Ordinary People as Mass Murderers – Perpetrators in Comparative Perspectives* (The Holocaust and Its Context Series, 2008, co-edited with Claus-Christian W. Szejnmann).

Rebecca Jinks has recently submitted her doctoral thesis, 'Representing Genocide: The Holocaust as Paradigm?' at Royal Holloway, University of London. Her interests include cultural representations and the aftermath of genocide, comparative genocide studies and the history of humanitarianism, and her next project will focus on urban 'misintegration' and urban violence in the break-up of the former Yugoslavia.

James Jordan is Karten Lecturer at the University of Southampton and member of the Parkes Institute for Jewish/non-Jewish Relations. He is the author of *From Nuremberg to Hollywood: The Holocaust in the Courtroom of American Fictive Film* (forthcoming, 2013), and co-editor of *Governments in Exile and the Jews of Europe* (with Jan Lanicek, 2013), *Jewish Journeys: From Philo to Hip Hop* (with Tony Kushner and Sarah Pearce, 2010) and *The Memory of the Holocaust in Australia* (with Tom Lawson, 2008). He is the co-editor of the journal *Holocaust Studies*.

Tony Kushner is Professor in History and Director of the Parkes Institute for the Study of Jewish/non-Jewish relations at the University of Southampton. He is the author of eight monographs, including *Remembering Refugees: Then and Now* (2006) and *Anglo-Jewry since 1066: Place, Locality and Memory* (2009). His most recent book is *The Battle of Britishness: Migrant Journeys since 1685* (2012). He is currently working on a study of the construction of ethnicity in the British armed forces and a longer term project on Holocaust journeys.

Tom Lawson is Professor of Holocaust Studies at the University of Winchester and co-editor of the journal *Holocaust Studies*. He is the author of *The Church of England and the Holocaust* (2006) and *Debates on the Holocaust* (2010) and the co-editor of several other books including (with James Jordan) *The Memory of the Holocaust in Australia* (2008) and (with Thomas Kühne) *The Holocaust and Local History* (2010). From 2011 to 2012, he was 'Mid-Career Fellow' of the British Academy and his new book *The Last Man: A British Genocide in Tasmania* will be published in 2014.

Duncan Little studied history at the University of Surrey from 1993 to 1996 before heading to Falmouth College of Arts where he qualified as a broadcast journalist in 1997. He researched, produced and directed the highly acclaimed ITV West Country Top Secret series which examined international, national and regional events during the Cold War. The six programmes won a 'Special Jury REMI Award' at the 2005 WorldFest International Film Festival. He continues to work both in news production and in the making of factual programmes.

Andy Pearce is Professional Tutor at the Centre for Holocaust Education, Institute of Education, University of London. He is involved in the delivery of the Centre's national CPD programme for school teachers, ITE programme and MA Module. He has collaborated on projects with the Imperial War Museum London, the UK delegation to the International Task Force and the Wiener Library, as well as teaching history and politics in London secondary schools. He is the author of the forthcoming book *Holocaust Consciousness in Contemporary Britain*.

Caroline Sharples is Lecturer in Modern European History at the University of Leicester. She is the author of *West Germans and the Nazi Legacy* (2012) and has also published on memories of the *Kindertransport*. She is currently researching the remembrance and representation of war criminals in the Federal Republic since 1945, and working on a synthesis of Holocaust engagement within the two German states between 1945 and 1990.

Dan Stone is Professor of Modern History at Royal Holloway, University of London. He is the author or editor of 14 books including, most recently, *Histories of the Holocaust* (2010), *The Oxford Handbook of Postwar European History* (ed., 2012), *The Holocaust, Fascism and Memory: Essays in the History of Ideas* (2013) and *Saving Europe: The Rise and Fall of the Postwar Consensus* (forthcoming).

Introduction

Caroline Sharples and Olaf Jensen

On Sunday 27 January 2013, an estimated 1500 events took place around Britain to mark Holocaust Memorial Day (HMD) and the 68th anniversary of the liberation of Auschwitz.[1] These events ranged from interfaith ceremonies to talks by Holocaust survivors, photographic exhibitions and film screenings. As has become common in recent years, the lead-up to HMD was characterised by Members of Parliament signing a Book of Commitment in the House of Commons, pledging their support for the occasion and demonstrating the extent to which Holocaust commemoration has become institutionalised. In keeping with the development of social media, Prime Minister David Cameron even took to Twitter, declaring, 'Memorial Day is a day to remember the innocent victims of the Holocaust and re-commit to combat all forms of racism and prejudice.'[2]

Public interest in the Holocaust continues to grow, aided by the relentless scheduling of television programmes depicting the Second World War and an enduring popular fascination with the Third Reich in general. Yet, while an element of anti-Germanism may be a long-standing feature of 'acceptable racism' in Britain, the Holocaust itself has not always received such levels of attention.[3] Indeed, as this collection of essays demonstrates, the path towards establishing a Holocaust consciousness in Britain has been protracted and politicised, and the manner in which the nation remembers this genocide remains imperfect. Encompassing representations of the Holocaust within film, art, newspapers, public exhibition space and state-sanctioned commemoration, this interdisciplinary study offers an exploration of some key moments in Britain's engagement with the Holocaust, and highlights the continued controversies surrounding the nation's complex relationship with the past.

Why Britain?

One might immediately question why the Holocaust *should* become a central part of British memory culture. Certainly, some scepticism was expressed when the notion of a national day of remembrance for victims of Nazi persecution was broached in 1999, and the matter was debated again on the flagship BBC programme *Newsnight* days before the inaugural event in 2001.[4] Likewise, the organisers behind the first HMD seemed at great pains to legitimise its establishment, a concern rendered all the more explicit when 'Britain and the Holocaust' became the central theme for the 2002 commemorations. Mainland Britain, of course, was geographically removed from the killing sites, unencumbered by occupying Nazi forces and neither perpetrator nor collaborator in the crimes of the Third Reich. As a result, the nation has not had to endure the same painful, soul-searching questions as Germany, Austria or the former occupied territories. In many ways the Holocaust was, and remains, a distant event for the British population.

Nevertheless, Britain does have considerable reason to consider the Holocaust part of its national history. Britain hosted thousands of unaccompanied child refugees in the wake of the 1938 *Kristallnacht* pogrom, as well as Holocaust survivors after the war. Far from being the temporary refuge that was perhaps initially envisaged, many of these people subsequently settled in this country and raised families. British troops liberated Bergen-Belsen concentration camp in April 1945 and provided crucial relief to survivors. Britain also played a leading role in the denazification of Germany and the initial prosecution of Nazi war criminals. Each of these factors illustrates the significance of the Holocaust for British audiences.

Looking beyond these specific connections, there are also much wider questions regarding intolerance and human behaviour that give the Holocaust a continued relevance for all nations. As David Cesarani has argued,

> [The Holocaust] provokes questions about Britain's contemporary responsibility as a member of the international community and about the responsibility of individual citizens towards members of other ethnic and faith groups, victims of prejudice and bigotry, immigrants, asylum seekers, or the citizens of other countries afflicted by racism or tyranny.[5]

An emphasis on humanitarian lessons is thus a regular feature of modern-day Holocaust remembrance; the phrase 'never forget' is similarly oft-cited. Cameron's statement for HMD 2013 offers just one example of such rhetoric, which arguably can reach a point where it seems rather trite. We might question whether any real memory work is being done as a result. Beyond these 'easy' platitudes, however, there are other reasons why Britain should be reflecting critically on this period of history that relate directly to Britain's own behaviour during the 1930s and 1940s.

Indeed, much of the existing historiography on Britain and the Holocaust points to a catalogue of failings or omissions. First and foremost is the issue of just how much the British government knew about the persecution of the Jews. Cesarani raises this point in the 2002 HMD theme paper, stating 'the British Government and public knew about the Nazi persecution of Jews, homosexuals, Sinti and Roma and political opponents of the regime, yet it maintained normal diplomatic and trade relations with the Third Reich'.[6] Tony Kushner has also explored levels of British knowledge of mass killings by 1942, suggesting that a commitment to liberal values precluded any emphasis on the fate of any one victim group. These values meant the government was reluctant to address publicly the 'Jewish dimension' to Nazi atrocities, and thus did not speak out as strongly as it might have done.[7] There is also an enduring popular fascination with the question of whether the Allies should have bombed Auschwitz to halt the killing process.[8]

Second is the issue of what might have been done to save more lives prior to the outbreak of the Second World War. The refusal to admit more refugees into Britain, or grant access to Palestine, has attracted a vast amount of scholarly criticism.[9] Likewise, the treatment of those refugees who did make it to British shores has come under significant scrutiny.[10] Such issues complicate Britain's conventional, celebratory narrative of the war. Pointing to the 'rescue' of Jewish children, for example, accentuates Britain's preferred self-image as a haven for the oppressed. Mythologising the notion of Britain 'standing alone' in the fight against Nazism offers something of a 'safe' story with clear-cut heroes and villains and a redemptive, victorious ending.[11] Here, Britain's physical remoteness from the Holocaust can be seen as facilitating a limited dialogue with the crimes: they happened in a different land, in a very different political climate; they could not possibly happen *here*. As a result, there is a tendency to gloss over some of the more uncomfortable moments in Britain's past. One example of this can be seen in Liverpool's rejuvenated waterfront. There, juxtaposed amid a whole series of memorial plaques to naval forces and merchant seamen who kept vital supplies coming into Britain, is a dedication to those who lost their lives on the *Arandora Star* in July 1940. The anonymity of the victims, described simply as 'non-combatants', and the detail that they were struck by a torpedo, lends itself to a familiar tale of German aggression against innocent civilians. The fact that these 'non-combatants' were actually refugees being deported from Britain as 'enemy aliens' is quietly omitted.[12]

Third, there is also the question of Britain's post-war handling and understanding of Nazi war criminals. By the late 1940s, the zeal for prosecuting suspected individuals within the British zone of occupied Germany had already begun to wane amid growing Cold War tensions, inadequate resources and manpower and a lack of public support at home. Donald Bloxham has been particularly prolific in this field, noting too the British reluctance to look upon former *Wehrmacht* generals as anything other than honourable soldiers.[13] Britain's relationship with Nazi war criminals, however, was not confined to the immediate post-war era. The issue was revived in the mid-1980s with the exposure of former SS personnel who had been allowed to settle in Britain. The fact that the government had actually favoured East European immigrants over Jewish survivors underscored Britain's failure to comprehend fully the nature of the Holocaust and prompted the passage of the War Crimes Act of 1991.[14]

As Cesarani and others have argued, it is precisely these sorts of problematic episodes and Britain's 'ambiguous' relationship to the Holocaust that underscore its relevance to the nation's history. Britain does have something to learn about itself here and the manner of its engagement with the Holocaust is thus worthy of further investigation.

British memories of the Holocaust

The extent to which the Second World War and the Holocaust have been recalled since 1945 has become an incredibly popular field of research, and a key element in the 'memory boom' that has characterised historical studies since the 1990s. As with conventional narratives of *Vergangenheitsbewältigung* (overcoming the past) in West Germany, or the formation of a collective Holocaust memory in the United States, works on Britain tend to depict the post-war period as one of lengthy silence or disinterest with regard to the Nazi genocide. This, in turn, has been explained by several factors including persistent anti-Semitism within Britain, or sheer incomprehension that anyone might be persecuted on the basis of race or religion. In the summer of 1979, Yehuda Bauer commented that 'in Britain, nothing at all has been done' to mark the Holocaust.[15] It is a statement frequently cited by historians trying to trace patterns of remembrance in this country and one which encourages an emphasis on the 1980s and beyond as the period in which the Holocaust really entered the public consciousness. Such developments as did occur during the 1980s and 1990s have been routinely subjected to critical analysis. Steven Cooke, for instance, offers a detailed account of Britain's first public memorial dedicated solely to the victims of the Holocaust. Eventually located in a corner of Hyde Park, this physical rejoinder to remember 'blends' into the landscape and can go completely unnoticed by passers-by. Initial proposals to locate the memorial near the Cenotaph or the river frontage of Lambeth Palace were similarly 'restrained' and symbolised the 'distancing of the Holocaust from the official history of British involvement in World War II'.[16]

By contrast, the inclusion of the Holocaust in the first History National Curriculum in 1991, the establishment of a permanent Holocaust exhibition at the Imperial War Museum, London, in 2000 and the introduction of annual HMDs have all been taken as indicators of a marked change in British responses. Along the way, historians have identified several key moments as fostering a heightened, albeit temporary, public engagement with the Holocaust. These include the sensational kidnap and televised trial of Adolf Eichmann in 1961, the screening of the 'Genocide' episode of *World at War* in 1975 and the impact of the American TV series *Holocaust* in 1978. Scholars have also pointed to the impact of the David Irving trial and the Oscar-winning *Schindler's List* in generating both interest in the Holocaust and the sense that Britain should be doing more to commemorate it.

The impetus for these developments stemmed from a variety of factors including the 40th and 50th anniversaries of the war's end in 1985 and 1995, and the growing sense of urgency attached to capturing survivors' testimonies before the Holocaust fades from living memory. It is also possible to point to a growing sense of multiculturalism and anti-racism within Britain since the 1970s.[17] External impulses cannot be ignored either. The establishment of the United States Holocaust Memorial Museum has been suggested as a further spur to the development of British Holocaust engagement (prompting a sense of 'we should have one too'), while more contemporary examples of mass killing in Rwanda and the former Yugoslavia have underscored the pedagogic arguments for increasing awareness of the Holocaust.

However, for all this, Britain's response to the Holocaust cannot simply be depicted as a linear path towards ever greater, more critical engagement. Instead, it may be more accurate to talk of 'ripples' of interest throughout the post-war era, moments that sparked brief yet intense public discussion about the legacy of the Third Reich. Just as scholars of Germany have now reached a consensus that the 1950s were far from an era of 'collective amnesia' with regards to the Nazi past, so too have notions of 'silence' within post-war Britain undergone serious challenges within recent historiography. Cesarani, for instance, convincingly points to the role of survivors, former refugees and Jewish ex-servicemen in maintaining a public discussion of the Holocaust after 1945.[18] Cooke also supports this with his exploration of the Board of Deputies of British Jews and the creation of the Hyde Park memorial.[19] Nor, it seems, was such discussion confined to representatives of Anglo-Jewry; there are also numerous examples of specialist engagement with the Holocaust throughout the post-war era, be they among historians, war crimes prosecutors or even members of the medical profession.[20]

Today, much of the scholarly debate centres on the purpose, significance and likely impact of HMD or the permanent exhibition within the Imperial War Museum. Historians are divided as to whether such events truly register with the wider British population, whether they facilitate or hinder acts of remembrance and whether the emphasis in each case should be on the universal or the particular. Some scholars believe that we have now reached a point where there is simply too much attention being paid to the Holocaust; others argue that what representation we do have remains partial.[21] Bloxham, for instance, notes that even amid the 2000 Stockholm Conference which enshrined the Task Force for International Cooperation on Holocaust Education, Remembrance and Research, Soviet civilians and prisoners of war (POWs) continued to be excluded from discussion of the victims of National Socialism. This omission, repeated in the programme for Britain's first HMD, demonstrates the politicised nature of remembrance activity.[22] There are also fears that making the Holocaust a part of Britain's national story will inevitably encourage a sense of Britain's moral superiority, thereby ensuring that representations of the Holocaust fail to progress beyond rhetoric of a glorious, heroic war against evil Nazism.

Debating British Holocaust consciousness today

The essays within this volume thus seek to explore the complexities of British memory culture in more depth and, by presenting a wide range of approaches, open and inspire a critical interdisciplinary discourse. By bringing together established scholars and rising academics in the field, this collection re-examines some of the most high-profile representations of the Holocaust and poses a series of questions regarding the state of British understanding of genocide today.

In the opening section, attention is focused on British experiences of Nazism during and in the immediate aftermath of the Second World War. Duncan Little explores the little-known story of hundreds of British POWs who were imprisoned at Auschwitz. These men witnessed the Holocaust and thus offer a fascinating example of its relevance to Britain's national story. Many had been transported in cattle trucks and suffered terrible abuse at the hands of their captors. Some lost their POW status and were reclassified as concentration camp prisoners, with a complete loss of rights as a result. Drawing upon oral testimonies and affidavits submitted to the Nuremberg trials, Little restores a voice to these men and highlights the various ways in which they sought to retain a distinctly 'British' way of life amid the horrors of Auschwitz.

Caroline Sharples then examines the popular resonance of the International Military Tribunal at Nuremberg, 1945–1946. Designed not only to bring the leading, surviving members of the Third Reich to judicial account, the Nuremberg trials also aimed to acquaint the world with the enormity of Nazi criminality and ensure it could never be repeated. Utilising newspaper reports as well as Mass Observation surveys and directives, Sharples questions the extent to which these lessons were actually embraced by the British public. Kushner then weaves together the relationship between these initial misunderstandings of the Holocaust and more recent distortions of the past, exploring the fabrication of British POW memoirs.

The middle sections of this book examine some of the key cultural representations of the Holocaust in Britain since 1945. Tim Cole examines the impact of the 1979 television series *Holocaust*, which became a massive media event in itself. Drawing on press reports, he reconstructs the debates that surrounded the BBC's decision to screen the series, as well as the response from critics and members of the public. James Jordan's overview of BBC Holocaust programming between 1945 and 1979 helps to contextualise Cole's findings, with particular emphasis on the long-running television series *This Is Your Life*. In the process, he gives new insights into just how many opportunities the British public had to learn more about the Holocaust during this period. In the context of Cole's and Jordan's essays, Olaf Jensen reflects and comments on the British perception of the Holocaust in light of British comedy and recent feature films.

Moving into the museum setting, Antoine Capet, Rebecca Jinks and Tom Lawson then discuss different elements of the Imperial War

Museum's depiction of the Holocaust. Capet explores the works of art held by the museum, yet seldom displayed to the public. Analysing a variety of striking images, he questions the reticence in hanging these paintings and the extent to which a 2008 exhibition constituted a new awareness of the Holocaust. Jinks assesses the permanent Holocaust and Crimes Against Humanity exhibitions, exploring the interactions between memories of the Holocaust and the growing awareness of other mass atrocities. Both exhibitions, she argues, marginalise the role of Britain throughout these tragedies and this, in turn, has significant impact on the forging of a specifically British memory of the Holocaust. Developing these themes, Lawson then offers a critical summary of the relationship between Britain, the Holocaust and Britain's imperial past.

The concluding section of this volume turns its attention to rituals and commemorative practices. Mark Donnelly focuses on how the 50th anniversary of the liberation of Auschwitz and the war's end was observed, conceptualised and described in Britain in 1995. He examines public discourses of Holocaust remembrance and their culturally sanctioned frameworks. Coming closer to the present day, Andy Pearce then considers the effects that the introduction of a national memorial day has had upon British awareness of the Holocaust. He notes the profound shift in the perceived importance and relevance attached to the Holocaust by the political establishment, and considers the extent to which this was part of a wider effort to develop a Holocaust consciousness in contemporary Europe. Finally, Dan Stone draws upon some of the overarching themes of this collection and reflects upon the current position of the Holocaust within British historical memory. He critiques the extent to which Britain has come to terms with this past and makes a plea for greater sensitivity in future discussions of this complicated period of modern history.

Notes

1. 'Commemorate Holocaust Memorial Day', Holocaust Memorial Day Trust, http://hmd.org.uk (accessed 4 February 2013).
2. @David_Cameron, 27 January 2013, https://twitter.com/David_Cameron/status/295473202015121409 (accessed 4 February 2013).
3. On the notion that Germans are 'fair game' for racist comments, see Tony Kushner, 'The Holocaust and the Museum World in Britain: A Study of Ethnography', *Immigrants and Minorities*, 21 (1–2) (2002), 14–16.
4. 'Remembering Genocide in the Twentieth Century', *Newsnight* transcript, 23 January 2001, http://news.bbc.co.uk/1/hi/events/newsnight/1136757.stm (accessed 4 February 2013).

5. David Cesarani, 'Britain, the Holocaust and Its Legacy: The Theme for Holocaust Memorial Day, 2002', 3, Holocaust Memorial Day Trust Theme Papers, http://hmd.org.uk/resources/theme-papers (accessed 4 February 2013).
6. Ibid., 1.
7. Tony Kushner, *The Holocaust and the Liberal Imagination: A Social and Cultural History* (Oxford, 1994), 168–201. Arguably, more is now being done to address the issue of British wartime knowledge of the persecution of the Jews. The National Archives, for example, runs workshops for schoolchildren to sift through relevant documentation for themselves – see National Archives, 'Britain and the Holocaust', http://www.nationalarchives.gov.uk/education/holocaust.htm (accessed 4 February 2013).
8. See, for example, Michael J. Neufeld and Michael Berenbaum (eds), *The Bombing of Auschwitz: Should Allies Have Attempted It?* (Lawrence, Kansas, 2003); David S. Wyman, *The Abandonment of the Jews: America and the Holocaust, 1941–1945* (New York, 2007), 288–307.
9. See, for example, Louise London, *Whitehall and the Jews, 1933–1948: British Immigration Policy, Jewish Refugees and the Holocaust* (Cambridge, 2000); Bernard Wasserstein, *Britain and the Jews of Europe, 1939–1945* (Oxford, 1979).
10. David Cesarani and Tony Kushner (eds), *The Internment of Aliens in Twentieth Century Britain* (London, 1993); Tony Kushner and Katharine Knox (eds), *Refugees in an Age of Genocide: Global, National and Local Perspectives during the Twentieth Century* (London, 1999).
11. On this theme, see Caroline Sharples, 'The Kindertransport in British Historical Memory', A. Hammel and B. Lewkowicz (eds), The Kindertransport to Britain, 1938/39: New Perspectives. *Yearbook of the Research Centre for German and Austrian Exile Studies*, 13 (2012), 15–28.
12. Interested visitors to Liverpool's waterfront can gain slightly more information if they take the short walk over to the Merseyside Maritime Museum in the Albert Docks. A first-floor exhibition on the Battle of the Atlantic includes a three-dimensional model of the *Arandora Star* and acknowledges the refugee status of many of these victims.
13. See Donald Bloxham, 'British War Crimes Trial Policy in Germany, 1945–1957: Implementation and Collapse', *The Journal of British Studies*, 42 (1) (2003), 91–118 and 'Punishing Soldiers during the Cold War: The Case of Erich von Manstein', *Patterns of Prejudice*, 33 (4) (1999), 25–45.
14. David Cesarani, *Justice Delayed: How Britain Became a Refuge for Nazi War Criminals* (London, 1992).
15. Yehuda Bauer cited in Kushner, *The Holocaust and the Liberal Imagination*, 258. The same statement is also reproduced in Andy Pearce, 'The Development of Holocaust Consciousness in Contemporary Britain, 1979–2001', *Holocaust Studies*, 14 (2) (2008), 72; Steven Cooke, 'Negotiating Memory and Identity: The Hyde Park Holocaust Memorial, London', *Journal of Historical Geography*, 26 (3) (2000), 452. For a further overview of Britain's engagement with the Holocaust see David Cesarani, 'How Post-War Britain Reflected on the Nazi Persecution and Mass Murder of Europe's Jews: A Reassessment of Early Responses', *Jewish Culture and History*, 12 (1–2) (2010), 95–130.
16. Cooke, 'Negotiating Memory and Identity', 453.

17. Tony Kushner, 'Too Little, Too Late? Reflections on Britain's Holocaust Memorial Day', *Journal of Israeli History Politics, Society, Culture*, 23 (1) (2004), 118.
18. David Cesarani and Eric J. Sundquist (eds), *After the Holocaust: Challenging the Myth of Silence* (New York, 2012).
19. Cooke, 'Negotiating Memory and Identity', 449–465.
20. Cesarani, 'How Post-War Britain Reflected on the Nazi Persecution', 95–130.
21. For a summary of this divide, see David Cesarani, 'Seizing the Day: Why Britain Will Benefit From Holocaust Memorial Day', *Patterns of Prejudice*, 34 (4) (2000) 61–66.
22. Donald Bloxham, 'Britain's Holocaust Memorial Days: Reshaping the Past in the Service of the Present', *Immigrants and Minorities*, 21 (1–2) (2002), 54–55.

Part I
Confronting the Holocaust

1

'No One Believed What We Had Seen': British Soldiers Who Witnessed Mass Murder in Auschwitz

Duncan Little

The Auschwitz extermination camp is synonymous with the Holocaust. Countless books and films have been made about its horrors and over one million people visit its site every year.[1] It is a lesser known fact, though, that hundreds of British men were imprisoned on its outskirts in camp E715, a site designated for POWs.[2] This was originally located in Auschwitz III, next to the Monowitz concentration camp and approximately two miles east of the gas chambers. In 1944, the camp was relocated by a short distance to be in closer proximity to the IG Farben plant that was engaged in the production of synthetic oil and rubber as part of the German war effort. The British soldiers held within this complex were thus in a unique position to observe Nazi crimes, and to try and ease the suffering of individual concentration camp prisoners by providing them with food and cigarettes. Some of these men would become key witnesses in the 1947–8 IG Farben trial at Nuremberg, helping to document industry's use of slave labour during the Second World War. The British public, however, remained largely unaware of the POWs' connections with Auschwitz and it is only relatively recently that details of their plight have started to receive greater media and academic attention. Drawing upon post-war affidavits, together with the author's own interviews with three POW survivors, this chapter sheds new light on their experiences.[3] In the process, it offers a compelling example of why the Holocaust can be considered very much a part of Britain's own national history.

Eyewitnesses to the Holocaust

Working in the IG Farben plant meant that the British POWs quickly became accustomed to the constant brutality of the Nazi regime. In his post-war affidavit to the Nuremberg hearings, Robert Ferris recounted one occasion where he witnessed the SS carrying 30 dead bodies through the main entrance of the factory and down 'into the cellar of the administration building'.[4] Frederick Davison also stated that he saw murder being 'committed on four or five different occasions' and that concentration camp prisoners would be killed 'in the streets of the factory grounds'. He added, 'I have seen the bodies themselves hundreds of times'.[5] More recently, Brian Bishop recalled similar scenes when he would return from the factory to the POW camp:

> There were four ropes on a makeshift gallows with four bodies hanging from them. No one seemed bothered that they were there; it was one of those things that happened and there's nothing we could do about it. It was no different from someone being shot down in the factory.[6]

Such testimonies clearly demonstrate an awareness of the casual executions that occurred among the slave labour force, yet the British soldiers have also spoken of the wider extermination process that was already underway by the time of their arrival in Poland. Bishop states, 'if the wind was blowing in the wrong direction then you could smell this awful, sickly smell. That upset me more than anything I think.'[7] The smell was not the only indicator of what was happening in Auschwitz; some of the Jewish prisoners the POWs came into contact with could speak English and would therefore converse with the British, relaying what they had heard or seen:

> They used to come in and one of them was missing and you used to say 'Where's so and so' and they used to say, 'Gone for a shower', and you used to say, 'Without a soap and towel?' They just used to nod their heads and you knew then that they had gone to the gas chambers.[8]

Such observations clearly highlight some of the difficulties that the Nazis faced in trying to keep their activities secret, especially when IG Farben officials also started to complain about the 'terrible smell' from the crematoria.[9]

The post-war affidavits from the British POWs share the same theme: everyone knew of the gas chambers and were aware that Jews especially lived under the constant shadow of death. Such narratives help to complicate existing scholarly arguments about the state of Holocaust awareness in Britain (and other Western democracies) both during and immediately after the war. While governments and early war crimes trials may have been reluctant, or simply unable, to comprehend the particular persecution of any one victim group, the example of the British POWs shows there was some knowledge of the true character of the Nazi extermination programme even if they were not necessarily given a chance to articulate it straightaway.[10] While hindsight and the subsequent emergence of more information about the Holocaust may obviously affect retellings of the E715 experience, Joseph White argues that the British POWs were nonetheless quick to make the connection between those 'stripees' wearing a Star of David on their uniforms, and those bearing the brunt of physical abuse. He claims, 'no one left Auschwitz with any doubt as to who perpetrated the Holocaust, or against whom'.[11]

Many of the British soldiers also made it their mission to learn as much about Auschwitz as possible. Leonard Dales, for instance, recalled how one Jew made him promise that he would survive so he might tell the outside world about the cold, calculated manner in which murder was being carried out.[12] Another POW, Charlie Coward, has also been credited with using his position as trustee and camp spokesman to pass information about the gassings to British and Swiss authorities. This included sending details of Jewish transports to the War Office.[13] For White, this desire to discover the facts and understand the racial hierarchy within Auschwitz exemplifies the 'humanity' of the British soldiers. He argues that, in their refusal to remain passive observers, the responses of the British POWs constitute a marked contrast to those of German bystanders.[14]

British reactions, however, went further than simply documenting what they had seen. Practical relief for concentration camp prisoners was also attempted, with POWs giving their own soup rations to the Jews. Bishop admits that the food was inedible – 'we always gave it to the Jews because it stank so badly you just couldn't drink it . . . [but] they were really thankful'.[15] The exchange, however, was not without some risk. Doug Bond records that 'if the SS spotted us offering soup to the Jews then they would kick the bucket over and threaten to shoot'.[16] As POWs, the British soldiers were in receipt of Red Cross parcels and were thus in a position to share other items with the Jews.

In his affidavit, Leonard Dales recalled an occasion where 'one of our boys' tossed a cigarette to a Jew 'who was loading some pipes'. In the 'scramble' to retrieve this gift, he injured his leg. What would normally have been a fully treatable cut became an instant death sentence. The Jew turned to Dales and stated, 'I guess this is the end. It means the gas chamber for me.'[17]

To some extent, the POW camp may be regarded as something of a mixed blessing for the British soldiers. In addition to occupying a position of 'relative privilege' in the Nazi racial hierarchy, many of these men also noticed material improvements in their conditions compared with previous spells of imprisonment in Italian POW camps.[18] In Italy, Red Cross parcels were shared between two or three men; in E715 Auschwitz there was a period when they would receive a single parcel each.[19] Similarly, when the POWs were moved closer to the IG Farben factory in February 1944, they found showers, better toilet facilities and a repair room for clothes and shoes. By contrast, POWs in one of the Italian camps only had a bar over a trench to act as their improvised lavatory. However, the reality of being housed in such close proximity to the Auschwitz crematoria negated most of these improvements. Brian Bishop insists that 'for the smell alone, I would have preferred to stay in the Italian POW camps'.[20]

It is also important to note that not all of the British soldiers at Auschwitz were classified as POWs; some were sentenced to live as concentration camp inmates themselves. Corporal Kenneth Lovell from the Durham Light Infantry was one such example. Initially imprisoned in Stalag 383 in Bavaria, he escaped only to be recaptured on 23 November 1944. He was then sent to Auschwitz, whereupon 'my head was shorn and I received a striped inmate suit with a black triangle and the letters XKGF [former prisoner of war]. I was not considered a prisoner of war anymore and was treated like any other concentration camp inmate.'[21] Stripped of the protection afforded by POW status, Lovell spent the rest of the war as a slave labourer.

Private Harry Ogden was also reclassified as a concentration camp prisoner and sent to Auschwitz. He endured various incidents of physical and mental abuse. He was kicked and beaten during interrogation, sentenced to 36 lashes and left in solitary confinement on a diet of bread and water. He remained in Auschwitz until the end of the war.[22] Ogden's case was later investigated by the United Nations War Crimes Unit, but it appears there was little (if any) interest in his wartime plight back in Britain. There remains a lack of specific data as to just how many more British men simply disappeared into the Nazi concentration camp system.

The British soldiers who retained their POW status were also far from immune from becoming the victims of war crimes. Brian Bishop recounts how the IG Farben camp manager, Gerhard Ritter, would fire his gun through the British huts to ensure prisoners were out of their bunks, on parade and ready to go to work at the crack of dawn. On one occasion, this performance resulted in one British man being injured by a stray bullet as he lay on his bed.[23] The POWs also held Ritter responsible for one of the few British deaths at E715 Auschwitz. Corporal Reynolds had refused an order to climb '70 feet up girders in the deep cold of the 1943 winter', fearing he would freeze to the metal unless he was supplied with appropriate protective clothing; Ritter executed him on the spot.[24] In a separate incident, another soldier, Private Campbell, was stabbed for helping a Polish girl carry a pail of soup. In this case, the man survived.[25] White names the perpetrator as Benno F, a German army sergeant, and states the same figure was responsible for the shooting of Reynolds.[26] Other witnesses remember his full name as Benno Franz and maintain Reynolds was killed by Ritter. Either way, some of the British POWs plotted to avenge these incidents by luring both men under a set of girders and dropping concrete slabs onto them.[27] Although this particular plan was never put into effect, there were other, more subtle, ways in which the British taunted their captors and tried to introduce aspects of their own culture into the surroundings.

One example of this was Arthur Gifford-England's garden. Unable to work in the factory after an accident, Gifford-England approached fellow POW Charlie Coward explaining that he wanted some plants. In exchange for cigarettes, these were duly obtained from the nearby town of Oświęcim and Gifford-England planted tomatoes and flowers in an area roughly six feet by six feet. He saw this garden as a very British act of defiance against the Nazis.[28] Another clear respite from the horrors surrounding the POWs was football. Sunday was their rest day and the Britons divided themselves into four separate teams, the majority of fixtures occurring in 1944 on a field outside E715's perimeter and a clear mile from the concentration camp. Local people and POWs alike would watch these matches. Back within E715, the POWs would also stage plays; surviving advertisements for two performances in December 1944 reveal productions of *Sweeney Todd* and *Night at an Inn*. It is unclear why these particular plays were chosen by the men, particularly given the macabre content of the former. White notes the introduction of a

'Shylock-type character' in *Night at an Inn* and suggests this might be seen as indicative of a 'cultural anti-Semitism' that had not been completely shaken by the scenes in Auschwitz. Whether or not this was the case, it is clear that any latent prejudice that may have existed did not impede efforts to try and help Jews.[29]

Football, gardens and plays offered a means of raising morale and alleviating stress among the POWs, as well as a form of protest against the Nazis. The latter was demonstrated when the camp authorities sent a censor to view one of the plays and ensure that the British were not making derogatory remarks about Adolf Hitler. The cast had been banned from singing *God Save the King* and so instead decided upon a rendition of *Land of Hope and Glory*. Gifford-England recalls that the British deliberately sat two burly POWs either side of the censor. When they stood to sing this replacement for the national anthem, they pushed themselves against the Nazi, forcing him onto his feet as well.[30]

Defiance, though, did not stop at potentially upsetting a censor during amateur dramatics. There are anecdotal stories that the British POWs, having already protested that being forced to help the German war effort was against the Geneva Convention, undertook various acts of sabotage around the IG Farben factory. Gifford-England recounts how the men swapped 'destination' signs on a number of wagons sited along train sidings, believing this would result in paint being sent to the Russian front instead of bullets.[31] In a separate incident, Doug Bond left the valves on the factory's acetylene bottles open overnight so they would be empty in the morning.[32]

Heroic untruths

Alongside the acts of petty vandalism, tales of dramatic heroism have also emerged from post-war POW testimonies. These again add up to a narrative of defiance and British courageousness and, as such, fit into longstanding, popular images of Britain's fight against Nazism. At the same time, though, these episodes highlight important questions over the reliability of memories and the purpose behind some of these accounts.

Charlie Coward was the British POWs' Red Cross trustee at E715 Auschwitz and acted as the liaison point between them and their captors. In his post-war affidavit, he described hearing the story of a Jewish ship's doctor from north east England who was sent to Auschwitz after the Nazis discovered his religion.[33] This doctor was able to get word of his predicament to the British POWs and asked them to notify his family back in Sunderland. Coward then apparently decided to try and find this doctor for himself, arranging with a guard to 'swap clothing with one of the inmates and to march into the camp with [them]'.[34] He did not succeed in his mission to find the Englishman, but he claimed he did enter the concentration camp at Auschwitz, spent a single night there, and ate potato soup with the other prisoners.

Coward's account recalled vivid details of the conditions in the camp. He explained how the SS counted them when they left IG Farben and again when they entered the camp itself, and how, in an effort to gain increased food rations, the living would 'hold up the dead' so the Nazis would include them in the head count.[35] Coward also described the layout of the huts with three tiers of bunk beds, each having to 'accommodate two or three inmates'. Tables were arranged in the middle of the hut where prisoners would fight to get their portion of soup. In the morning, they were woken by the Capos who would 'kick and beat' people who had 'not gotten up'; those 'who could not get up were just carted away'.[36]

As a result of this escapade, Coward was one of the few E715 POWs to achieve post-war fame. He wrote a book outlining his experiences and a related film, *The Password Is Courage*, was produced in 1962. The same year also saw Coward being recognised on an episode of the long-running BBC television programme, *This Is Your Life*. Questions, however, have been raised over the accuracy of Coward's account. Given the better treatment and Red Cross parcels afforded to the POWs, some have wondered how a reasonably 'healthy' looking person could be surrounded by 'skeletal' inmates and yet not be spotted by the SS. As George Longdon wrote in his affidavit, '[Concentration camp prisoners] looked three parts dead. They were all skin and bones ... their thighs were as thin as my arms'.[37] This physical contrast between the POWs and the concentration camp inmates is underscored by a set of images of the E715 prisoners, organised by Coward himself with a local photographer. One of these clearly depicts Coward with the camp football team, smiling and posing with his hands resting on the shoulders of another member of the group. He certainly does not look thin or gaunt, although it may have been possible for him to pass himself off as a recent arrival at the camp. Another former POW, David Alexander, testified at Nuremberg that 'for the most part the new ones looked pretty much the same as we did, like normal, healthy human beings. After they were there for a month or so, a great change ... would take place.'[38]

Regardless of Coward's physical appearance, though, there are other lingering questions over his story. White asks the fundamental question: 'why would anyone sneak into a Nazi concentration camp when so much could go wrong, and especially when the price of discovery would be so great?'[39] Even Coward's fellow POWs have voiced their scepticism. Doug Bond insists,

> [Coward] was the man in charge of the camp so he couldn't afford to go missing could he? When we were on parade, he was always there as he was in charge. He was always on parade when the German officer came on parade so he could never afford to go missing really.[40]

Bishop, meanwhile, comments:

> When I was in the camp, I heard that a Jew had replaced Charlie Coward for a night and that he was staying in E715. I don't know if it was true. I used to talk to Charlie Coward all the time but he never mentioned it.[41]

A remarkably similar tale of an E715 POW controversially claiming to have exchanged places with a Jew is that of Denis Avey who published his experiences in the 2011 work *The Man Who Broke into Auschwitz*.[42] Like Coward, he noted how the 'living were counted with the dead' and described how he 'gagged on the foul air' as he entered the huts in the concentration camp.[43] Avey claims that the man he exchanged places with was then hidden from the Nazis in the POW huts and that only two British men, Bill Hedges and Jimmy Fleet, were aware of the swap:

> They told me I was an idiot but they went along with it. Bill's bunk was above mine in the back corner of the hut and he handled most of the subterfuge. It was his job to secrete Hans away. To the rest, the story was to be that I was ill and had taken to my bed.[44]

The Man Who Broke into Auschwitz has become an international bestseller and Avey was also among the 27 recipients of the British Hero of the Holocaust award issued in March 2010.[45] However, there are inconsistencies in Avey's story. Guy Walters has been especially vocal in his criticisms, highlighting, among other aspects, Avey's claim that 'he made the swap in an attempt to make contact with an Australian POW who claimed to have been incarcerated in Birkenau and forced to stoke the crematoria'.[46] The man in question was Donald Watts and his postwar book, *Stoker*, has been widely dismissed as untrue. Walters thus concludes that 'given this, and the various conflicting versions of Avey's supposed "swap", it is almost impossible to take *The Man who Broke into Auschwitz* at face value'.[47] He adds, 'the chance that two British POWs [Coward and Avey] both independently thought up the life endangering idea to swap places with an inmate of Auschwitz stretches credibility to breaking point'.[48]

Former POW Brian Bishop also refutes Avey's account. He stresses that the huts at E715 Auschwitz consisted of a number of rooms with each one containing around 20–25 men. He says the idea that an imposter

> could simply take to a bed and that nobody would notice that he was not the same man who they had been sharing a room with for a number of months is quite simply not possible. How did he get to the toilet for a start? Someone would surely have noticed a stranger get out of a bunk and walk past them to the communal toilets.[49]

Why, though, might some of these former POWs feel compelled to 'beef up' their stories in this manner? Arguably, it may simply have been a means to gain some interest and kudos in a post-war society that cared little for yet more war stories, or at least those lacking a sense of heroism.

Another notable example of the fragility of POW memories comes with the depiction of the camp's evacuation in 1945. It was clear by the start of that year that the war was over. Following a night of substantial bombing by the Russians, the Nazis ordered the British soldiers to walk back to Germany. It is at this point that the recent recollections of Bishop and Bond, who were on the same route together, start to differ from the testimonies of some of their fellow former inmates. Neither of them can remember any type of brutality by the guards; Bond recalls them as being 'all old blokes who were in the First World War and they didn't want to march anyway'.[50] Yet the post-war affidavits signed by other former POWs cast a different light on the 520-mile trek from Auschwitz to Landshut.

The journey lasted four months and there were a number of incidents which were subsequently reported to the United Nations War Crimes Commission. These included men being forced to stand in the freezing cold so the Germans could eat a meal in a warm house, and being billeted in a field from 'seven o'clock in the morning till seven o'clock at night ... in intense cold without food'.[51] Each episode caused immense suffering to the POWs, with one document stating that there were more than '100 cases of frostbite, many of them quite serious'.[52] One POW, Andrew Porteous, also recorded an occasion when a German guard lifted 'the butt of his rifle ... [to] strike two men on the back'. Porteous pushed the guard away whereupon the guard pointed the gun at him and fired. Portcous threw himself to the ground to avoid the bullet.[53]

Despite these clear testimonies of abuse, both Bond and Bishop maintained that these incidents did not happen on their march to Germany. It is uncertain if their memories have been blocked by the trauma of what occurred – or if they have both forgotten what had happened over the passage of time. It is also possible that in the chaos of war, they somehow ended up in a separate group – away from these particular members of E715 Auschwitz.

'No one believed what we had seen'

The majority of men from E715 Auschwitz tried to create a normal life for themselves upon their return to Britain in 1945, yet the memories of what they had witnessed would haunt them for years to come. Many would not – or could not – talk about their experiences in Auschwitz. Like some of the Holocaust's survivors, these men felt their tales would simply be dismissed as untrue. Arthur Gifford-England states, 'I didn't talk about it for a long time, no one believed what we had seen.'[54] Likewise, Brian Bishop notes,

> I didn't even tell my wife. She knew I had been there but I never told her the details of what happened at E715. After the war, people were only interested in heroes. If you escaped from a prison camp then you became a hero. If you didn't escape then you became forgotten. In Auschwitz, it was practically impossible to escape as every bush had a soldier hiding behind it.[55]

Such reasoning may again help to account for Coward and Avey's attempts to enhance their wartime stories.

There are several reasons why post-war Britain may have 'forgotten' or ignored its troops who had been imprisoned in Auschwitz. Firstly, it is worth noting that the camp's liberation by Soviet troops may have meant little to British audiences in January 1945, focused as they were on their own, ongoing war effort. Furthermore, the men of E715 had already left Auschwitz by this point, forced onto their march to Germany. They would not be found by American forces until April and thus their connection to Auschwitz was not immediately apparent. In addition, the birth pangs of the Cold War were starting, with Britain and the United States becoming increasingly distrustful of the Soviet Union. There were few, if any, Western reporters, photographers or film cameras embedded with the Soviet army and thus little opportunity for full details of the liberation of Auschwitz to reach Western audiences. The empty remnants of E715 would effectively disappear behind the Iron Curtain.

Instead, it was the camps in the west of Europe, liberated by the British and the Americans, that had the biggest impact and arguably cemented the imagery of overcrowded, disease-ridden concentration camps into the mindset of the British public. Tony Kushner and Joanne Reilly have already demonstrated the apparent difference in the way eastern and western camps were reported upon by the British media with their analysis of Bergen-Belsen.[56] Soon after the camp's liberation, by British forces, in April 1945, the *Daily Mail* produced a collection of photographs, entitled *'LEST WE FORGET'*. Kushner and Reilly argue that

> the particular role of the western camps was [not] understood at the time. *'LEST WE FORGET'* was actually unusual in mentioning, if only in one sentence, Auschwitz.... although it was equally believed in 1945 that the western camps, without the apparatus of mass murder, were by far the worst in the Nazi system.[57]

Kushner and Reilly also argue that *Lest We Forget* effectively dehumanised people liberated from the camps:

> Who were these victims? In *LEST WE FORGET*, as in so much else of the instant atrocity material of 1945, they were simply identified through the concentration camp in which they had been liberated – there are no names, personal histories or anything else that would undermine their use merely as illustrators of the true nature of Nazism.[58]

The same might be said of the British POWs who had witnessed aspects of the Holocaust. They rarely learnt the personal histories of the people around them and, upon their return, some of them effectively became the 'British illustrators' at Nuremberg, underlining the criminal nature of National Socialism to the court. Even these testimonies did not resonate far beyond the courtroom. In the aftermath of the lengthy International Military Tribunal of 1945–6, subsequent war crimes trials (and particularly those unrelated to the British zone of occupation) struggled to gain significant media attention; the British press was dominated by more immediate stories happening at home. The domestic situation was chaotic: potatoes had just entered the ration list for the first time, meat rations were being decreased and the country was still recovering from some of the most extreme weather it had seen for generations with a hard winter followed by widespread flooding in the spring. The country's monetary woes also continued; sterling convertibility was suspended in August 1947 and the resulting economic chaos saw Hugh Dalton resign as Chancellor of the Exchequer in November. A trial happening hundreds of miles away in another country simply did not register on the collective consciousness.

This combination of economic woes and social change, as well as memories of a very different wartime experience back home, may also account for returning POWs' inability to speak out about their time in Auschwitz. Those Britons who had stayed at home and survived the Blitz appeared hardened by years of aerial bombardment, bad news, death and a shortage of food together with a lack of other key supplies for the home front. As Bertie Harwood, who arrived at Liverpool in 1945, commented, 'It was not the same England I had left in early 1940. There was a tense, workmanlike atmosphere. Everyone was going about his or her business with utterly weary faces but with grim purpose.'[59] It could be argued that the 'Blitz spirit' united the country to create a new, tougher Britain. One woman who survived the air raids wrote, 'each one of us, no matter to what class of society we belonged, instinctively rebelled against allowing Hitler – that silly little man with a toothbrush moustache – to rule our lives. It was a feeling that united the nation as never before or since.'[60] To go through so much death and destruction surely created a hardened attitude to life. Combine this 'toughening up' of attitudes and the notion that being a POW meant that you had 'been captured by the enemy and so had brought shame on your country', then it is perhaps not surprising that so few people took any real notice of these men upon their return.[61]

Consequently, the British POWs who had been imprisoned in Europe received a muted response. Returning POWs from Japan had, legitimately, secured the national interest as details of the horrific conditions they had endured were revealed. In a superficial comparison, at least, POWs from German camps appeared to have been treated with greater respect and dignity; isolated cases of inhumane treatment against POWs in German custody remained under-reported.

The apparent disinterest in the fate of the E715 POWs can be further explained in terms of the rapid transition from war to peace. It could be argued that after six years of fighting, the nation wanted to quickly forget the suffering caused by conflict and focus on the future. As the diplomat Sir Robert Bruce Lockhart observed, 'Seventeen days since VE Day, and never have I seen a nation change so quickly from a war mentality to a peace mentality.' About the continuing conflict with Japan, he added, 'The war has disappeared from the news ... sport and election now fill the front pages.'[62] The population's war weariness is further reflected by the lack of its celebratory mood in May 1945. Photographs showing massive celebrations in Piccadilly Circus have entered the national consciousness as demonstrating a huge outpouring of joy and relief at the end of the conflict – but the truth may have been rather different. David Kynaston argues that the celebrations were actually quite 'low key' and quotes Mass Observation reports which show that, overall, 'crowds were too few and too thin to inspire much feeling'.[63] With such a lack of apparent interest in the country's victory, perhaps it is not surprising that few were prepared to ask about or listen to the experiences of returning servicemen and POWs.

Perhaps the biggest cause for this perceived lack of interest would be the huge list of new problems faced by the country. The cost of war had been high and the country had 'run up debts amounting to £3,500 million, compared with less than £500 million back in 1939'.[64] If British POWs who had been in German captivity had ever been part of the immediate post-war headlines then the country's new focus of rebuilding, and sorting out its war debt, meant these men would quickly become yesterday's news. Austerity had become the day's watchword. Keynes had warned of a 'financial Dunkirk' in August 1945 and, by October the same year, troops were being used to unload food during dock strikes.[65] Bread rationing began a year later in 1946. Britain may have defeated Nazism, but it was at a huge cost, and Attlee's new Labour government had a very long 'to do' list. The experiences of British POWs were simply not important in the consciousness of a nation which faced such severe problems.

An example of the post-war mood can be gleaned from the reflections of former POW Jim Witte, who recounted his experience of a train journey from London to Essex shortly after the war's end:

> It was all very unreal and I began to get the feeling of an anti-climax. Although I had written home to say that I had arrived safely in England, there was no one at the station to meet me. So much for the 'hero's return', I thought. I found myself queuing for a bus amongst a lot of women chattering about the availability of bananas.[66]

Sergeant W.P. Wood expressed similar sentiments:

> I suppose the most common sensation of a returning prisoner was one of anti-climax. It had been a long time in coming and the

imagination had created a sort of mirage. Life in England fell far short of this illusion of course.[67]

These men had been 'regular' POWs. For the men of E715 Auschwitz, the situation was far worse. They had witnessed unimaginable horrors yet no one understood what would today be described as post-traumatic stress disorder. The emerging military threat posed by the Soviet Union, together with the need to rebuild a shattered country and strengthen a weakened economy, meant that the government lacked the money, time and inclination to be able to treat veterans properly. When Bishop arrived back to Britain in 1945, he found it 'difficult' to cope and was soon discharged on medical grounds from the army. He was paid an allowance on the condition of visiting a psychiatrist every Friday. This gave him a financial incentive to visit the doctor but he gained little from the treatment and felt the exercise was 'fruitless' as the doctor seemed disinterested in what he had seen at Auschwitz. He stopped the treatments after two years, although his nightmares continued and his mental health did not improve until the middle of the 1950s.[68]

A rare case of a former E715 POW actually being invited to talk about his experiences comes in the reminiscences of Arthur Dodd. He recalls how, upon returning to this country, he was asked to speak alongside a parachutist at the local cinema. The parachutist recounted to the assembled crowd his own tales of daring adventures and afterwards was swamped with admirers from the audience. Dodd, however, was left alone and quietly left the stage. He would wait another five decades before speaking out again, when his biography was published by Colin Rushton in 1999.[69] Brian Bishop also kept quiet:

You got fed up with people bragging about what they did in Army and I didn't really feel my experiences mattered that much. All we were interested in was surviving. Everyone else wrote their stories about what a smashing time they had. I didn't.[70]

Such comments again help to explain the 'silence' surrounding the POWs from E715 Auschwitz for most of the post-war era. If people only wanted to hear from heroes, and not from the men who had been captured, then the opportunities simply did not exist for these individuals to have their accounts heard, let alone recorded for future generations. As any desire to share their experiences diminished, so did the opportunities for historians to record eyewitness testimonies.

Of course, it was not just British POWs from Auschwitz who were finding it hard to tell their stories to a world adjusting to images of horrific suffering. Primo Levi's account of his life as a Jewish man sent to Auschwitz, *If This Is a Man*, has become required reading for those studying the Holocaust, yet even this was initially rejected by publishers in 1947. Levi explained that this lack of interest in his work was because post-war Europe had been through 'difficult times of mourning and reconstruction and the public did not want to return in memory to the painful years of the war that had just ended'.[71] It is perhaps for this reason that the book was not an immediate success. Levi found a new publisher in 1958 and 'from then on the interest of the public has never flagged. In Italy, the book has sold more than 500,000 copies.'[72]

In the final analysis, the experience of POWs in Auschwitz was just so different to the conditions that other British POWs had undergone that, quite simply, no one could believe the horrors of what they had witnessed. As one former E715 prisoner, Eric Doyle, wrote, 'their [the inmates] condition and treatment was so bad that it is impossible to explain it to people in England'.[73] Furthermore, it is clear that, while the trauma of what they had witnessed would remain with them for the rest of their lives, the men of E715 also wanted to try and forget the past and have a fresh start. As White points out, 'upon demobilization, the British government implored veterans to get on with their lives and to forget the past, something they took as an order'.[74] Such an approach meant these men never had a real opportunity to discuss what they had witnessed. Because they did not discuss their experiences, the public remained largely unaware that these men were ever at Auschwitz, which in turn meant 'no one believed that we were (there) and no one believed what we had seen'.[75] All of this makes a comment made by Doug Bond in 2007 all the more poignant. While assisting in the research for my book, *Allies in Auschwitz*, he said, 'Would anyone have ever thought about writing it as a story? I don't suppose anyone gave it a second thought.'

Notes

1. Annual visitor numbers are available on the Auschwitz-Birkenau Memorial and Museum website: http://en.auschwitz.org/z/index.php?option=com_content&task=view&id=56&Itemid=24.
2. Estimates as to the precise number of British soldiers who were imprisoned at E715 Auschwitz vary from 900 to 1500 within different post-war accounts.
3. My conversations with Bond and Gifford-England happened predominately during the course of 2008 when I was writing *Allies in Auschwitz*. Both men

had spoken with former comrades about their experiences (but not with each other) and their memories appeared, in the main, to be reliable as I cross-referenced their recollections with the affidavits written shortly after the war. My interviews with Bishop started in 2006. It was the first time he had ever spoken about his time at E715 Auschwitz and his comments were again cross-referenced with the other sources.

4. Robert Ferris, Testimonial statement for Nuremberg IG Farben hearings, 1947–1948, Imperial War Museum (IWM) Documents section. Item ref: NI 11693.
5. Frederick Davison, Testimonial statement for Nuremberg IG Farben hearings, 1947–1948 IWM Documents section. Item ref: NI 11694.
6. Duncan Little, *Allies in Auschwitz* (Forest Row, 2009), 28.
7. Ibid.
8. Ibid., 29.
9. Christian Schneider, Testimonial statement for Nuremberg IG Farben hearings, 1947–1948. IWM Documents section. Item ref: NI 7604.
10. On the reluctance to note the particular suffering of the Jews, see: Tony Kushner, *The Holocaust and the Liberal Imagination: A Social and Cultural History* (Oxford, 1994), 205–342; John P. Fox, 'The Jewish Factor in British War Crimes Policy in 1942', *The English Historical Review*, 92 (362) (1977), 82–106; Donald Bloxham, 'The Missing Camps of *Aktion Reinhard*: The Judicial Displacement of a Mass Murder', in Peter Gray and Kendrick Oliver (eds), *The Memory of Catastrophe* (Manchester, 2004), 118–131.
11. Joseph Robert White, ' "Even in Auschwitz...Humanity Could Prevail": British POWs and Jewish Concentration-Camp Inmates at IG Auschwitz, 1943–1945', *Holocaust and Genocide Studies*, 15 (2) (2001), 284.
12. Leonard Dales, Testimonial statement for Nuremberg IG Farben hearings, 1947–1948. IWM Documents section. Item ref: NI 11695.
13. White, ' "Even in Auschwitz...Humanity Could Prevail" ', 279.
14. Ibid., *passim*.
15. Little, *Allies in Auschwitz*, 38–39.
16. Ibid.
17. Leonard Dales, Testimonial statement for Nuremberg IG Farben hearings, IWM Documents NI 11695.
18. On the POWs and the racial hierarchy, see White, ' "Even in Auschwitz...Humanity Could Prevail" ', 267.
19. For further details on the conditions in the Italian camps, see Ibid., 270.
20. Author's notes, interview with Brian Bishop, 2008.
21. Kenneth Lovell, Testimonial statement for Nuremberg IG Farben hearings, 1947–1948. IWM Documents section. Item ref: 11702.
22. Harry Ogden, Report to United Nations War Crimes Investigation Unit, National Archives, WO 311/149.
23. Little, *Allies in Auschwitz*, 34.
24. War Crimes Investigation Report, National Archives, WO 309/1063.
25. Ibid.
26. White, ' "Even in Auschwitz...Humanity Could Prevail" ', 266.
27. Little, *Allies in Auschwitz*, 34–35.
28. Author's notes, interview with Arthur Gifford-England, 2008.
29. White, ' "Even in Auschwitz...Humanity Could Prevail" ', 282–283.

30. Little, *Allies in Auschwitz*, 42.
31. Ibid., 32.
32. Ibid.
33. Ibid., 77.
34. Charles Coward, testimonial statement for Nuremberg IG Farben hearings, 1947–1948. IWM Documents section. Item ref: NI 11695.
35. Ibid.
36. Ibid.
37. George Longdon, Testimonial statement for Nuremberg IG Farben hearings, 1947–1948. Source: IWM Documents section. Item ref: NI 11703.
38. David Alexander, Testimonial statement for Nuremberg IG Farben hearings, 1947–1948. IWM Documents section. Item ref: NI 11698.
39. White, ' "Even in Auschwitz … Humanity Could Prevail" ', 279.
40. Little, *Allies in Auschwitz*, 78.
41. Ibid.
42. Denis Avey with Rob Broomby, *The Man Who Broke into Auschwitz* (London, 2011).
43. Ibid., 137.
44. Ibid., 132.
45. This award, issued on 9 March 2010, recognised those who had helped save lives during the Holocaust. Of the 27 recipients, only two were still alive at the time of issue: one was Denis Avey, the other was Sir Nicholas Winton, who orchestrated the Czech Kindertransport.
46. Guy Walters, 'The Curious Case of the "Break into Auschwitz" ', *New Statesman*, 17 November 2011.
47. Ibid.
48. Guy Walters, 'Did This British PoW Really Smuggle Himself into Auschwitz to Expose the Holocaust … or Is His Account Pure Fantasy and an Insult to Millions Who Died There?', *Daily Mail*, 8 April 2011.
49. Author's notes, interview with Brian Bishop, 2008.
50. Little, *Allies in Auschwitz*, 61.
51. Statements provided by E715 POWs as part of post-war investigation by United Nations War Crimes Unit. National Archives, item ref: WO 311/112.
52. Ibid.
53. Ibid.
54. Little, *Allies in Auschwitz*, 67.
55. Ibid., 66.
56. See, for example: Jo Reilly, David Cesarani, Tony Kushner and Colin Richmond (eds), *Belsen in History and Memory* (Oxford, 1997); Joanne Reilly, *Belsen: The Liberation of a Concentration Camp* (London, 1998).
57. Reilly et al., *Belsen in History and Memory*, 6.
58. Ibid., 5.
59. Cited in Adrian Gilbert, *POW: Allied Prisoners in Europe, 1939–1945* (London, 2006), 316.
60. Juliet Gardiner, *The Blitz: The British under Attack* (London, 2010), 371.
61. Author's notes, interview with Brian Bishop, 2008.
62. David Kynaston, *Austerity Britain 1945–48: A World to Build* (London, 2007), 60.
63. Ibid., 13.

64. Robert Pearce, *Attlee's Labour Governments 1945–1951* (London, 1994), 33.
65. Ibid., x.
66. Gilbert, *POW: Allied Prisoners in Europe*, 317.
67. Ibid.
68. Little, *Allies in Auschwitz*, 64–65.
69. Colin Rushton, *Spectator in Hell* (Chichester, 1999). This book told of Dodd's abuse by SS guards and the hard labour he was forced to undergo. It also highlighted Dodd's apparent role in plans to aid Jewish prisoners to escape from Auschwitz. As with the Coward and Avey examples, then, there remained some emphasis on British bravery and acts of resistance.
70. Ibid., 66.
71. Primo Levi, *If This Is a Man* (London, 1979), 381. The first publication run was limited to 2,500 copies.
72. Ibid.
73. White, ' "Even in Auschwitz...Humanity Could Prevail" ', 285.
74. Ibid.
75. Little, *Allies in Auschwitz*, 67.

2
Holocaust on Trial: Mass Observation and British Media Responses to the Nuremberg Tribunal, 1945–1946

Caroline Sharples

On 21 November 1945, six months after the end of the Second World War, 21 former high-ranking members of the Nazi state entered Court-room 600 in the Nuremberg Palace of Justice to face charges of con-spiracy, crimes against peace, war crimes and crimes against humanity.[1] The subsequent proceedings before the four Allied powers lasted for almost a year, fill over 20 volumes and have become known as one of the most famous courtroom dramas in history. The legacy of the International Military Tribunal (IMT) is multifaceted; aside from its sig-nificance in terms of the development of international criminal law and, in particular, the concept of 'crimes against humanity', the trial was also responsible for the preservation and translation of a wealth of primary source material from the Third Reich which remains an important tool for historical research. In popular culture too, the IMT – and the sub-sequent Nuremberg proceedings – has left its mark, including the 1961 film *Judgment at Nuremberg* and the 2000 production *Nuremberg*. Further-more, the courtroom itself has become something of a tourist attraction, receiving 13,138 visitors in 2005 alone. It now houses a permanent exhibition on the tribunal.[2]

Given the immense scale of the proceedings, it is not surprising that the IMT has also long proved a source of intense scholarly interest. Much of this existing secondary literature focuses on procedural issues and points of law.[3] Other works concentrate on the psychology of the defen-dants, or particular moments within the trial, such as the screening of footage from the liberated concentration camps, or the holding up of the notorious 'Shrunken Head of Buchenwald'.[4] Whatever the primary area of enquiry, though, significant claims have been advanced for the impact of the IMT. Michael Marrus, for example, emphasises its historical importance in comprehensively documenting the Holocaust for the first time for a non-Jewish audience.[5]

More recently, though, a number of more critical studies have been produced which challenge the ability of the IMT and, indeed, war crimes trials in general to effect popular understandings of the past. A growing canon of literature is developing on the relationship between judicial processes, history and memory.[6] Again, questions of legal and moral legitimacy tend to come to the fore, but the IMT's representation of the Nazi genocide has also been subjected to particular scrutiny. In the aftermath of the Second World War, much of the focus within Britain and the United States, for example, rested firmly on the concentration camps in Western Europe, places such as Bergen-Belsen and Dachau that Western forces had liberated. These sites were held up as constituting the very worst of Nazism – a theme that was continued throughout the Nuremberg proceedings, with little attention being afforded to the *Operation Reinhard* camps in Poland. A blurring of the camp system, coupled with a refusal to particularise the fate of any one victim group, thus precluded an accurate understanding of the enormity of the 'Final Solution'. Erich Haberer sums up many of the criticisms that have subsequently been levelled at the trial, arguing, 'it minimised the Holocaust, marginalised the victims and misrepresented the complexity of the continent-wide implementation of the Nazi genocidal policies'.[7]

Even if, as Tony Kushner suggests, the IMT did prompt the figure of six million murdered Jews to gain currency, its ability to sustain public interest was limited. 'In Britain and the United States', Kushner argues, 'the public soon tired of the meticulous attention to detail in the trials and there was relief when they finally finished nearly a year later'.[8] Donald Bloxham similarly cites the lack of public support for war crimes trials as a key factor in Britain's reluctance, in the wake of the IMT, to launch further prosecutions within its own occupation zone of the now divided Germany.[9]

It seems, therefore, that despite the lofty educational ideals bound up in the Nuremberg proceedings, there remained significant omissions or distortions, and the trial did not necessarily have the desired impact on the 'ordinary' people at the grass roots of post-war European society. Despite the enormous volume of literature on the IMT, though, little has been done to explore these responses in any depth. Such investigations as there are focus mainly on popular notions of victors' justice and German victimhood which help characterise the immediate post-war period as one of widespread (West) German silence, reticence or even 'collective amnesia' about the recent past. As a result, German responses to the IMT are also frequently dismissed as one of general disinterest.[10] The question remains, though, how far we can reasonably expect the people of a defeated, devastated nation to follow such a lengthy court case. Before condemning the delay in Germans' 'coming to terms with the past', it is, perhaps, worth considering just how much attention was being paid to the IMT by people in other countries. The British population, for example, was unencumbered by any issues of guilt or responsibility, and facing less urgent problems in terms of day-to-day survival in the immediate months after the war's end. To what extent did they engage with the events in Nuremberg? Is it simply a case of growing boredom with the protracted nature of the legal proceedings, as Kushner suggests, or can we identify any further modes of response to the trial? To try and answer some of these questions, this chapter explores the ways in which the tribunal was relayed to a wider audience through the press and analyses responses to a series of Mass Observation (MO) surveys and directives.

Nuremberg and the British press

In 1942, the Allies announced their intention to punish Nazi war crim-inals amid growing reports of systematic violence and mass murder taking place in occupied Europe. Just what form this 'retribution' would take, however, remained unclear and it was not until the summer of 1945, with the war in Europe officially concluded, that agreement was reached regarding the creation of a four-power international tribunal to prosecute the leading, surviving members of the Nazi hierarchy.[11] Some figures within the British government, including Churchill, had expressed some scepticism over these plans, and even initially echoed Stalin's call for the summary execution of major Nazi figures. The prospect of a trial, as favoured by the United States Secretary of War, Henry Stimson, was viewed with some unease. Aside from the fact there was no legal precedent for the type of trial envisioned, there was also a very real sense that the guilt of those concerned was simply too obvi-ous to warrant a trial, together with fears that any courtroom setting could very quickly become a platform for the dissemination of National Socialist ideology. Many were also wary of repeating the mistakes that had occurred at the end of the First World War.[12]

Responses generated by both the 1942 Declaration and the 1945 London Charter revealed that the wider British public was also unsure about the best way to deal with Nazi war criminals. Initially, many appeared to favour the idea of making those responsible for atrocities answer before a court of law; a reader of the *Manchester Guardian* urged the Allied governments to temper their indignation in the face of the reports emerging from war-torn Europe and exercise a degree of caution, begging 'let us not also have the blood of the innocent on our hands'.[13] The rule of law, it was felt, must be upheld. A reader of the *Daily Telegraph*, fearing that the victims of Nazism might take matters into their own hands, similarly declared that 'retribution [should] be arrayed under legal process so that true justice shall be done and the truly guilty discovered and an impressive demonstration of the law be made to the world'.[14] Others, though, proved more sceptical, with one reader arguing:

What further records or siftings of evidence against the Axis criminals are required? The whole of butchered Europe now lies agonised in terrible testimony. What judicial processes or judges and juries will be necessary?[15]

Similar sentiments would be expressed repeatedly during the IMT itself.

The British newspapers themselves, meanwhile, seized upon the Allied Declaration and called for 'spectacular' punitive measures to be implemented against the Nazis. Under the headline 'They Must Not Escape', the *Sunday Express* sensationally denounced Hitler, Göring, Himmler and Hess as 'the greatest murder gang ever known in history'.[16] A more measured tone was adopted by the London publication *News Chronicle*, which also proved notable for drawing its readers' attention to one particular group of victims, stating:

They should, for example, include some special reparation for the crimes committed against the Jews. Cold-blooded massacres of Jews is Germany's greatest act of barbarism. War on civilian populations and shooting of hostages as reprisals...can be defended as Acts of War which may weaken the enemy's will to go on fighting. For the Jewish massacre there is no such defence. They, like the murder of prisoners of war are an affront to the humane impulses which are at the basis of civilisation.[17]

This recognition of the specific persecution of the Jews was unusual both during and immediately after the Second World War. Kushner has already examined Western tendencies to depict the Holocaust in 'universal' terms after liberation, and it is also important to note the infrequency with which the word 'Jew' appeared in the liberation news-reels footage, IMT indictment or the subsequent trial transcripts. While this clearly hindered the development of a Holocaust 'consciousness' in post-war Britain, the example of *News Chronicle* suggests there were pockets of knowledge and understanding among the population and better-informed journalists.

As the final arrangements for the Nuremberg Tribunal were being put into place in the autumn of 1945, the British press were already dis-playing signs of great interest in the forthcoming case, with a series of reports anticipating just who would be standing trial and setting out in minute detail the conditions that the former Nazis were now facing in custody. When the indictment was finally made public on 20 October 1945, it was reproduced in all the leading newspapers.[18] By the time the trial began a month later, the media could hardly contain its excite-ment, with *The Times* proclaiming it 'the greatest trial in history, an international precedent to which the eyes of the world are turned'.[19] The *Daily Telegraph* engaged in similar high-flown rhetoric, announc-ing the IMT's opening as 'Humanity's Day of Wrath when upon a score of evil men shall be done the justice for which the blood and tears of tortured millions cry out from beyond the grave'.[20]

There was, however, a clear expectation that the proceedings would be short-lived affairs. The *Daily Telegraph*'s special correspondent, Ossian Goulding, for example, insisted that it would last 'an absolute minimum of three months'.[21] Even as the trial dragged over into the New Year, the initial wave of journalistic interest began to wane, and the num-ber of column inches dedicated to the tribunal began to dwindle from half page spreads at the start of the case to instances of just a few sim-ple paragraphs. A reader's letter to the *Jewish Chronicle* underlined the inconsistency in the coverage afforded to the trial by different elements of the British press:

> Last week I read the magnificently written column in *The Times* on the revelations at the Nuremberg trials of the Nazi use of anti-Semitism as a political weapon and the Nazis' deliberate murder policy which culminated in the epic stand of the Warsaw Ghetto. But to my astonishment, there was not one single word of the trials

in the *Daily Sketch*, nor does there appear to have been since. Presumably so important a proceeding historically as the arraignment of the arch-villains of Nazism and Fascism who plunged the whole world into the most terrible war in human record is no longer 'news' to a 'national' newspaper, nor is enlightenment on the most potent weapon they ever used – anti-Semitism.[22]

While the attention of the British tabloids may have wavered over the course of the trial, they were certainly not alone; the *Jewish Chronicle* itself failed to give the IMT detailed, regular exposure. Having greeted the opening of the trial with great acclaim at the end of November 1945, praising the fact that 'the picture of the Nazi conspiracy and of the misdeeds of the Hitler regime already far exceeds in clarity of description and analysis anything hitherto spoken or written in any language or in any place', the newspaper quickly grew restless with the slow pace of the proceedings.[23] A week later, it was noted how the presentation of the British case had managed to speed things up: 'it is hoped that the increased tempo of the trial, which has departed from the somewhat documentary character it assumed in the initial stages, will now be maintained'.[24] A fortnight on, the *Jewish Chronicle* devoted two pages to the American prosecution case for the persecution of the Jews.[25] However, it is the accompanying editorial which proves notable here. Having cited excerpts from Hans Frank's 1941 diary, submitted as evidence for the prosecution, the *Chronicle* declared:

> When, round about this time, this paper ventured to assert that as many as two million Jews might by then have perished, it was met with humming and hawing and in one case by the pitiful reservation that in our intense anxiety we were probably putting out an exaggeration which was condescendingly described as 'understandable'. The Nuremberg court has now been told by responsible counsel that the actual balance sheet of the massacre was 'on a conservative estimate' not two million, but 5,700,000. Do not the circumstances demand that those papers and publicists who sought to belittle the magnitude of the Nazis' crime during the war should offer a manly retraction and an admission that the Nazi 'monster' was much blacker than it was painted? . . . . In any case, we hope those who are so prone to ease their conscience and favour their own convenience by denouncing as 'Jewish exaggeration' every new report we carry of ill-treatment of Jews will feel the sting of the Nuremberg revelations – even through the pachydermatous envelope of what remains of their conscience.[26]

This opportunity to respond to wartime critics marked the high point of the *Jewish Chronicle*'s interest in the trial. Thereafter, little else was published on the IMT until the proceedings neared their end in autumn 1946. The intervening months witnessed a debate over the translation of Jewish texts, following on from Julius Streicher's defence claim that his actions were based upon a mistranslation of the Talmud, and a note from Peter Calvocoressi that Nuremberg was notable for marking the end of the 'Big Power' coalition between the Allies.[27] Rather than following the IMT avidly, the *Jewish Chronicle* placed an overwhelming – and understandable – emphasis on the need to look towards the future, rather than dwelling on the recent, traumatic past. An article in August 1946, for example, took pleasure in highlighting how a group of young Jews had formed a collective farm on Streicher's old estate in Nuremberg, thus offering a symbolic act of defiance against the defeated regime and enabling a more positive identification to be made with a city so closely associated with National Socialism. For the most part, though, foreign news was dominated by the Palestine question; events in Germany received relatively little attention. Such discussion as there was of the past surrounded the issue of restitution and fears of any fascist or anti-Semitic revival.[28] Nor was the *Jewish Chronicle* alone in this approach; the Association of Jewish Refugees (AJR) also largely ignored the proceedings. Following a front page report in January 1946 that rendered explicit the link between the trial's location, the 1935 Nuremberg Laws and the setting for the former Nazi Party rallies, the case received no further mention until September, when the AJR began to anticipate the verdict.[29] Instead, the emphasis was on the more pressing needs of helping Jewish refugees and tracing the missing.

Rationing, of course, was still very much in effect in Britain and thus affected the availability of newsprint during this period and, by extension, just how much could actually be said about the events in Nuremberg by any publication. In February 1946, as the IMT was still underway in Nuremberg, Stafford Cripps ruled out easing restrictions on newsprint, despite pressure to alleviate growing unemployment within the newspaper industry. Food supplies, he argued, had to take priority. In the end, newsprint rations would not be lifted until March 1956.[30] Given these constraints, newspaper editors obviously had to make careful choices as to the best use of these precious resources. More often than not, the IMT was vying for attention alongside more immediate stories 'back home'. In February 1946, for example, *The Times* relegated the Soviet presentation of the case for crimes against humanity to a small, seven-paragraph article on the edge of page four; the biggest story on this page (some 26 paragraphs) focused on British food shortages.[31]

Each day of the IMT proceedings did, however, continue to receive some note (although never front page headlines) in the leading British broadsheets, and there remained key moments in the case which managed to pique interest and generate a little more coverage, most notably the testimony of Hermann Göring in March.[32] Indeed, Göring proved a particular subject of fascination throughout the IMT. Some of this interest may be accounted for in terms of his responsibility, as Head of the Luftwaffe, for the air raids on Britain, as well as his general high profile within the Third Reich. This was a name that arguably had greater currency for British audiences than figures like Ernst Kaltenbrunner or Arthur Seyss-Inquart. Göring's loss of weight while in Allied custody also generated numerous press reports.[33]

In fact, much of the press attention at the start of the IMT proceedings focused on the physical appearance and demeanour of the accused, especially since, after all the media build-up, the eventual sight of the defendants in the dock proved somewhat disappointing or disconcerting for observers. The *Daily Telegraph* struggled to link the image of 'these little men' to the 'bombastic figures' of the Nazi state, and had to content itself with references to Hans Frank's 'thin sneering mouth and cold eyes'.[34] Similarly, *The Times*, having described the behaviour of Göring, Hess and Frank during the reading of the indictment, commented, 'as for the others, they might almost have been attending some business convention. Dr Schacht has never looked more benign, or the chiefs of the German army and navy more Prussian and stolid'.[35] The London *Evening Standard* also fixated on the 'dark, sinister-looking' Hans Frank, referring to him as a 'butcher' and concluding 'he is the only one who really seems untamed'.[36] In an effort to fill in some of the psychological gaps, several newspapers had, by the end of the trial, resorted to printing pictures of the defendants in uniform during their 'glory days' in the Third Reich.[37] Similar inabilities to reconcile the sight of ageing, 'ordinary-looking' defendants with the crimes under discussion would be increasingly evident in later war crimes proceedings, while efforts to demonise the accused or draw out peculiar physical traits would also quickly become a trope of media reporting on war crimes trials.[38] Both facets of trial coverage indicate a general bewilderment regarding the perpetrators' motivation, as well as a desire to impose a reassuring sense of distance between these 'monsters' and the rest of the human population.

Throughout the IMT, press reports remained very much oriented towards the perpetrators of Nazi crimes, rather than their victims. Even the screening of the documentary film *Nazi Concentration Camps* received little attention at the time; the *Daily Telegraph*, for example, devoted just two short paragraphs to this event before spending the rest of the article discussing Göring's wartime activities.[39] This, however, was in keeping with the nature of the proceedings themselves; these relied heavily on a documentary approach, utilising Nazi sources to make their case rather than survivor testimony, which was regarded as less reliable. Not only did this deny a voice to those who had suffered under the regime, but the endless submission of affidavits and official documents could be seen as imbuing the proceedings with a rather sterile air, prompting many people to lose interest in them. That patience with the IMT was declining by the spring of 1946 was evidenced in a piece penned for the *Daily Telegraph* by the Earl of Birkenhead. Noting that the trial 'can hardly be finished by June, and will probably take longer', the author took issue with those elements of the population who either did not want a trial in the first place, or were feeling increasingly frustrated at its dragging on for so long, stressing that 'ordered systems of justice are essential to freedom, happiness and comfort' and that adopting the alternative suggestion of summary execution would have 'placed ourselves in a hopeless moral position and on the same judicial level as the men we are trying, to the joy of future generations of German propagandists'.[40]

At the same time, it is clear from readers' letters to the newspapers that it was not just the sheer length of the trial that was proving a cause for concern among sections of the British population. A series of letters in *The Times* throughout April and May 1946 discussed the extent to which the defendants were receiving a fair trial, and whether media reporting on the proceedings was prejudicing the case against them.[41] While these epistles centred predominantly on points of procedure, there were correspondents in both *The Times* and the *Manchester Guardian* who revealed a closer reflection on the crimes themselves. One letter-writer bemoaned the silence and 'apparent indifferen[ce]' of his fellow readers to 'the peculiar horrors of Buchenwald and the unparalleled crime of genocide – the deliberately attempted and nearly successful annihilation of an entire race', suggesting that many people still believed it was 'all "just propaganda" '.[42] Another correspondent, meanwhile, revealed a sense of unease over the whole war crimes issue, arguing, 'surely we who agreed to the dropping of these atomic bombs should be the last to condemn brutality and inhumanity in others, or speak of stains on a nation's shame?'[43] Similar arguments, of course, would be frequently advanced by elements of the German population angry at what they saw as 'victors' justice' after 1945.

At the end of the trial in October 1946, two London newspapers took it upon themselves to ask local passers-by for their thoughts on the proceedings. The majority of contributors quickly affirmed their approval of the sentencing, although again there appeared to be a common 'wondering regret that so much time should have been spent on the trial of obviously guilty men'.[44] Claims that the accused should have been executed straightaway were also accompanied by a clear sense of British victimhood. Conjuring up memories of the Blitz, a photographer from Harrow Road declared, 'I am delighted, especially in the case of Göring. His sentence is fair retribution for what he and his Luftwaffe did to London.'[45] Similarly, a 47-year-old kitchen porter insisted: 'I'd hang the lot of them, and it wouldn't have taken me ten months to decide on that. We in England knew they were guilty six years ago' – a dating that coincides with the Battle of Britain.[46] The London *Evening News* also conveyed notions of the suffering experienced on the British Home Front during the war, noting how a tobacconist from Camberwell Green, who regretted the fact the accused had not been 'hanged right away', had lost her husband in a 1940 air raid.[47]

The brief surveys conducted by the local press offer some insights into public attitudes towards the Nuremberg defendants, yet it remains unclear how far these people were simply adopting the quick and easy course of agreeing with the death sentences handed down by the court, and how far their comments were the result of careful engagement with the details of the IMT. Two people questioned were able to elaborate a little further on the trial; one was a businessman from Harrow who commented that the acquittal of three defendants was illustrative of a 'a genuine desire to mete out simple justice'[48]; the other was a Polish warrant officer who had experienced Nazi persecution first-hand before escaping to Britain and serving with the RAF. The latter argued there was a distinction to be made between 'Göring and the rest [who] were just doing their duty' and figures like Josef Kramer who ran Belsen. It can obviously be argued that this man's personal experience of the Third Reich made him far more inclined to follow the details of the trial.[49] It is also questionable, of course, how far the small number of participants in these surveys, and those who had felt compelled to write letters to the press, were representative of wider public opinion at this time. Similarly, the comments reproduced in the press were subject to editing, and may have been governed by the phrasing of questions posed by roving reporters. The question thus remains: what can we determine about popular British responses to Nuremberg war crimes proceedings?

Nuremberg and Mass Observation

In 1937, a social research institution was founded with the aim of uncovering everyday experiences in Britain. Known as Mass Observation, this institution invited non-professional writers to participate in a series of open-ended questionnaires, or directives on a wide variety of issues ranging from topical news stories to leisure activities and dietary habits. Information was also gleaned through opinion surveys and observations of people's conversations and behaviour within various public arenas. In the autumn of 1946, as the IMT was nearing its end, MO began to turn its attention to investigating just what the 'ordinary Briton' was thinking about these proceedings, canvassing around 150 individuals on the streets of London, either as part of a direct interview or through more discreet, indirect conversations in shops or people's places of work.[50]

The results of this survey are summarised in the chart below Figure 2.1. It is clear that the vast majority of those questioned felt that the whole trial had been rather futile. The reasoning behind this ranged from the idea that it was a 'waste of money' to the 'fact' that the defendants had clearly been guilty from the very start – both themes echoing the sentiments expressed within the press. The protracted nature of the IMT was also routinely seized upon. One man summed up the whole proceedings succinctly with the simple comment, 'it's been going on so long you get tired of it. They should be shot.'[51]

However, despite the large proportion of people claiming to have lost interest in the case, it is notable that a significant number still remained sufficiently informed about the proceedings to hazard a guess as to when the verdict would be delivered. MO staff themselves underscored this fact, remarking,

> In March this year, two out of every five people asked said that they were taking no further interest in the trials at all, yet in September, three out of five gave a guess as to the exact day of the announcement of the verdict, and all but two per cent of these were within a week of the right date.[52]

Indeed, 17 people questioned advanced an exact date for the trial's conclusion, the majority of whom opted for 23 September 1946. At least

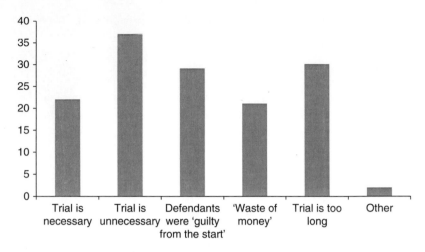

Figure 2.1   Public Responses to the IMT (September 1946)
Source: Mass Observation Archive, University of Sussex, Topic Collections 25/15/E: Nuremberg (September 1946).

two people, though, went further, acknowledging that while this had been the original date set for the verdict, it had now been postponed for another week.[53]

Once the verdict of the IMT was finally announced on 2 October 1946, MO conducted another survey on the streets of London, and again, some of the replies revealed that a certain amount of knowledge about the trial had been acquired among the British population. That three of the accused were acquitted became a particular topic for conversation, with most able to name Schacht and von Papen in the process (Fritzsche, on the other hand, was usually referred to simply as 'the other one'). A 25-year-old man stated:

> I cannot think why they don't hang them all – they're far worse than ordinary murderers... They were all involved in the bestiality and cruelty – some more than others – but by the enormity of their crimes, all deserve to die. Von Papen who looks like a wily old fox was intriguing in all the capitals of Europe. There is just a shadow of doubt in Schacht's case – his interests were entirely financial.[54]

The overwhelming consensus among Londoners was that all of the defendants should have been punished, a result which is perhaps unsurprising, given the earlier, popular insistence that the men in the

Nuremberg dock had 'always' been guilty. Most favoured the use of the death penalty, although a few felt more ingenious or symbolic methods of making them suffer were required.

Throughout these surveys, the cost of the trial was repeatedly emphasised by the people of London, and is perhaps understandable not only given the public's perennial interest in how their taxes are being spent, but also in terms of the need for domestic reconstruction, a factor that would have been particularly apparent within the bomb-damaged capital. In part, these responses may have been rendered more apparent by the very structure of the MO survey. The IMT was not the only area of interest in September 1946, and the initial questions that were put to participants actually concerned the current problem of squatting across the city – a clear reminder of the war's legacy which, when juxtaposed with subsequent questions on the IMT, may have encouraged people to question the government's sense of priorities. A 35-year-old builder, for instance, denounced the trial as 'a waste of public money and good men's time'.[55] Similarly, it was hoped that the end of the IMT would, in turn, bring to an end the whole issue of the Nazi past and enable people to move on with their lives. A 40-year-old man commented, 'I think the sooner they're hanged the better so we can concentrate on the job of reconstruction and world peace. Trials of this sort only sidetrack the issue.'[56]

The sense of hardship, deprivation and loss experienced by the British during the Second World War also continued to hold sway. During a subsequent survey at the start of October 1946, when the results of the IMT had finally been made known, a 60-year-old ticket collector, for example, noted, 'I think how we all suffered during the war: you couldn't go home and get a decent night's sleep and always in fear, weren't you?'[57]

Those who did support the need for a war crimes trial tended to frame their response in terms of the importance that it afforded the reputation of British justice abroad, and saw it as in keeping with the British humanitarian tradition, with one participant commenting, 'the English people always stick up for the rights of a people'.[58] It is, however, unclear just who is being included under this umbrella term 'people'; whether this is indicative of the government's representation of universal suffering under Nazism or whether there is, actually, an awareness of the particular fate of the Jews under the Third Reich. The blurring of victim groups was, however, apparent in the comments of a 40-year-old woman: 'I'd say every one of those men on trial have been responsible for the deaths not only of soldiers, sailors and airmen, but thousands of innocent civilians.'[59]

Others stressed the educational value that the trial posed for future generations – and future warmongers. A 31-year-old man noted, 'the purpose of them surely is to set an example to the German people so that they realise what has been going on all the time'.[60] A 40-year-old man stated:

> It'll tend to make irresponsible gangsters think hard before plunging the world into war. I think this trial will set a precedent because they know they won't be allowed to go unscathed if they do lose the war – it'll serve as a lesson for all.[61]

At the same time, though, there were those who raised concerns as to just where all this might lead in the future:

> They've created a precedent by hanging these war leaders – they've never done it before. Men like Keitel are soldiers first, they just obey orders...It'll lead to the winning country in future wars not just shooting leaders, but shooting the armies as well.[62]

The idea that figures like Keitel were simply following orders was shared by other observers among the British population, with several individuals taking pains to distinguish between 'Jew baiters' and 'war leaders'. While anticipating the verdict in September 1946, for example, one man remarked, 'in my opinion, one can surely only allow the three Service Chiefs to be acquitted'.[63] Once again, this is a sentiment that was in keeping with responses being generated among the West German population, many of whom appeared very reluctant to countenance the involvement of the Armed Forces in the perpetration of Nazi atrocities and clung instead to longstanding rhetoric of the 'honourable soldier'.[64]

In addition to stopping people in the streets or engaging them in casual conversation, MO staff also introduced the IMT into one of their regular directives, asking people to record their thoughts and feelings on the trial for themselves. This, though, came at the end of the hearings in September 1946 and was tacked onto a series of questions relating to spiritualism and newspaper reading habits. Over 200 people responded to this request although even the most cursory glance at the results reveals that it was the former issue, on themes such as fortune telling, telepathy and astrology, which generated the greater interest among participants. Most people produced several pages on these subjects, with the Nuremberg trial, in contrast, appearing as something of an afterthought at the end, often receiving little more than a paragraph. Once again, the primary responses were those that stressed the cost and lengthy nature of the trial, with several writers dismissing the IMT as a 'farce'.[65]

The results gleaned by MO also demonstrate that knowledge about Nazi crimes was circulating among the British population not simply as a result of having heard about or seen the atrocity newsreels on the liberation of the western concentration camps, but also from having friends or relatives returning home from the war. A 56-year-old man, for example, said:

> I have only read bits of it in the newspaper before the trial came to a head so I've got a sort of general idea of it all, mixed up with football results! I don't think they should let any of 'em go free, you know, after what happened in Germany. My son was out there and he saw some terrible things.[66]

For the most part, though, the comments recorded by MO reveal people's primary focus as having rested firmly with the perpetrators, with little mention of the crimes they were actually charged with committing. The Nazi genocide is largely ignored, as is the specific persecution of the Jews. The September 1946 directive did generate a couple of exceptions to this trend, but largely as a means of affording some sort of comparison between Nazi actions and those of the Allies and the media. One person noted, 'I think the Nuremberg trials were conducted fairly as regards the responsibility for mass extermination of the Jews, but some of the "crimes against humanity" of which the people at Nuremberg were accused were committed by all the belligerents during the war'.[67] Another stated, 'by allowing these miserable men to be persistently photographed and exhibited like animals in a zoo . . . we indulge our sadistic tendencies in a way that only differs in degree from the German tortures of the Jews'.[68] One of the most judicious responses in the whole MO investigation also continued to blur the identity of the Nazis' victims, reflecting:

> The cause of the shooting of the 50 airmen should undoubtedly have died, also Frank, also whoever gave the order or caused the order to be given for the burning of women and children in a church in France . . . I agreed with the trial and conviction of the murderers in the concentration camps.[69]

A rare moment of engagement with the Holocaust came in the following statement by a 45-year-old woman which shows how it could sometimes take more than a trial or newsreel footage to shape public opinion. For her, the defining moment was when she made a personal connection to one of the victims:

> First I pitied them Germans because I also have a young boy of 27 who had to fight, but now that I have met a woman with my own eyes who has had her husband, parents and sisters burnt alive in a gas chamber, I have no sympathy left at all. At first I used to think all this stuff in the papers about the Germans used to be for propaganda, but now that I have seen this Czech lady, who was young and good looking, with a great big scar across her face which the Gestapo made, I can't feel sorry for them any longer, I must say. I don't know if it's everyone of them that is guilty, but quite likely.[70]

Indeed, earlier research conducted by MO had already revealed that the revelations emerging with the liberation of the concentration camps in the spring of 1945 did not always serve to foster close, critical engagement with the crimes of the Third Reich among the British population. A 30-year-old woman from Hampstead, for instance, noted on 2 May:

> I'm beginning to get fed up with all these pictures in the papers. I know it's very terrible, and I was as horrified as anyone at the beginning, but honestly, you can't keep *on* feeling emotional about it. I do think they've overdone it. I certainly shan't go and see the film. I don't think it would mean anything to me now. I feel quite hardened. I mean, you keep on looking at pictures of dead bodies heaped on top of each other – well, you just get used to it; just as we've had to get used to the idea of death all through this war.[71]

Conclusion

If the British public were becoming desensitised to the Nazi atrocities while the Second World War was still, officially, raging, it certainly becomes questionable what level of sustained interest they would be able to take in a complex, year long war crimes proceeding. 'Trial fatigue' set in very rapidly, aided, no doubt, by the ultimately frustrated optimism that the charges against the former Nazis would be a relatively open and shut case, and that the trial would be over in three months. While many recognised the moral and educational imperatives bound up in such a prosecution, people struggled to understand just why these figures warranted so much time and expense, particularly when Britain still needed to rebuild itself. However, the failure to fully comprehend the suffering of the Jews under Nazism cannot simply be accounted for in terms of popular disinterest or even apathy about the events in Nuremberg; it is clear that the IMT did generate a range of responses, and some level of reflection about the recent past, albeit one which often focused on points of law or Britain's own war losses. Rather, the very structure of the tribunal itself ensured that the Holocaust was never really at the forefront of the case for the prosecution. The murder of 'civilians' was simply one of a number of indicators of Nazi evil, and it would take another 20 years or so before the enormity of the 'Final Solution' really began to be addressed.

Acknowledgements

I thank the Mass Observation Archive (MOA) for permission to cite source material in this chapter.

Notes

1. Martin Bormann, Head of the Party Chancellery, was tried in absentia. Robert Ley, head of the German Labour Front, committed suicide before the start of the IMT; Gustav Krupp was ruled too ill to stand trial. For details of the indictment against the Nuremberg defendants, see: *The Trial of German Major War Criminals: Proceedings of the International Military Tribunal Sitting at Nuremberg, Germany. Part 1, 20th November, 1945 to 1st December, 1945* (London, 1946).
2. Municipal Museums of Nuremberg, *Memorium: Nuremberg Trials. Initiative to Establish a Memorial in the Nuremberg Palace of Justice* (January 2006), 6.
3. See, for example: George Ginsburgs, *The Nuremberg Trial and International Law* (Dordrecht, 1990); John and Ann Tusa, *The Nuremberg Trial* (London, 1983); Bradley F. Smith, *Reaching Judgement at Nuremberg* (London, 1977); Robert K. Woetzel, *The Nuremberg Trials in International Law* (London, 1962); Robert Wolfe, 'Flaws in the Nuremberg Legacy: An Impediment to International War Crimes Tribunals' Prosecution of Crimes against Humanity', *Holocaust and Genocide Studies*, 12 (3) (1998), 434–453.
4. See, for example: Richard Overy, *Interrogations: Inside the Minds of the Nazi Elite* (London, 2002); Hannah Caven, 'Horror in our Time: Images of the Concentration Camps in the British Media, 1945', *Historical Journal of Film, Radio and Television*, 21 (3) (2001), 205–253; Susan Twist, 'Evidence of Atrocities or Atrocious Use of Evidence: The Controversial Use of Atrocity Film at Nuremberg', *Liverpool Law Review*, 26 (3) (2005), 267–302; Lawrence Douglas, 'Film as Witness: Screening Nazi Concentration Camps before the Nuremberg Tribunal', *The Yale Law Journal*, 105 (2) (1995), 449–481.
5. Michael Marrus, 'The Holocaust at Nuremberg', *Yad Vashem Studies*, 26 (1998), 5–41, 5.
6. See, for instance, Donald Bloxham, *Genocide on Trial: War Crimes Trials and the formation of Holocaust History and Memory* (Oxford, 2001);

Devin O. Pendas, *The Frankfurt Auschwitz Trial, 1963–1965: Genocide, History and the Limits of the Law* (Cambridge, 2006); Lawrence Douglas, *The Memory of Judgement: Making Law and History in the Trials of the Holocaust* (New Haven, 2001); Mark Osiel, *Mass Atrocity, Collective Memory and the Law* (New Brunswick, 1997); Rebecca Wittmann, *Beyond Justice: The Auschwitz Trial* (Cambridge, MA, 2005).

7. Erich Haberer, 'History and Justice: Paradigms of the Prosecution of Nazi Crimes', *Holocaust and Genocide Studies*, 19 (3) (2005), 487–519, 493. See also D. Bloxham, 'The Missing Camps of Aktion Reinhard: The Judicial Displacement of a Mass Murder', in Peter Gray and Kendrick Oliver (eds), *The Memory of Catastrophe* (Manchester, 2004), 118–134, and Donald Bloxham, *Genocide on Trial*, 88–9, 124–126; Tony Kushner, *The Holocaust and the Liberal Imagination: A Social and Cultural History* (Oxford, 1994), 205–342; John Fox, 'The Jewish Factor in British War Crimes Policy in 1942', *English Historical Review*, 92 (362) (1977), 82–106.

8. Kushner, *The Holocaust and the Liberal Imagination*, 226.

9. Donald Bloxham, 'British War Crimes Trial Policy in Germany, 1945–1957: Implementation and Collapse', *Journal of British Studies*, 42 (2003), 91–118.

10. For narratives of German responses to the IMT, see: Wilbourn E. Benton, *Nuremberg: German Views of the War Trials* (Dallas, 1955); Christoph Burchard, 'The Nuremberg Trial and its Impact on Germany', *Journal of International Criminal Justice*, 4 (2006), 800–829.

11. These intentions were rendered explicit in the London Charter of the IMT, 8 August 1945.

12. Bloxham, 'British War Crimes Trial Policy in Germany, 1945–1957', 91–118.

13. *Manchester Guardian*, 'Justice or Revenge?', 13 January 1942.

14. *Daily Telegraph*, 'Retribution or Revenge?', 16 January 1942.

15. Ibid.

16. *Sunday Express*, 'They Must Not Escape', 24 September 1944.

17. Sir Walter Layton, 'How to Deal with Germany 2: Punishing the Criminals', *News Chronicle*, 13 September 1944.

18. See *Manchester Guardian*, 'The First List', 30 August 1945; *Evening Standard*, 'Secret War Crime Witnesses in Nuremberg Gaol', 12 September 1945 and 'Murder Lists Read Out', 20 October, 1945; *Sunday Express*, 'Silent Men of Nuremberg', 7 October 1945.

19. *The Times*, 'The Nuremberg Trial', 20 November 1945.

20. *Daily Telegraph*, 'Trial of 20 Nazi War Chiefs Opens Today', 20 November 1945.

21. *Daily Telegraph*, 'Nuremberg Trial Will Make History', 20 November 1945.

22. *Jewish Chronicle*, 'Playing down Nuremberg Trials?', 21 December 1945, 15.

23. *Jewish Chronicle*, 'The Nuremberg Trial', 30 November 1945, 1.

24. *Jewish Chronicle*, 'The Nuremberg Trial', 7 December 1945, 9.

25. *Jewish Chronicle*, 'The Nuremberg Trial', 21 December 1945, 1, 9.

26. *Jewish Chronicle*, 'Out of their Mouths', 21 December 1945, 10.

27. *Jewish Chronicle*, 'Streicher and the Talmud', 29 March 1946, 10; 'Nuremberg: The End of an Era', 13 September 1946, 11.

28. *Jewish Chronicle*, 'Kibbutz Nili Nuremberg', 16 August 1946, 11.

29. AJR *Information*, 'Nuremberg', 1 (January 1946), 1; 'The Trial of Nuremberg', 9 (September 1946) 65.

30. For discussion on newsprint rationing, see *The Advocate*, 'Hopes British Clothes Rationing will End in Present Lifetime', 20 February 1946; *Sydney Morning Herald*, 'Rationing of Newsprint', 2 June 1954; *Glasgow Herald*, 'Newsprint Rationing Ends in March', 15 August 1955.
31. *The Times*, 'German Crimes in East Europe', 15 February 1946. The article on food shortages ('Minister's Warning on Food Shortage', Cols. A and B) also continued onto p. 8. Earlier articles within this edition of the newspaper similarly focused on food, fuel and housing shortages within Britain, as well as elections in Greece and disturbances in Syria and Argentina.
32. See, for example, *The Times*, 'Göring in the Box'; *Daily Telegraph*, 'Goering Gives Evidence at Nuremberg'; *Evening Standard*, 'Goering: "I Urged all Aid for Franco"', 14 March 1946.
33. See, for example, *The Times*, 'The Nuremberg Trial' and *Manchester Guardian*, 'War Trials Start Today', 20 November 1945.
34. *Daily Telegraph*, 'Nuremberg Trial Opens', 21 November 1945.
35. 'Great Nuremberg War Trial Opens', *The Times*, 21 November 1945.
36. 'Goering and Co Jump Up and Speak', *Evening Standard*, 21 November 1945.
37. *Evening Standard*, 'Goering Was the "Moving Force for War"', 1 October 1946.
38. See, for example, Caroline Sharples, *West Germans and the Nazi Legacy* (New York, 2012). The Belsen Trial had already set the tone for sensational reporting with frequent references to Josef Kramer as the 'Beast of Belsen'. Subsequent trials, particularly from the 1960s, would see a growing emphasis on 'excess perpetrators' who were seen as harbouring a peculiar blood lust. For more on this theme, see Wittmann, *Beyond Auschwitz*.
39. *Daily Telegraph*, 'Secret of Nazis' Austrian Invasion', 30 November 1945.
40. *Daily Telegraph*, 'Nuremberg Trial Is for all Time', 26 March 1946.
41. *The Times*, 'The Nuremberg Trials', 10 April–13 May 1946.
42. *Manchester Guardian*, 'Nuremberg', 28 October 1946.
43. *The Times*, 'Judgement at Nuremberg', 29 October 1946.
44. *News Chronicle*, 'London Is Satisfied. Justice Was Done', 2 October 1946.
45. Ibid.
46. Ibid.
47. *Evening News*, '"We Should Hang 'em All"', 1 October 1946.
48. *News Chronicle*, 'London Is Satisfied. Justice Was Done', 2 October 1946.
49. *Evening News*, '"We Should Hang 'em All"', 1 October 1946.
50. MOA, University of Sussex, Topic Collections 25/15/E: Nuremberg, September 1946.
51. Ibid.
52. MOA, File Report 2424A: Note on Nuremberg, 27 September, 1946.
53. MOA, Topic Collections 25/15/E: Nuremberg, September 1946.
54. MOA, Topic Collections 25/15/E: Nuremberg, October 1946.
55. MOA, Topic Collections 25/15/E: Nuremberg, September 1946.
56. Ibid.
57. MOA, Topic Collections 25/15/E: Nuremberg, October 1946.
58. MOA, Topic Collections 25/15/E: Nuremberg, September 1946.
59. Ibid.
60. Ibid.
61. Ibid.
62. MOA, Topic Collections 25/15/E: Nuremberg, October 1946.

63. MOA, Topic Collections 25/15/E: Nuremberg, September 1946.
64. See Sharples, *West Germans and the Nazi Legacy*, 20–21. There were particular complaints that the convicted members of the Armed Forces were to be hanged like common criminals, rather than given the 'honour' of facing a firing squad. The reluctance to accept the Wehrmacht's involvement in crimes against humanity was further underscored by the controversy surrounding the touring 'Crimes of the Wehrmacht' exhibition in the 1990s – see, for example, Hannes Heer and Jane Caplan, 'The Difficulty of Ending a War: Reactions to the Exhibition "War of Extermination: Crimes of the Wehrmacht 1941 to 1944" ', *History Workshop Journal*, 10 (46) (1998), 187–203.
65. MOA, University of Sussex, 'The Mass Observation Directive Questions, 1939–1951 and 1955', September 1946.
66. Ibid.
67. Ibid.
68. Ibid.
69. Ibid.
70. Ibid.
71. MOA, University of Sussex Topic Collection, 'Political Attitudes and Behaviour, 1938–1956'. TC25/15/C: Atrocity Stories, May 1945. For more on British responses to concentration camp footage, see Caven, 'Horror in our Times', 243–250; and Kushner, *The Holocaust and the Liberal Imagination*, 217–219.

3
Loose Connections? Britain and the 'Final Solution'

Tony Kushner

Howards End, E.M. Forster's classic Edwardian novel, may seem an unlikely starting point for a commentary on post-war Britain and its confrontation with the Holocaust. But as Oliver Stallybrass noted,

> 'Only connect...'... is the epigraph of a novel much concerned with the relationships, and the possibility of reconciliation, between certain pairs of opposites: the prose and the passion, the seen and the unseen, the practical mind and the intellectual, the outer life and the inner.[1]

Is the bond between Britain and the Holocaust threadbare, illusory, insignificant and contrived? Alternatively, is it intricate, subtle and, in its unique way, powerful and important? From the point of view of memory work, including historiography, Britain has been treated as a backwater and as such largely ignored. If she *is* considered, it is largely within precise, though emotionally loaded, historical moments. One disturbing and uncomfortable connection with a deep past is Britain's responsibility as the Mandatory authority in Palestine after the First World War. It relates especially to Britain's increasingly restrictive policy towards the entry of Jews escaping persecution during the Nazi era and, even more controversially, after the Second World War.[2] More positively and recently celebrated is the linkage made through the United Kingdom as a place of exceptional refuge during the 1930s in the form of the *Kindertransport* in which close to 10,000 children were given (temporary) refuge.[3] For the most part, however, overviews of post-war confrontation with the Holocaust simply ignore Britain.[4]

For many years, the reverse was also true – collective memory in Britain associated with the war tended to ignore what is now widely known as the Holocaust. Again, there were exceptions, most notably the liberation by British troops of the Bergen-Belsen concentration camp in April 1945 – even here, the detail that most of its victims were Jewish was ignored or downplayed.[5] More recently, however, as the Holocaust has become recognised as one of the defining events, if not *the* defining event of the twentieth century, greater efforts have been made to connect the British war effort and experience to that of the persecuted Jews on the continent in what is an uneven and ongoing process.

For Mark Connelly, the 'myth of the Second World War... is deeply implanted in the heart and minds of the British people'. It is, as he adds, 'public and shared and has its own conventions.... It is a memory which tends to marginalise moments of misery, fear and loss and value episodes of bravery, resolution and humour.'[6] At its heart is Dunkirk, the Battle of Britain and the Blitz. The Second World War, according to cultural historian Patrick Wright, is for Britain still 'that over-riding moment of national dignity and worth', remaining 'the still living memory of a righteous war that "we" won'.[7] The Blitz especially, Angus Calder highlights, 'supports a myth of British or English moral pre-eminence, buttressed by British unity'.[8]

The work of Wright and Calder is rooted in the 1980s and early 1990s, but their analysis carries the validity of British collective memory of the Second World War into the new millennium. Nevertheless, it will be argued here that Britain's morally untarnished and unproblematic referencing of the war is potentially challenged by the increasing attention given to the Holocaust which, by the end of the twentieth century, became *the* philosophical focal point for discussing issues of morality and modernity – including, of deep significance here, the role of the 'bystander'.[9] Indeed, according to Rainer Baum, Holocaust 'moral indifference' is '*the* form of modern evil'.[10] As a result of such perspectives, crude ethical readings of the Holocaust have now permeated the sphere of pedagogy in Britain. Thus the draft 'National Curriculum in England', produced by the Department for Education in February 2013, includes the Second World War and within it 'Nazi atrocities in occupied Europe and the *unique evil* [my emphasis] of the Holocaust'.[11]

The potential for tension with regard to 'rival' memory work connected to the Second World War – Jewish suffering on the one hand, and 'Britain alone' on the other – is even greater in the light of a growing body of research and popular awareness that the British government did not do all it could have done to help the Jews of Europe in their time of greatest need. One response to such allegations has been to reply to the (sometimes polemical) literature accusing Britain (and America) of inaction, indifference and even antipathy towards the persecuted Jews with equally simplistic accounts that provide exoneration and suggest that nothing could be done to help other than winning the war.[12] Another has been to emphasise what *was* done to help (hence the effort made to eulogise the *Kindertransport*) and, in other ways, to directly link the British war experience with that of European Jewry. Both were present in an initiative sponsored in the last days of the 'New Labour' government when the former prime minister Gordon Brown presented the first 25 awards to Britain's 'Heroes of the Holocaust'.[13]

Amongst them were two living recipients. One was Sir Nicholas Winton, dubbed the 'British Schindler' for his role in helping to bring hundreds of Czech Jewish children to Britain in early 1939 as a discreet part of the *Kindertransport*.[14] The other was Denis Avey, a British POW who, along with up to 1400 others, arrived in the Auschwitz camp complex from Italy 'in autumn 1943 and winter 1944 to form subcamp E715'.[15] Of these, Avey has become the more famous. A year after his 'Heroes of the Holocaust' award, Avey, with the assistance of ghostwriter Rob Broomby, a BBC Radio broadcaster, published *The Man Who Broke into Auschwitz*, a book that has become an 'international bestseller'.[16]

Avey's testimony had already been taken in 2001 by the Imperial War Museum, which a year earlier had opened its permanent Holocaust exhibition and carried out many interviews of survivors and other witnesses to the Nazi persecution of the Jews.[17] It was part of a wider confrontation with the Holocaust in British society from the late twentieth century onwards and manifest, beyond the exhibition, in the form of war crimes legislation (1991), integration into the National Curriculum (also 1991), and the institution and institutionalisation of Holocaust Memorial Day (2000 onwards).[18]

Avey's narrative of his Auschwitz POW experiences was also in the public domain. He was interviewed and featured in Diarmuid Jeffrey's *Hell's Cartel: IG Farben and the Making of Hitler's War Machine* (2008), where the British POW appears on the same pages as the writer, chemist and slave labourer in the Auschwitz 3 (Monowitz) Buna factory, Primo Levi.[19] Avey's account of life in camp E715 was then relatively consistent and it conformed to the narrative of misery and dislocation experienced by his fellow British POWs who had given their testimony at different points in the post-war era. This came first in the post-1945 trials through the Nuremberg Military Tribunals relating to Nazi industrialists in 1947 via affidavits collected in the previous two years.[20] More recently their life stories have appeared in several collective and individual biographies, including Duncan Little's *Allies In Auschwitz* (2009 and 2011) and his contribution to this volume.[21] It is clear that they suffered much at the time – more through the close proximity of mass murder than sustained ill-treatment (Red Cross food parcels ensured that they were relatively well-nourished). Even so, some were subject to physical punishment and one, Corporal Reynolds, was killed for disobeying an order by a German Army officer administering the sub-camp.[22] Moreover, the journeys *after* the departure from Auschwitz as the Germans abandoned the camp and forced the inmates and POWs west were the most traumatising for many of these men.[23] But of equal if not greater significance is the feeling of post-war neglect experienced by the British POWs, even though a sizeable number gave their evidence at Nuremberg. As Joseph White (so far the only academic historian to study their story) notes, little empathy and less interest greeted veterans of E715, because their testimonies were fundamentally at variance with British experience. Eric Doyle (one of the British POWs) expressed their frustration to a Nuremberg investigator: 'Their [the inmates'] condition was... so bad that it is impossible to explain it to people in England.'[24] Interviewing another POW, Arthur Gifford-England, Little was told 'I didn't talk about it for a long time, no one believed that we were at Auschwitz and no one believed what we had seen'.[25]

Following revisionist work on post-war America, David Cesarani has argued for a critique of the idea that with regard to Britain there was a ' "silence" [with regard to the Holocaust] in the first 15 years after the war and that the subject, in any form, was absent from the public sphere'.[26] Whilst acknowledging that many Jewish survivors who came to Britain after the war felt that 'their [particular] experiences were not recognised in the public arena for decades', he concludes that as Nazi atrocities were 'lodged in the popular imagination and featured in public discourse... [w]hether Jews were specifically identified as victims may not have mattered'.[27] It mattered, however, to those such as Kitty Hart who survived Auschwitz and the death marches and was liberated in Salzwedel before coming to Birmingham after the war. Hart wrote in her memoir that in both the Jewish and non-Jewish worlds,

> everybody in England would be talking about personal war experiences for months, even years, after hostilities had ceased. But we, who had been pursued over Europe by a mutual enemy, and come close to extermination at the hands of that enemy, were not supposed to embarrass people by saying a word.

She adds, starkly, that 'People didn't understand. In some ways the suffering I endured in the early post-war years was worse than in the KZ. Personally, I certainly found that time more traumatic.'[28]

What unites the collective and individual accounts of the British POWs of E715 is the lack of space to tell and reflect on their war experiences in Auschwitz when they returned to domestic lives. Indeed, the work that has been produced recently on them explicitly attempts to correct that earlier vacuum of interest and empathy. There are clearly similar processes at work with regard to the 'puzzle' of why there was a 'demonstrable reluctance' to hear the stories of the Jewish survivors of the Holocaust.[29] Gena Turgel, who had also survived Auschwitz, then the death marches and finally Belsen, provides a clue to solving this 'puzzle'. In her memoir, she notes that when she came to Britain 'people seemed very preoccupied with themselves. Some said: "We also had a hard time. We were bombed and had to live in shelters. We had to sleep in the Underground." ' She concludes that 'These people lived in a different world.'[30] Rather than provide shared empathy, the parallel narratives of suffering in Blitz and Holocaust created at best distance and at worst irritation to those that had experienced the dangers and discomfort of the Home Front.

What the post-war isolation of the POWs of E715 highlights is the need for a more nuanced approach to the reception of Holocaust survivors in Britain, which needs to be placed in a wider, more comparative context. As Little notes, POWs in general struggled to find a place when returning home, fitting into the heroic narrative of neither Blitz nor battle. Those that had endured the co-presence of the 'Final Solution' experienced a double marginality in terms of collective war memory – their stories simply did not fit and, as with the majority of Holocaust survivors, there was no attempt to deal with the trauma they had experienced, albeit in this case as intimate witnesses rather than as direct victims. In this respect, they faced some of the same problems as those British soldiers (and later doctors and nurses) who had liberated Belsen in April 1945, but with the additional burden of being perceived as 'only' POWs.[31]

Such feelings of marginality perhaps partly explain the distortion that has occurred in the testimony and representation of two E715 POWs relating to the help they gave to Jewish victims of Auschwitz. The cases are interrelated in that the second relies very heavily on the romance of the published life story of the first. The result is that they produce remarkably similar narratives, albeit constructed more than half a century apart. Inevitably, however, the *context* of these falsifications – given the 57-year gap – is markedly different and reveals much about changes in Holocaust consciousness in post-war Britain.

The Password Is Courage was first published in 1954 and has been republished regularly since, most recently in 2011. It is the ghostwritten account of Sergeant Major Charles Coward, the self-styled 'Count of Auschwitz'.[32] Coward is presented as saving hundreds of Jews whom he helped escape. In addition, in what might be described as a melding of Woody Allen's Zelig with Steven Spielberg's Oskar Schindler with the British POW omnipresent in all forms of Holocaust resistance and rescue, Coward helps plot the *Sonderkommando* uprising in October 1944, alerts the Allies to the 'Final Solution' and, most remarkably, exchanges places with a Jewish inmate of Monowitz so that he could search for a British POW.[33] None of these claims stands up to scrutiny and they have no supporting evidence. Yet in 1962 Coward was the first British person to be awarded the title of 'Righteous Among the Nations' by Yad Vashem in Jerusalem, without, as White suggests, any 'extensive corroboration'. There is a strong possibility, as White argues, that international politics after the Eichmann Trial and Coward's relationship with Shimon Peres' father played a decisive role in this decision.[34]

It is undoubtedly the case that Coward was appalled by the treatment of the Jews at Auschwitz and in his small way, as with the other British POWs of E715, did his best to help through acts of everyday kindness such as giving food, clothing and cigarettes from Red Cross parcels to those they labelled (somewhat ambiguously) as 'stripees'.[35] Leon Greenman, who was born in the East End of London but stranded in Holland at the outbreak of war and unable at the decisive moment to be able to prove his British nationality, was transferred from Birkenau to Monowitz and experienced the POWs on a daily basis. He is not sentimental about his co-nationals. Trying to mix with the 'Tommies' as much as he could, he found that 'Some of the soldiers were kind, others just indifferent.'[36] Coward was in the former category and went further than most to show empathy and practical support. But his alleged grander gestures to save the Jews of Auschwitz were simply fantasy and reflect the 'boy's own' tone of the rest of *The Password Is Courage* and its tales, before transfer to E715, of constant and audacious escape. But the Coward myth extended further in the public sphere. In 1960 he was honoured by a *This Is Your Life* episode which focused heavily on his Jewish rescue activities in Auschwitz, providing a background to the Yad Vashem award.[37] A film version of *The Password Is Courage*, with Dirk Bogarde as Coward, was released by Metro-Goldwyn-Mayer (MGM) two years later.[38]

But it is within the marketing history of *The Password Is Courage* that the changing focus of collective memory can be located. Initially, as a cheap paperback published by Souvenir Press and then Corgi, the emphasis was on the Coward narrative as a POW escape account. It was in the mould represented later most famously by Steve McQueen in *The Great Escape* (1963) but already firmly established by *The Wooden Horse* (1950). The film version of *The Password Is Courage* was presented *solely* as a POW escape narrative and the story ends in 1943, before the transfer to Auschwitz.[39]

Further placing the memoir in a particular genre, it was endorsed by military figures such as Lt. Col. F. Spencer Chapman, who extolled it with the words 'Of all the escapes I have read of the last war, this is the most outstanding.'[40] As late as 1975, it still contained a quote from one of the original reviews stating that *The Password Is Courage* was 'an epic among escape stories'.[41] Only with a new edition in 2001 was the focus changed with the back cover given the title 'The Man Who Broke *into* Auschwitz'. The description emphasised Coward's role in helping Jews to escape and in organising resistance. 'Finally', it added, Coward 'smuggled himself *into* the Auschwitz compound and mingled with its doomed inmates – until he was forced to flee from certain execution himself'.[42] Here, at the turn of the millennium, we can clearly detect a shift from a classic war narrative of POW escape, as portrayed in Anglo-American filmic versions throughout and beyond the 1950s (and reaching perhaps its most absurd level with *Escape to Victory* (1981), starring Pele, Bobby Moore, Mike Summerbee and other footballers alongside Sylvester Stallone), to a Holocaust narrative and the attempt to share victimhood with the Jewish prisoners of Auschwitz.[43]

It is this later Auschwitz-centred model that Coward's fellow E715 POW, Denis Avey, exploited from the late 2000s. Rather than be one amongst many of these former British soldiers in the Auschwitz complex, Avey, in his ghosted memoir, *The Man Who Broke into Auschwitz*, borrowed both the story and the later nomenclature of Coward's account. Published in 2011 by the mainstream Hodder & Stoughton (contrasting to the small local publishers who were responsible for the earlier collective accounts of these men), it carried an enthusiastic foreword from Sir Martin Gilbert who commented that 'The honesty of this book heightens its impact.'[44] Avey replicates almost exactly Coward's story of swapping places with a Jewish inmate.[45]

There are Holocaust memoirs that are completely fabricated, most famously Binjamin Wilkomirski (or as he was, Bruce GrosJean and then Bruno Dosseker) and his *Fragments* (1996).[46] More common, however, are deliberate distortions to provide the right kind of redemptive ending.[47] Avey's memoir, whilst that of a witness rather than a victim of the Holocaust, is unique in that it is built upon two earlier distortions – that by Coward, as noted, but also the false Holocaust memoir *Stoker* (1995) by Donald Watt, as revealed by journalist Guy Walters.[48]

What then were the motives of Denis Avey? One explanation is basic finance and a way of selling more copies of the book, or as one commentator posted, 'Sounds like someone's a bit short of a few bob in his old age.'[49] Yet whilst this dishonourable motive cannot be fully discounted, I would suggest it is not fully convincing and it is more revealing to explore the underpinning ideological and cultural reasons behind the fictional aspects of his memoir. Using a heroic model, and before *The Man Who Broke into Auschwitz* was published, White has argued that the positive response of the British POWs to the Jews in their midst reflected the near impossibility of escape (many of these men had previous records in this respect) and thus an even greater desire to 'help Hitler's ideological "enemies", the concentration-camp inmates' to do their 'bit' for the war effort.[50] If this model is extended, first Coward and then Avey aggrandised their role out of a frustration that they could do no more. But one can go further, and suggest that with Avey and the last edition of Coward's book, the increasing awareness of the horrors of the Holocaust creates a narrative challenge to more traditional British readings of the conflict. It is no longer enough to present it purely as a military battle, albeit one where 'good' fought against 'evil'. As a result, there has been an impulse (and demand) to move from the presentation of the POWs in E715 from *witnesses* to *fellow sufferers* in Auschwitz.

Sensitivity towards the Holocaust has enabled an understanding, if not quite complete, that it happened to millions of individuals, not just to a mass of faceless victims. In the recent collective and individual accounts of the British POWs, including that of Denis Avey, there is an emphasis on individual Jews in Auschwitz and the help that was given to them – *The Man Who Broke into Auschwitz* focuses on Hans, a Dutch Jew, and Ernst Lobethal, a German Jew.[51] Whilst this personalisation was also present in *The Password Is Courage*, a significant shift in representation and focus has occurred.

Coward, as White suggests, in the post-war period was 'eager to tell what he thought the audience wanted to hear'.[52] In this respect, Coward's 1954 memoir, alongside tales of his heroic escape, contained detailed and harrowing descriptions of violence and an element of sexual titillation relating to the Auschwitz complex. It followed a similar pattern, therefore, to Lord Russell of Liverpool's *The Scourge of the Swastika* published the same year. Subtitled *A Short History of Nazi War Crimes*, Russell's bestselling book was illustrated with graphic photographs and was intended by the author 'to provide the ordinary reader with a truthful and accurate account of... German war crimes' distilled from the post-war prosecutions at Nuremberg and elsewhere.[53] At times the book comes close to a pornography of violence, especially in its illustrations of naked victims, including most gratuitously a photograph of naked women being forced to run during an inspection at an unnamed concentration camp.[54] As with the post-war film footage and other imagery associated with the newly liberated concentration camps, *The Scourge of the Swastika* framed what would later be known as the Holocaust through the prism of atrocity. As Caroline Sharples' contribution to this volume illustrates, the press and public responses (as represented by Mass Observation [MO]) to the Nuremberg Trials focused on the criminality and the responsibility of those charged. There was only rarely a deeper engagement with the *impact* of their crimes against humanity and especially the fate of the major victims, the Jews. The trials failed to gain sustained interest and as Sharples notes, one major reason for this was the domination of a domestic narrative over the events on the continent beyond the more conventional war: 'The sense of hardship, deprivation and loss experienced by the British during the Second World War... continued to hold sway.' As a result, the 'Nazi genocide [was] largely ignored, as [was] the specific persecution of the Jews'.[55]

Holocaust scholars Donald Bloxham and Michael Marrus differ over the impact of the Nuremberg Trials on the understanding they generated of the Holocaust and how central it was to the prosecutions.[56] Bloxham's extensive research shows how the desire to show intent, the shortcomings of documentation and the American desire to avoid the witness testimony of victims warped scholarship for several decades. He also makes a strong case that the Holocaust was not the major focus of the trials taken as a whole. But the Nuremberg Trials were still, as Marrus highlights, part of a slow process of growing awareness of a specific genocidal crime, including the widespread dissemination of the figure of six million Jewish victims.[57]

Indeed, another MO directive in summer 1946 on attitudes to Jews, whilst revealing a profound and disquieting level of anti-Semitism, perversely illustrated a crude understanding of the 'Final Solution'. Two extreme, but not isolated responses, illustrate the point shockingly: 'The only thing I disapproved of with regard to the Hitler's Gas Chamber was that there was not enough' and 'I am inclined to agree with Hitler that the best solution of the Jewish problem, for the Gentiles, that is, would be to gas the lot.'[58] Such comments were prompted, however, by the domestic impact of events in Palestine and were not evident in the survey work carried out by MO on the response to the Nuremberg Trials. And with regard to the specific experiences of the Jews, it is significant in the light of this study as a whole that the immediate post-war trials (and early Holocaust historiography which owed much to the material generated by them) largely avoided the testimony of the Jewish survivors, especially those from Eastern Europe. Instead – as with those from E715 and the smaller number who were concentration camp inmates – it was those who were British nationals who were given prominence in the Belsen Trials, Nuremberg Trials and beyond.[59]

To bring this overview together, it is helpful to engage with a phrase – 'the domestication of violence' – employed by Dan Stone to understand how the collective memory of the Holocaust was forged in immediate post-war Britain. The horror, he argues, was 'domesticated ... in order to make its narration bearable'.[60] This approach of seeking out the mechanisms of 'cognitive control' has been developed and nuanced by Aimée Bunting, who highlights how

> Then and now, British people have always drawn the Holocaust within the reassuring parameters of their own national narrative, creating an active link between themselves and the destruction process, and exposing the diverse and complicated nature of British identity.[61]

Stone's model, in the light of Bunting's intervention, needs modification, especially in relation to British engagement during the Second World War – that is the period preceding his study. Activists such as Victor Gollancz and Eleanor Rathbone, both of whom campaigned intensively on behalf of the persecuted Jews, did indeed domesticate the Holocaust, but in the process they did *not* attempt to make its narrative more palatable. Gollancz especially, in his remarkable pamphlet *Let My People Go* (written on Christmas Day, 1942, and published a week later) did not spare his readers from the horrors that were taking place:

> The murders have taken the form of random shootings, mass shootings, mass electrocutions [sic], mass poison-gassing, and transportation in conditions which inevitably involve death during the journey. This is over and above slow starvation by the allotment of hopelessly inadequate rations, or no rations at all.

He warned his readers not to assume any discrimination had been made in favour (in fact the reverse) of 'pregnant women, babies, the sick or the very old'.[62]

Gollancz then called upon the public not to 'pass by on the other side', invoking local patriotism: 'I cannot believe that you will, because that would be contrary to the very essence of the British character'. If that was not enough, Gollancz then attempted to bring the Holocaust literally home:

> If you saw a child playing in your own street, and knew that, unless you took some action within your power, it would be sent to a torturing death before the day was out, would you fail to act? No: then will you fail to act *now*? Does a little child in Warsaw suffer less and God forgive us, *fear* less than a child in London, or Leeds, or whatever your town or village may be? [63]

Demanding a degree of empathy that he himself employed, having been told about the details of the 'Final Solution' by Polish courier Jan Karski, Gollancz asked that just for a few moments his reader '*be* just one of those human beings' rather than the cold abstraction of 'six million', and

> then be another, and another. Be the mother flinging her baby from a sixth-story window: be a girl of nine, torn from her parents and standing in the dark of a moving truck with two corpses pressed close against her: be an old Jew at the door of the electrocution chamber.[64]

His pleas did not fall on deaf ears. A quarter of a million copies of his pamphlet were circulated and tens of thousands of ordinary people, including those in the armed forces, sent letters to their Members of Parliament (MPs) and signed petitions to the Foreign Office demanding action from the British government.[65] And there were those that went beyond such actions and fulfilled the obligation of close identification required by Gollancz: 'I cannot write what I feel about all this evil. My soul cries out in distress. I am a Jew, a Pole, a Greek. I am all women who are tortured, all children who are hurt, all men who die in agony', wrote one Mass Observer in her war diary.[66]

This then was a contemporary and passionate British relationship with the Holocaust – albeit one, as Eleanor Rathbone bitterly noted after what she saw as the wasted opportunity of the Anglo-American Bermuda conference on refugees in spring 1943, that was encouraged from above. She asked

> whether Ministers who show impatience with their critics and who assure us that everything possible is being done, would feel quite so certain about that if their own wives, children or parents were among these people; were in imminent danger not merely of death, but of such agony of fear and pain that death is longed for as a merciful release.[67]

There is a curious irony that in the belated attempt to connect Britain to help given to the Jews of Europe through 'Heroes of the Holocaust' and other memory work, Gollancz, Rathbone and others, such as James Parkes, who campaigned throughout the Nazi era, have been neglected and forgotten. A more direct route, it seems, is needed to the Holocaust, insisting upon co-presence as witnesses to the destruction process and more – help given in the places of destruction themselves. Announcing the 'Heroes of the Holocaust' scheme in 2009, which as with the Yad Vashem 'Righteous Gentile' awards, requires the risking of one's own life in saving Jewish lives, Prime Minister Gordon Brown stated that he was determined to give 'proper recognition for those who made extraordinary contributions to protect others during the Holocaust. Their brave actions form a critical part of our nation's wartime history.'[68]

In relation to the POWs of E715 – those closest to the 'Final Solution' – none of them actually risked their lives to help the Jewish inmates of Monowitz. Their contribution was more mundane but nevertheless important. It is also important not to romanticise the group as a whole – not all the British in Auschwitz were sympathetic. Leon Greenman, looking for moral support from a British POW, followed him into a latrine only to be given a diatribe against the Jews of Britain and their alleged unpatriotic black market activities (particularly stinging to the Jewish inmate as his two brothers were serving in the British army). As a result, 'I felt lonelier than ever. One of my own had talked like the Nazis.'[69] In *Survival in Auschwitz*, Primo Levi was also unsentimental about the British POWs he encountered in Buna. They feature in relation to Henri, a man whose survival Levi puts down to his clinical and cold approach and to whom the great chronicler of Auschwitz has no empathy. Emotionless, Henri 'seduces' the English POWs for food and cigarettes: 'his instrument of penetration, with the English and others, is pity'.[70] These POWs appear only at one other point in Levi's classic testimony. In what turned out to be his last winter in Auschwitz, he refers to the cold and snow. Levi is in his summer outfit, the 'Germans and Poles go to work in rubber jack-boots, woollen ear-pads and padded overalls; the English have their wonderful fur-lined jackets'.[71] In short, the British occupy a different world even if located in Auschwitz.

To conclude, we expect far too much of the POWs of E715 if they are presented as 'extend[ing] a lifeline to the drowning' and as the last sign of 'humanity'.[72] They were powerless to stop the destruction process and, for some, their inability to do so has haunted them thereafter. Yet equally their experiences during the war must not be dismissed as inconsequential just because they were not 'Britain's Schindlers'. This is also true of the many thousands of others who were witnesses to mass murder, including the Mass Observer's son, cited by Caroline Sharples, who 'was out there and ... saw some terrible things'.[73]

In Britain there was contemporary engagement with the Holocaust in the everyday world. There were also the direct connections as with the POWs at Auschwitz and those that liberated Belsen – these were real places which, by accident, were seen by ordinary British people. As Little rightly notes in relation to camp E715, it 'offers a compelling example of why the Holocaust can be considered very much a part of Britain's own national story'.[74] And finally to return to the question posed at the beginning of this overview: 'Only connect...'? For too long linkages to the Holocaust have been forgotten or marginalised as a narrow collective memory of 'Britain alone' prevailed. But in rediscovering the multilayered and complex relationship between the British and persecuted Jewry, balance is required and, as with the narratives of Charles Coward and Denis Avey, there is a need now in the twenty-first century to avoid the fiction that these POWs too were victims of the Holocaust or, alternatively, its heroes. As Primo Levi noted, the British were the ones wearing the winter coats and eating the Red Cross food, ensuring their survival. Analysis of Britain's relationship with the Holocaust has to have, as its starting point, a humility that accepts that gulf in experience.

Notes

1. Oliver Stallybrass, 'Editor's Introduction', in E.M. Forster (ed.), *Howards End* (Harmondsworth, 1980 [1910]), 10.
2. Louise London, *Whitehall and the Jews 1933–1948: British Immigration Policy and the Holocaust* (Cambridge, 2000); Ruth Gruber, *Destination Palestine: The Story of the Haganah Ship Exodus 1947* (New York, 1948) for a contemporary account that reveals the tension over war memory between the Jewish world and Britain.

3. See Tony Kushner, *Remembering Refugees: Then and Now* (Manchester, 2006), chapter 4; and *The Battle of Britishness: Migrant Journeys, 1685 to the Present* (Manchester, 2012), chapter 6.

4. Judith Miller, *One, By One, By One: Facing the Holocaust* (New York, 1990) is an important intervention which confronts post-war memory work in a variety of countries but does not mention Britain.

5. See Joanne Reilly, David Cesarani, Tony Kushner and Colin Richmond (eds), *Belsen in History and Memory* (London, 1997); David Cesarani and Suzanne Bardgett (eds), *Belsen 1945: New Historical Perspectives* (London, 2006).

6. Mark Connelly, *We Can Take It! Britain and the Memory of the Second World War* (London, 2004), 1, 3, 5.

7. Patrick Wright, *On Living in an Old Country: The National Past in Contemporary Britain* (London, 1985), 25, 245.

8. Angus Calder, *The Myth of the Blitz* (London, 1991), 2.

9. Norman Geras, *The Contract of Mutual Indifference: Political Philosophy after the Holocaust* (London, 1998); Jonathan Glover, *Humanity: A Moral History of the Twentieth Century* (London, 1999); David Blumenthal, *The Banality of Good and Evil: Moral Lessons from the Shoah and the Jewish Tradition* (Washington, DC, 1999).

10. Rainer Baum, 'Holocaust: Moral Indifference as the Form of Modern Evil', in Alan Rosenberg and Gerald Myers (eds), *Echoes from the Holocaust: Philosophical Reflections on a Dark Time* (Philadelphia, 1988), 53–79.

11. Department of Education, *The National Curriculum in England: Framework Document for Consultation* (London, 2013), 171.

12. For polemics and counter-polemics, see William Rubinstein, *The Myth of Rescue: Why the Democracies Could Not Have Saved More Jews from the Nazis* (London, 1997); Theodore Hamerow, *Why We Watched: Europe, America and the Holocaust* (New York, 2008). For an overview of the shape of such debates, see Tony Kushner, 'Britain, America and the Holocaust: Past, Present and Future Historiographies', *Holocaust Studies*, 18 (2–3) (Summer/Autumn 2012), 35–48.

13. See *The Times*, 10 March 2010; *The Guardian*, 10 March 2010. For the origins of the scheme, see Simon Rocker, 'New award for Britain's Shoah Heroes', *Jewish Chronicle*, 1 May 2009.

14. Robin Rosen, 'British Schindlers on Brown's List', *Jewish Chronicle*, 12 March 2010. For a more balanced account of Winton's activities in Prague and London which emphasises that he was part of a larger team, see William R. Chadwick, *The Rescue of the Prague Refugees 1938/39* (Leicester, 2010), especially chapter 2.

15. Joseph White, ' "Even in Auschwitz…Humanity Could Prevail": British POWs and Jewish Concentration-Camp Inmates at IG Auschwitz, 1943–1945', *Holocaust and Genocide Studies*, 15 (2) (2001), 270. There are lower estimates with no consensus yet emerging of the number of British POWs in Auschwitz. A figure of 1,200 is given by Robert Jan Van Pelt and Deborah Dwork, *Auschwitz 1270 to the Present* (New Haven, 1996), 233. The first arrivals were housed in E711 before being transferred a few weeks later in 1943 to E715. See Colin Rushton, *Spectator in Hell: A British Soldier's Story of Imprisonment in Auschwitz* (Chichester, 2007 [1997]), 53–58.

16. Taken from the cover of Denis Avey with Rob Broomby, *The Man Who Broke into Auschwitz* (London, 2011).
17. Imperial War Museum oral history interview, 16 July 2001, Catalogue no. 22065. More generally for the Imperial War Museum's pioneer role in carrying out Holocaust-related interviews, see Tony Kushner, 'Oral History at the Extremes of Human Experience: Holocaust Testimony in a Museum Setting', *Oral History*, 29 (2) (2001), 83–94.
18. Andy Pearce, 'The Development of Holocaust Consciousness in Contemporary Britain, 1979–2001', *Holocaust Studies*, 14 (2) (2008), 71–94.
19. Diarmuid Jeffreys, *Hell's Cartel: IG Farben and the Making of Hitler's War Machine* (London, 2008), 233–235, 287–289 and esp. 287.
20. See White, ' "Even in Auschwitz...Humanity Could Prevail" ', which uses these affidavits extensively.
21. Rushton, *Spectator in Hell*, which focuses on the story of Arthur Dodd but also gives brief accounts of other British POWs in Auschwitz; Duncan Little, *Allies in Auschwitz: The Untold Story of British POWS held captive in the Nazis' Most Infamous Death Camp* (Forest Row, 2011 [2009]) which focuses on three men: Doug Bond, Arthur Gifford-England and Brian Bishop.
22. Little, *Allies in Auschwitz*, 33–34.
23. Little, chapter 4. Even then, their experiences cannot be compared to the Jewish and other former inmates of Auschwitz and the appalling mortality rate of the 'death marches'.
24. White, ' "Even in Auschwitz...Humanity Could Prevail" ', 285.
25. Little, *Allies in Auschwitz*, 67.
26. David Cesarani, 'How Post-war Britain Reflected on the Nazi Persecution and Mass Murder of Europe's Jews: A Reassessment of Early Responses', in Tony Kushner and Hannah Ewence (eds), *Whatever Happened to British Jewish Studies?* (London, 2012), 99–135, here 101. Cesarani builds on Lawrence Baron, 'The Holocaust and American Public Memory, 1945–1960', *Holocaust and Genocide Studies*, 17 (1) (2003), 62–88 and Hasia Diner, *We Remember with Reverence and Love: American Jews and the Myth of Silence after the Holocaust, 1945–1962* (New York, 2009).
27. Cesarani, 'How Post-war Britain', 126–127.
28. Kitty Hart, *Return to Auschwitz* (New York, 1985), 11–12.
29. Cesarani, 'How Post-war Britain', 128.
30. Gena Turgel, *I Light a Candle* (London, 1988), 177.
31. Joanne Reilly, *Belsen: The Liberation of a Concentration Camp* (London, 1998).
32. John Castle, *The Password Is Courage* (London, 1954), 203.
33. Ibid., chapters 14–21.
34. White, ' "Even in Auschwitz...Humanity Could Prevail" ', 281.
35. See Little, *Allies in Auschwitz*; Rushton, *Spectator in Hell*, *passim* for such everyday acts of solidarity and support.
36. Leon Greenman, *An Englishman in Auschwitz* (London, 2001), 75.
37. It was broadcast on BBC television, 24 October 1960. See *Jewish Chronicle*, 28 October 1960 and *AJR Information*, 15 (12) (December 1960), 3 as well as James Jordan's contribution to this volume.
38. *The Password Is Courage* (MGM, 1962).

39. In the version of *The Password Is Courage* shown in cinemas, the story ends in 1943 and 'A potentially difficult portrayal of the events at Auschwitz was replaced by voice-over information at the end of the film', using drawings. See Wollheim Memorial through (www.wollheim_memorial.de/en/die_geschichte_des_romans_the_password_is_courage_von_john_castle; accessed 20 March 2013). The television version of *The Password Is Courage* removes this section.

40. John Castle, *The Password Is Courage* (London, 1962 [Corgi reprint]).

41. Corgi 1975 edition, inside cover from the *Yorkshire Evening Press*.

42. Souvenir Press edition, 2001 and reprinted in 2011.

43. To be fair to *Escape to Victory*, there is reference to the suffering of Slavs when the English players demand that they should be allowed to recruit Polish footballers so as to save them from starvation and persecution. A turning point in representation is perhaps found in the award-winning animation by Aardman Animations' *Chicken Run* (2000), which parodies such POW escape films but, presumably out of good taste, does not provide a parallel with the concentration camps even though the chickens are escaping from mechanised and systematic slaughter.

44. Martin Gilbert, 'Preface', in Avey, *The Man Who Broke into Auschwitz*, vi.

45. Gilbert, chapters 12 and 13.

46. Binjamin Wilkomirski, *Fragments* (Basingstoke, 1996). See Blake Eskin, *A Life in Pieces* (London, 2002) and Elena Lappin, 'The Man With Two Heads', *Granta*, 66 (Summer, 1999), 9–65 for the background to this remarkable story.

47. See Tony Kushner, 'Holocaust Testimony, Ethics and the Problem of Representation', *Poetics Today*, 27 (2) (2006), 275–296.

48. Guy Walters, 'Did this British POW Really Smuggle Himself into Auschwitz to Expose the Holocaust ... or Is His Account Pure Fantasy and an Insult to Millions Who Died There?', *Daily Mail*, 9 April 2011; 'The Curious Case of the "Break into Auschwitz"', Guy Walters blog in *New Statesman*, 17 November 2011 (http://www.newstatesman.com/print/blogs/guy-walters/2011/11/avey-book-holocaust; accessed 12 March 2013). Sue Vice is working on a project exploring not only false Holocaust testimony but others from traumatic moments of history. Its preliminary work is summarised in her 'False Testimony', in Richard Crownshaw, Jane Kilby and Antony Rowland (eds), *The Future of Memory* (Oxford, 2010), 157–66.

49. 'Alan', 9 April 2011 (http://www.dailymail.co.uk/news/article-1375018/Denis-Avey-broke-Auschwitz-expo...; accessed 4 March 2013).

50. White, ' "Even in Auschwitz ... Humanity Could Prevail" ', 267.

51. Rushton, *Spectator in Hell*; Little, *Allies in Auschwitz*; Avey, *The Man Who Broke into Auschwitz*, 3–4, 125–126.

52. Avey, *The Man Who Broke into Auschwitz*, 281.

53. Lord Russell of Liverpool, *The Scourge of the Swastika* (London, 1954), viii.

54. Russell, facing 213. I have been informed that the book was sold in the 'back room' of bookshops selling pornography.

55. Caroline Sharples, contribution to this volume.

56. Donald Bloxham, *Genocide on Trial: War Crimes Trials and the Formation of Holocaust History and Memory* (Oxford, 2001); Michael Marrus, 'The Holocaust at Nuremberg', *Yad Vashem Studies*, 26 (1998), 5–41.

57. Marrus, 'The Holocaust at Nuremberg', 18.

58. University of Sussex, Mass-Observation Archive, Directive on Jews, July 1946, DR Jam 11 and Pin 1 and similarly Cle 2.
59. Bloxham, *Genocide on Trial*, 99 on the Belsen Trial and the prominence of 'British' evidence.
60. Dan Stone, 'The Domestication of Violence: Forging a Collective Memory of the Holocaust in Britain, 1945–1946', *Patterns of Prejudice*, 33 (2) (1999), 13–29, here 13.
61. Aimée Bunting, 'Britain and the Holocaust: Then and Now' (Unpublished PhD thesis, University of Southampton, 2006), abstract and conclusion.
62. Victor Gollancz, *Let My People Go* (London, 1943), 1.
63. Ibid., 8.
64. Ibid., 9. See also Ruth Dudley Edwards, *Victor Gollancz: A Biography* (London, 1987), 375.
65. For a summary of public agitation, see Eleanor Rathbone, *Rescue the Perishing* (London, 1943).
66. Mass-Observation Archive: D5460, 24 October 1944.
67. Rathbone, *Rescue the Perishing*, 17.
68. Brown quoted by Rocker, 'New award'.
69. Greenman, *An Englishman*, 81–82.
70. Primo Levi, *Survival in Auschwitz* (New York, 1961), 90–91.
71. Ibid., 123.
72. White, ' "Even in Auschwitz...Humanity Could Prevail" ', 266, 267.
73. Caroline Sharples, contribution to this volume.
74. Duncan Little, contribution to this volume.

Part II
The Holocaust on Screen

4

'Marvellous Raisins in a Badly-Cooked Cake': British Reactions to the Screening of *Holocaust*

Tim Cole

This most British of analogies, 'marvellous raisins in a badly-cooked cake', came at the end of a mixed review of *Holocaust* by *The Listener's* TV critic Joseph Hone when the four-part miniseries was screened on BBC1 in September 1978.[1] First shown on American television in April 1978, *Holocaust* told the story of the fictional German-Jewish Weiss family alongside that of an unemployed lawyer, Erik Dorf, who embarks on a career within the SS. The members of the Weiss and Dorf families are followed through a variety of Holocaust landscapes and the duration of the Nazi regime, with the story of the European-wide murder of Jews told through the Weiss family members' varied experiences. Such a telling was, Hone concluded, not entirely successful. He was far from alone in criticising *Holocaust*, even if the analogy he drew was somewhat eccentric. Indeed, his criticisms were relatively restrained compared to those of two colleagues at *The Listener*. The week before, David Wheeler had dubbed *Holocaust* 'history for idiots'.[2] The week after, it was dismissed by Jack Duncan as 'the daftest show I have ever seen on television'.[3]

In featuring *Holocaust* in three successive issues, *The Listener* was broadly representative of the press coverage generated by the premiere of this miniseries on British television. In early September 1978, the screening of *Holocaust* was a media event, although one that was relatively short-lived. *Holocaust* was reviewed multiple times within the same publication and coverage extended beyond the TV pages to appearances as news story, opinion piece and the focus of readers' letters. However, the reaction in the British press was less voluminous than in either the United States or West Germany. The extent and intensity of media debate generated by *Holocaust* in the United States can be seen in the coverage afforded in the *New York Times*. Over 20 articles appeared in this single publication when the miniseries was first screened on NBC in April 1978, alongside tens of letters to the editor.[4] No single British publication had anything approaching that level of coverage. In West Germany, the premiere of *Holocaust* in January 1979 resulted in several months of press coverage,[5] while in Britain the story tended to be confined to the days immediately before and after broadcast. But the screening of *Holocaust* still left a trace within the pages of the press as well as within the BBC archives, and it is both that I draw upon to uncover the nature of the debates that *Holocaust* generated when it was first shown on British television in the late 1970s.

Hone's review in *The Listener* is broadly representative of British press reactions in three ways. Firstly, Hone reflects the ambivalence that greeted the screening of *Holocaust* within large sections of the British press, as well in internal debates within the BBC. At the meeting of the Television Weekly Programme Review during the week that *Holocaust* was shown, BBC managers engaged in lengthy discussion over the decision of the BBC to screen the series. While the Head of Music and Arts, Television dismissed the series as 'ghastly, schmaltzy and inadequate', his assistant was glad that the BBC was showing this 'important story', even though 'he accepted it was often quite schmaltzy'. This divided reaction within the BBC was one developed by the Head of Plays, Drama, Television who portrayed older producers as expressing 'great indignation' at the screening of *Holocaust*, while there was 'cautious approval among younger producers'.[6]

Secondly, Hone's review provides a useful starting point as it raised many of the major themes that dominated British debates over *Holocaust*. Although he highlighted some positives – those 'marvellous raisins' – Hone started with a litany of criticisms levelled at this made-for-TV miniseries:

The real problem with *Holocaust* lay not in its historical inaccuracies and fictional improbabilities (bad – but could have been worse); its alarmingly high cliché and sugar content (this mass extermination was made for a mass audience, after all) its 'raking up old sores' (in this instance, a very necessary exercise, I should say); its rampant Zionism (understandable – acceptable even, given this background) – no the fault lay at a simpler, more basic level: it was badly made – often incompetently written and, more often, badly acted and directed.[7]

These faults represented many of the major arguments levelled against *Holocaust* in the pages of the British press, as well as finding echoes in a longer history of criticisms levelled at the so-called 'Holocaust Industry'.[8]

But, and here is the third way that *The Listener* can be seen as broadly representative, debate over *Holocaust* was generated within publications, extending to the letters pages where readers took TV critics to task and directly countered their dismissals of *Holocaust*. An example comes a few pages on from Hone's mixed review of *Holocaust* in the pages of *The Listener*. One reader, in response to David Wheeler's dismissal of Holocaust as 'history for idiots', wrote that they 'refuse[d] to be called an idiot because I found *Holocaust* both moving and significant' and 'the finest thing on television I have ever seen and timely as only true art can be'.[9] But before I turn to the letters pages that directly contradicted the position articulated within the pages of the same publication, I begin with the news and TV pages, alongside internal discussions taking place within the BBC, as *Holocaust* was purchased and shown.

Screening *Holocaust*

Holocaust was seen both within the 'ratings conscious BBC' and the press as an important coup for the Corporation in its battle for ratings against ITV in the all-important autumn schedule.[10] The British TV rights to *Holocaust* had generated a bidding war between the BBC and ITV in the second half of 1977 and early 1978, with the BBC finally offering $550,000 for the show.[11] The eagerness to screen *Holocaust* on British television contrasted, as Ian Ball noted in the *Sunday Telegraph*, with the situation on the Continent, where 'most of the programme buyers in European television were of two minds about acquiring "Holocaust" ',[12] resulting in delays and controversies over airing the show in France, Germany or Denmark.[13] While *Holocaust* was seen within the BBC as must-show TV,[14] whether it was also must-see TV was something debated within the British press in the immediate run-up to its screening over four nights in early September 1978.

The British press had been invited to a pre-screening of *Holocaust* a couple of weeks prior to transmission and began reporting the forthcoming 'TV marathon' as a news event.[15] They offered *Holocaust* to readers with its backstory of massive success in the United States marred by critical reaction, in particular the much cited dismissal by Elie Wiesel in the *New York Times*.[16] *Holocaust* was, according to the BBC's in-house publication, the *Radio Times*, 'the series that shook America'[17] and had, the *Sunday Times* informed readers, brought about 'the biggest controversy in television history' when aired on NBC.[18] Given that *Holocaust* had been contentious in the United States, the press assumed that the response in Britain would be similarly divided. It was, the *Sun* claimed, television that 'could split the nation'.[19] The *Daily Mail* went further, asserting that *Holocaust* was a 'TV epic which will split the nation' and 'provoke argument in almost every home in the land'.[20]

The press sought to generate debate by asking its readers to choose between the binaries of *Holocaust* as 'hokum or history' or plump for one or the other of side-by-side opinion pieces arguing in favour of and against the miniseries.[21] A few days before transmission, the *Daily Express* offered two diverging opinions on 'The TV Series Everyone Will Be Talking About'. James Murray was pitted against Geoffrey Levy, with Murray arguing that 'we need films like "Holocaust" at least every ten years to remind each new generation that the unbelievable is always possible', while Levy argued that 'we ought not to watch Holocaust. It will create hate, violence and ultimately doubt.'[22]

Although the *Daily Mirror* claimed on 4 September that 'furious viewers protested last night' after the first programme was shown,[23] the direct viewer response to the show was less than the press hype in the run-up to screening *Holocaust* suggested and sought to generate. The BBC received only 262 phone calls about the miniseries between 3 and 11 September, fairly evenly split between those who rang in to complain about *Holocaust* and those who praised it.[24] The *Radio Times* published a sample of the close to 200 letters about the miniseries that it received, which it claimed were 'roughly equally divided between praise and criticism'.[25] The level of direct viewer response to the BBC was 'about average for any programme'[26] and nothing like the level of response in West Germany and the United States. In the former, more than 35,000 telephone calls were received by television stations, alongside 'an equal number of letters and telegrams'.[27] In the latter, the numbers of viewer responses was in the thousands rather than the hundreds.[28]

The TV critics' responses

However, while the direct response of viewers was different in Britain, press criticisms shared much with themes dealt with elsewhere. The concern raised by the centre-right press in Italy and Germany that *Holocaust* would dredge up the past and tarnish the image of West Germany was repeated in sections of the British press.[29] Writing in the *Daily Express*, Geoffrey Levy reminded viewers:

> We know what the Germans did to six million Jews. We mustn't forget it, either. But we cannot go on fighting the war interminably. In the years immediately after 1945 the battles continued to rage on celluloid. The war goes on, on videotape. German youth twitches with guilt complexes about the icy savagery of their parents' generation. Television series depicting stiff-necked and evil Germans seem never to be off our screens.[30]

Levy was not alone in his fears about the potential damage done by *Holocaust*. These fears were articulated in the letters pages,[31] but they were also found in the German embassy in London. In the summer prior to the British screening of *Holocaust*, the cultural attaché at the German embassy tried to ameliorate the impact of a miniseries which, he was sure, 'certainly will do us – I mean the new Germany and my personal aims since 1945 – harm'.[32] He sought to persuade the BBC to schedule a panel discussing 'the new Germany since 1949 . . . not to contradict "Holocaust" but as a balance'.[33] He was reassured that there were plans for a discussion show and that, 'on the wider point, you should know that the Board of Governors and Board of Management have been discussing the image of Germany as presented by BBC programmes in general, and for that reason alone there is a fair amount of pressure to see Holocaust put in perspective'.[34]

But these more broadly shared concerns over the danger of stereotyped representations of the Nazi past tarring contemporary West Germany spun off a British side-debate given that, as critics were quick to point out, 'all the Gestapo thugs were played by Englishmen'.[35] Sometimes this led to the incongruity of famous names from British television dramas cast in new, and more unsettling, roles. Under the headline, 'Achtung, Achtung, Achtung. What's going on here as that sweet P.C. Wilmot turns into a nasty Nazi?', James Murray was bewildered by the transformation of Tony Haygarth from 'sex-mad comic policeman, P.C. Wilmot in the BBC comedy series "Rosie"' into 'a vicious Nazi'.[36] Another British actor, Tom Bell, who played Eichmann, was highly critical of *Holocaust* in British press interviews, including the decision to give all the 'nasty parts to the English'.[37] According to William Hickey, writing in the *Daily Express*: 'For years, we led the world in smooth-talking actors who played kings and Roman emperors. Now I fear we have cornered the market in playing Nazi monsters.'[38]

If the European centre-right was concerned about the impact of *Holocaust* on contemporary West Germany, the left was more concerned about contemporary Israel.[39] The *Guardian's* TV critic Nancy Banks-Smith described the 'message' of *Holocaust*, 'that Jews must fight', as 'pernicious', particularly in the context of 'Begin and Sadat even now at Camp David, *Holocaust* sounds bellicose and bloody-minded'.[40] More explicit was Christopher Booker's questioning of 'whether we should go on, in the light of the events in the Middle East in the past thirty years, seeing the Jews collectively in quite so unambiguously heroic a moral light'. Writing in the *Spectator*, Booker drew parallels between Nazi Germany and contemporary Israel, claiming that when he saw an 'anti-Semitic mob on Kristallnacht... shouting "Jews Out! Out! Out!," the image which now almost inevitably rose to mind was of Mr Begin and a group of today's Israelis shouting "Palestinians out! Out! Out!" '.[41]

But more significant within the British press were not these more monolithic leftist or rightist positions that characterised much of the Italian and German media reaction, but concerns with the representation of the Holocaust that had taken centre-stage in the United States. There, a major anxiety had been with the inadequacy of television – and in particular TV drama – in representing the subject matter. Foremost among *Holocaust's* critics in the American press was Elie Wiesel, who bemoaned the 'trivializing' effect of the attempt to turn 'an ontological event into soap-opera'.[42] That the TV miniseries 'trivialized' the Holocaust – as Wiesel claimed – was widely asserted by British critics, with one bemoaning 'this schmaltzy, trivialised soap opera treatment' of the history of the Second World War.[43] More tasteless were the words of the *Guardian* TV critic Nancy Banks-Smith, who wrote that 'It has been said that where Hitler rendered the Jews down into soap, *Holocaust* has turned them into soap opera.'[44] The view of *Holocaust* as little more than generic TV soap opera was underlined with mocking parallels drawn by critics who dubbed *Holocaust* 'Eichmann Meets the Waltons',[45] 'Peytonplatz'[46] or 'Peyton Place with Nazis'.[47] These references to American shows reflected a tendency, as was the case in Italy, not simply to point to failings of television in representing the Holocaust, but more specifically the failings of American TV drama.[48] 'Are American television audiences so dumb', asked David Wheeler in *The Listener*,

that they cannot sustain an interest in one of the cataclysms of history unless it is packaged and wrapped for them in the old familiar way? If they are, then who is responsible? The family formula is the starting point for a series of dramatic contrivances which cheapen and distort. As portrayed in 1930s Berlin, the Jewish Weiss family are too sanitised and saintly to be believable. They do not live in historical time at all, but in the cliché-ridden tradition of American television family series. Not sit.com., of course. Perhaps sit.trag.com. would be the right classification.[49]

Although united in pointing out the failings of the miniseries to tell the story of the Holocaust as American soap opera, critics were divided over whether *Holocaust* was, on its own terms, good or bad soap opera. Some saw it as 'unwatchable'[50] with 'unbelievably bad' and 'trance-like' acting and 'banal' dialogue,[51] which had critics reaching for the off button.[52] The failings of the show – in particular the banality of the script – were also cause for concern amongst a number of department heads at the Television Weekly Programme Review meeting held on 13 September 1978.[53] However, other critics claimed that 'the case against "Holocaust" is not that it is bad soap opera, but worse – much worse – that it is very good soap opera. It was well made, often well acted, skilfully mounted, beautifully shot...'[54] According to David Wheeler,

> Its shortcomings are in many way disguised by the magnificence of the production – a distinguished cast and no expense spared in the sets... Somehow, seeing star actors emoting in this way adds to the conviction that what the producers wanted above all was entertainment, to be able to tell the annual general meeting, 'They said it couldn't be done – but we made a profit.'[55]

Wheeler hinted at an issue that others picked up on, which had been one element of American debates. The question of the commercialisation of *Holocaust* was particularly vexed in the United States given the inter-cutting of the miniseries with – sometimes ill-timed – commercials on NBC.[56] One thing that critics agreed on was that screening by the BBC without commercials meant that *Holocaust* could be seen 'as its makers intended' without the inappropriate commercials that had been criticised by commentators in the United States.[57] However, despite this, one critic suggested that 'the Madison Avenue odours linger on, in content and packaging'.[58] Others posed a series of rhetorical questions: 'isn't commercial treatment of Belsen and Buchenwald, Treblinka and Babi Yar, a sort of profanity?';[59] 'is it right to make millions of pounds out of this disgusting episode of history?';[60] 'should millions of pounds be made out of human suffering?'.[61]

Whether *Holocaust* was Hollywood at its best, or its worst, was a point of debate for critics, but that it was a Hollywood product was taken as accepted, and seen as the core of the problem.[62] The end result was, as a large number of critics noted – as they had in the United States[63] – that Hollywood airbrushed out the harsh realities of the Holocaust in a TV-set world where those living in the Warsaw ghetto were 'not only well-nourished, clean, and decently clad but meticulously shaven'[64] and 'the inmates of Buchenwald are American-plump and garbed in incredibly-clean and unkempt [sic] uniforms'.[65] *Holocaust* portrayed a world, wrote Rosalie Horner in the *Daily Express*, where 'the deathly hand of Tinsel City is ever present. The Buchenwald concentration camp looks almost out of "Ideal Homes." The natty striped uniforms of the inmates are bandbox bright enough for "The Pyjama Game," detracting from the darker horrors of the script. It all jars as surely as the American accent of the very bankable Joseph Bottoms as young hero Rudi Weiss.'[66]

With its well-fed, well-dressed actors, *Holocaust* was seen as domesticating the scale of the event,[67] and easing its violence. Sean Day Lewis claimed in the *Daily Telegraph* that 'the scenes so far shown in the concentration camps made one conscious only of actors in air-conditioned studios, not even remotely of the unthinkable squalor and degradation which must have reigned in those human hells'.[68] For most critics, *Holocaust* was simply not horrific enough.[69] Yet a widely reported news story in the days after screening suggested that for one viewer, the scenes were too horrific to bear. The suicide of a 'Jewish widow', Fanny Gedall, who was found dead after watching the first episode of the miniseries, was widely reported.[70] The claim was, as the *Daily Express* reported, that 'the horrors shown in the TV epic "Holocaust" were too much', citing her daughter-in-law who reported that her suicide notes said 'that after seeing such a terrible programme on Sunday night she did not want anything more to do with this world'.[71]

But, despite *Holocaust* appearing all too real for Gedall, it was dismissed by Holocaust survivor Reuben Ainsztein, writing in the *Sunday Times*, as riddled with 'incongruities and historical inaccuracies' and betraying 'a typical Hollywood contempt for facts'.[72] Ainsztein found these inaccuracies not simply irritating, but, to his mind, potentially dangerous, writing that 'in the Buchenwald scenes . . . the inmates look so well-fed and well-dressed that I would not be surprised if the stills are reproduced one day in a neo-nazi pamphlet as proof of how decent conditions were in Buchenwald and other Nazi concentration camps'.[73] He was not alone in seeing a danger of the fictions of *Holocaust* feeding into the fictions of denial. This danger was highlighted by others, who saw the dangers of mixing fact and fiction as *Holocaust* did with its presentation of fictional characters in factual places.[74] Levy's conclusion was to 'Let history tell the story of the holocaust, intellectually and factually. Let the *Diary of Anne Frank* remain the most profound, personal record of Nazi inhumanity...*Holocaust* is not like that. It is fiction woven into fact' and thus liable to be held up as a 'propagandistic lie. It would be an ironic way for future generations to question the historical accuracy of the Hitler years.'[75]

This preference for Anne Frank over *Holocaust* – 'Anne Frank who was real and who died is a thousand times more eloquent than the characters of this shoddy scenario'[76] – was repeated by a number of critics.[77] But more widespread were assertions of the superiority of the genre of documentary over drama, and in particular one recently aired TV documentary: *The World at War*. One unique element to British press criticisms of *Holocaust* were reminders that British TV had already done the Holocaust, and so it was claimed, done it better than Hollywood. In 1973–4, the Thames Television documentary series *The World at War* aired on ITV. One episode focusing on 'Genocide' was often mentioned in British reviews of *Holocaust*.[78] In his damning review of *Holocaust*, Peter Fiddick praised the 'masterly' treatment of this 'chapter of history' by British television makers in *The World at War* series, 'whose painstaking documentary techniques were applied to the whole wretched story, reaching a dreadful climax in the scenes of death and suffering which met the troops liberating Auschwitz and its wretched fellows. I was not the only viewer in the land who wept.'[79] A few days later, an even more damning review in the same paper again drew the same contrast: 'There were parts of Thames' *World at War* I could not see for tears. There were parts of *Holocaust* I could not hear for yawning.'[80]

Contrasting *Holocaust* unfavourably with *The World at War* was in part about asserting documentary portrayals over drama, as well as British TV over an American import. Even those who were broadly positive about *Holocaust* felt that the BBC would have done a 'better' job with the subject matter than American television producers,[81] which were sentiments shared within the BBC itself.[82] But there was more to the parallels drawn with *The World at War* than simply that British TV had done the Holocaust better than Hollywood could or would. There were also claims that Britain had already done the Holocaust and therefore did not need to do it again so soon. *Holocaust* was, for some critics, not necessary in Britain, where 'over the past 20 years there has been much including Thames TV's "World at War" series, which has seriously documented not only the genocide directed against the Jews but the historical context of this and other agonising events'.[83]

However, for its advocates, *Holocaust* was a miniseries which, despite its faults, had to be shown in late 1970s Britain. Supporters of *Holocaust* were quick to confess that they 'found it by no means faultless'.[84] It was a flawed, popular telling, which advocates argued – in echoes of Hilene Flanzbaum's later critiques of 'gatekeepers' of Holocaust representation[85] – 'should be judged within its own terms and not by standards applicable to other productions which it is not and does not pretend to be'.[86] Offering 'six million reasons' 'why they had to make a television drama out of Holocaust', the former editor of the *Jewish Chronicle*, William Frankel, was convinced that 'even a flawed picture is better than no picture, particularly at this distance from the events and at a time when neo-Nazis all over Europe and the USA are producing a mass of publications denying that the holocaust ever took place'.[87] In direct contrast to those critics who viewed *Holocaust* as fodder for deniers, Frankel saw contemporary denial as the context for the necessity of *Holocaust* garnering a mass audience.

The Holocaust was seen by many as subject matter that demanded a TV showing 'from time to time',[88] 'at least once every generation',[89] 'at least every ten years'[90] or 'every two to five' years.[91] In particular, there was stress placed on the importance of telling this story to those born since the war, who had 'difficulty in grasping the idea of such barbarism in the twentieth century'.[92] But there was also, as one survivor wrote to the press, an urgency to screening *Holocaust* in the autumn of 1978 given that the far-right National Front party was 'about to field over 300 candidates in the forthcoming elections'[93] and, as a critic noted, 'the Swastika can be seen on the streets of Europe and America'.[94] In that context, *Holocaust* was interpreted as a universal story about prejudice and racism.

The universalisation of *Holocaust* as an anti-racist tool was widely articulated by those who stressed the importance of the subject matter being shown on British television. Arguing in favour of *Holocaust*, Rosalie Horner claimed that 'we cannot remind ourselves often enough that when prejudice, extracted out of poverty, lack of employment and an amoral leader, it can become the most potent weapon, eroding everything which represents a civilised society'.[95] For her, and she was not alone, *Holocaust* was important because it was a universal story about prejudice and racism. Writing in *The Times*, Frankel asserted that 'however inadequate the instrument, serious efforts to keep the tragedy in the public consciousness must surely continue for the grim memory of the holocaust is vital if a recurrence of the catastrophe is to be prevented. The Jews are not the only possible victims of genocide.'[96] According to press reports, the Board of Deputies engaged in a similar universalisation of the lessons of Holocaust, stating that it was 'valuable and good that people should be reminded of the terrible events of World War Two and all that happened to people, and it should be taken as a warning of what can happen in a society when things get out of hand and racialist policies are pursued'.[97]

This universalisation of *Holocaust* as an anti-racist tool is striking. Reading the British press, it is clear that the screening of *Holocaust* did not result in in-depth engagement with the historical specificity of the 'final solution'. Unlike in Germany, where in the aftermath of the screening 'newspapers and magazines were filled with diaries of concentration camp survivors, interviews with former Auschwitz guards, and articles on the history of German-Jewish relations',[98] there was very little of that engagement with the history of the Holocaust or the experiences of survivors in Britain. Survivors were drawn upon only to ascertain their response to *Holocaust* as TV event, not to tell their own stories.[99] The one exception to the lack of any attempt to situate the miniseries within a broader historical context was the *Jewish Chronicle*, which published a guide for readers which offered 'the facts behind the TV fiction'.[100] This extract from the booklet prepared by American-Jewish organisations when *Holocaust* aired in America provided a glossary of key individuals, places and terms referenced in the miniseries.[101] This supplement within the pages of the *Jewish Chronicle* was not the only supporting material to the miniseries. 50,000 copies of an eight-page booklet to accompany the series were published by the Holocaust Remembrance Group, which distributed the booklet through synagogues and Jewish organisations.[102] However, in general terms the British press did not see the screening of *Holocaust* as the jumping-off point for broader discussion of the Holocaust as historical event, but a discrete cultural product and media event that featured in the TV pages, news pages and letters to the editor for a couple of weeks in late August and early September 1978.

This suggests a need to see the British response to *Holocaust* as an exception to the more general picture painted by Judith Doneson, who suggested that *Holocaust* 'furthered the penetration of the event in the American popular consciousness and had stirred the conscience of the European audience'.[103] Her view of *Holocaust* as a 'huge success'[104] is one that Emiliano Perra cautions against from his own study of Italian responses, where the screening of *Holocaust* in 1979 'did not stand out as a watershed in the process of memorialization of the Holocaust'.[105] Reading through the British press suggests that the response to *Holocaust* in Britain shared the muted and ephemeral reception seen in Italy, rather than the more extensive and far-reaching response seen in West Germany or the United States.[106]

Readers' responses

I want to nuance the picture I have painted so far by turning a few pages within the newspapers published in September 1978 to look at the letters pages. I do not seek to use these as a way to measure popular reactions to *Holocaust*, but see them as suggestive of the need to move beyond the criticisms levelled by the majority of TV critics precisely because the most severe of these were countered by readers. Although in the *Radio Times* the large number of letters received and published were broadly split between those in support of and those against *Holocaust*, this was not the case in those publications which reviewed *Holocaust* in the harshest terms. This can be seen, as I have already suggested, in the case of *The Listener*, but it is something that emerges more broadly within the British press. Pamela Manson wrote to the *Daily Telegraph*, whose critics had been dismissive of *Holocaust*, to specifically attack 'television critics who sit comfortably in their armchairs and castigate the producers of "Holocaust" for not showing the full horrors of the murder of six million Jews' who had, she suggested, 'surely missed the point of this timely series'.[107]

Reading the letters pages of those newspapers and magazines which were the most critical of *Holocaust*, it is clear that readers reacted directly to what they saw as sneering criticism. For example, Mary Malone's dismissal of the characters in *Holocaust* as 'hollow' 'puppets' in the *Daily Mirror* 'inspired a barrage of comments'.[108] A selection of five letters were printed. Only one criticised the film, although on different grounds to the aesthetic charge levelled by Malone.[109] More numerous and more prominent were letters directly criticising Malone's view. Placed most prominently as the lead letter, under the headline 'My Family Were Killed in a Nazi Hell', were the comments of a survivor who wrote that 'for me these people on the screen are real, not the puppets Miss Malone called them'.[110] All four critical letters published drew specifically on the wording of Malone's original review, countering her claims that *Holocaust* was filled with 'puppets', was 'absurd' and 'unreal'.[111] Likewise, two damning reviews in the *Guardian* by

Peter Fiddick and Nancy Banks-Smith were directly countered in letters to the editor.[112] Most critical were three letters that responded to
Nancy Banks-Smith's 'tasteless puns about Jews being turned into "soap"
and "soap opera"', her 'offensive witticisms' and description of the
miniseries as 'toothpaste'.[113]

Readers picked up on what they saw excessively harsh criticisms
and intemperate language, which they mocked in their letter. In his
damning review, Dennis Potter had concluded his critique of naked
Hollywood actors tastefully hiding their genitals with the sentence,
'It also meant – and pardon me if I splash you with my vomit –
that not all the extras needed to be circumcised.' An angry reader
responded,

> Before heading for the bathroom to rid myself of Dennis Potter's
> vomit, may I suggest that his smug intellectual criticism of Holo-
> caust as "tasteless," "irrelevant" and "Bestseller-Yuk," ignores the
> major justification for this rather unsatisfactory sugary production,
> i.e. that it will have been seen in millions of homes where, alas, BBC2
> and *The Sunday Times* do not intrude. If only one supporter of the
> National Front has now had second thoughts, then Holocaust was
> worthwhile.[114]

Whatever the TV critics said – and they said plenty of negative things –
Holocaust was watched in millions of British homes in September 1978.
How many million was a contentious and debated issue, given that the
BBC and ITV operated different systems of estimating viewing numbers.
The BBC estimated that 14.5 million watched the first episode, rising
to 15 million for the second, and 19 million each for episodes three
and four. ITV estimated figures of 8.5, rising to 9.5, 12 and then dropping slightly to 11.5 million. However, both were broadly in agreement
that numbers of viewers had risen, rather than fallen off, across the four
episodes.[115] What those viewers made of *Holocaust* was something that
the BBC sought to ascertain through a specially commissioned 'Audience Research Report'. This suggested that the press pre-publicity given
to *Holocaust* had played a part in stimulating individuals to watch the
show. But from the responses of this sample of viewers it would seem
that while the press coverage given over to *Holocaust* was one important
reason for the show's success, the tone of that press coverage – which as
I have suggested was largely critical – was not reflected by the majority of those who chose to watch the show and were largely positive
towards it.[116]

However, while *Holocaust* did garner a mass and largely appreciative audience, it does not seem that watching the miniseries equated to engagement with the Holocaust past. In an article published on the basis of this BBC audience review, the authors concluded that

> while the series itself mainly evoked a strong "gut reaction," the historical event was perhaps seen as a thing of the past, relating exclusively to Germany. It is arguable, therefore, that 'Holocaust' was seen first and foremost as a story, the impact of which was heightened by the knowledge that the events portrayed were substantially true.[117]

September 1978 seems a moment when far from *Holocaust* stimulating deep engagement with the wartime past, both British audiences and the press responded more to *Holocaust* as TV drama. For the British press, the screening of *Holocaust* was an opportunity to debate the (im)possibility of representing the Holocaust through soap opera. In the process, they covered most of the areas of later debate over the so-called 'Holocaust Industry'; issues that continue to be the focus of controversy.[118]

Acknowledgements

I thank the BBC Written Archive and Immediate Media Co. for permission to cite source material used in this chapter.

Notes

1. Joseph Hone, 'Television: Saints and Sinners', *The Listener*, 4 September 1978, 342. In Italy, the most common culinary analogy offered when critiquing *Holocaust* was *polpettone* (meatloaf), see Emilano Perra, 'Narratives of Innocence and Victimhood: The Reception of the Miniseries *Holocaust* in Italy', *Holocaust and Genocide Studies*, 22 (3) (2008), 420.
2. David Wheeler, 'Television, History for Idiots?', *The Listener*, 7 September 1978, 310.
3. Jack Duncan, 'Langham Diary. Post "Holocaust"', *The Listener*, 21 September 1978, 368.
4. Jeffrey Shandler, *While America Watches: Televising the Holocaust* (New York, 1999), 164–165.
5. Jeffrey Herf, 'The "Holocaust" Reception in West Germany: Right, Center and Left', *New German Critique* 19 (1) (1980), 30, 49.
6. BBC Written Archive, T41/508 Holocaust TV Registry, Extract from the Minutes of Television Weekly Programme Review, 6 September 1978.
7. Hone, 'Saints and Sinners', 341.
8. See most controversially Norman Finkelstein, *The Holocaust Industry* (London, 2000). On this longer history of criticism see Tim Cole, ' "The

Holocaust Industry"?: Reflections on a History of the Critique of Holocaust Representation', in Konrad Kwiet and Jürgen Matthäus (eds), *Contemporary Responses to the Holocaust* (Westport, CN, 2004), 35–57.

9. David Bulwer Lutyens, 'Letters to the Editor. History for Idiots?', *The Listener*, 14 September 1978, 339.

10. BBC Written Archive, T41/508 Holocaust TV Registry, Extract from the Minutes of Board of Governors, 21 September 1978; R78/2074/1 BBC Records Management Services – Management Registry, Extract from the Minutes of Board of Management, 25 September 1978; James Murray, 'BBC Joins Saturday Night TV Fever', *Daily Express*, 17 August 1978, 7; Grant Lochart, 'Same Old Names in the TV Battle', *South Wales Evening Post*, 24 August 1978; Ian Ball, 'Holocaust', *Sunday Telegraph*, 3 September 1978. [Where press cuttings are from the cuttings file at BBC Written Archives, no page references are given for those articles where page numbers are missing.]

11. BBC Written Archive, T41/508 Holocaust TV Registry, Letter from Alasdair Milne to the Director General of the BBC, 8 September 1978.

12. Ball, 'Holocaust'.

13. Ulf Zander, 'Holocaust at the Limits: Historical Culture and the Nazi Genocide in the Television Era', in Klas-Göran Karlsson and Ulf Zander (eds), *Echoes of the Holocaust. Historical Cultures in Contemporary Europe* (Lund, 2003), 277–280.

14. BBC Written Archive, R78/2074/1 BBC Records Management Services – Management Registry, Extract from the Minutes of Board of Management, 4 September 1978.

15. Gareth Parry, 'Slaughter of Jews Is TV Marathon', *Guardian*, 16 August 1978, 2.

16. Elie Wiesel, 'Trivializing the Holocaust: Semi-Fact and Semi-Fiction', *New York Times*, 16 April 1978, 29.

17. David Blundy, 'The Anger and the Pity', *Radio Times*, 2–8 September 1978, cover, 60.

18. 'Pick of the Day. Seven Hours of Darkness', *Sunday Times*, 3 September 1978.

19. Philip Phillips, 'The Greatest Horror Story of All Time', *Sun*, 2 September 1978.

20. Shaun Usher, 'The Holocaust – History or Hokum?', *Daily Mail*, 29 August 1978.

21. Ibid.

22. 'When Does Hate End and History Begin?', *Daily Express*, 29 August 1978, 10.

23. 'Fury over Nazi TV Series', *Daily Mirror*, 4 September 1978, 3.

24. BBC Written Archive, T41/508 Holocaust TV Registry, Information Department memo, 13 September 1978.

25. 'Was "Holocaust" Timely or Trashy?', Letters, *Radio Times*, 23–29 September 1978, 77.

26. Gareth Parry, 'Holocaust Meets Low-key Response', *Guardian*, 5 September 1978, 3.

27. Andrei Markovits and Christopher Allen, 'The German Conscience', *Jewish Frontier*, April 1979, 13–17 cited in Herf, 'The "Holocaust" Reception', 30.

28. Herf, 'The "Holocaust" Reception', 30.

29. Perra, 'Narratives of Innocence', 424; Herf, 'The "Holocaust" Reception, 31ff.
30. Geoffrey Levy in *Daily Express*, 29 August 1978, 10.
31. HLH, in 'Public Opinion', *Daily Mirror*, 8 September 1978, 13.
32. BBC Written Archives, T41/508 Holocaust TV Registry, letter from Herbert Sulzbach to Ludovic Kennedy, 25 July 1978.
33. Ibid.
34. BBC Written Archives, T41/508, Holocaust TV Registry, letter from Richard Francis to Ludovic Kennedy, 10 August 1978.
35. William Hickey, 'These Names Make News', *Daily Express*, 8 September 1978, 13.
36. James Murray, 'Achtung, Achtung, Achtung', *Daily Express*, 2 September 1978, 15.
37. 'The Jackboot Trial of Tough Tom', *Sunday People*, 3 September 1978.
38. Hickey, 'These Names', 13.
39. Perra, 'Narratives of Innocence', 422; Herf, 'The "Holocaust" Response', 44–45.
40. Nancy Banks-Smith, 'Last Night: Television. Holocaust', *Guardian*, 7 September 1978, 8.
41. Christopher Booker, 'The Lessons of "Holocaust" ', *Spectator*, 9 September 1978.
42. Wiesel, 'Trivializing the Holocaust'.
43. 'Soap Opera History Designed to Make Money', *Morning Star*, 6 September 1978.
44. Banks-Smith, 'Last Night', 8.
45. *Sunday Times*,10 September 1978.
46. Ruth Hall, 'After the Holocaust . . .', *Sunday Times*, 10 September 1978.
47. 'Your Best TV Guide to the Weekend. Sunday by Jack Bell', *Daily Express*, 2 September 1978, 13.
48. See Perra, 'Narratives of Innocence', 421; and Shandler, *While America Watches*, 167–170.
49. Wheeler, 'History for Idiots?', 310.
50. Banks-Smith, 'Last Night', 8.
51. Richard Last, 'Abysmal Standards Mark "Holocaust" ', *Daily Telegraph*, 4 September; Richard Last, ' "Holocaust" Proves a Dismal Failure', *Daily Telegraph*, 5 September 1978.
52. Richard Ingram, 'Television. For Kicks', *The Spectator*, 9 September 1978.
53. BBC Written Archive, T41/508 Holocaust TV Registry, Extract from the Minutes of Television Weekly Programme Review, 13 September 1978.
54. Dennis Potter, 'Holocaust: A Book of the Dead in the Style of Best-Seller', *Sunday Times*, 10 September 1978.
55. Wheeler, 'History for Idiots?', 310.
56. Shandler, *While America Watches*, 171–3.
57. Chris Dunkley, 'Television: Holocaust', *Financial Times*, 5 September 1978.
58. Wheeler, 'History for Idiots?', 310.
59. 'Let Evil Speak for Itself', *Daily Express*, 5 September 1978, 8.
60. 'Terrible Truths with a Tinsel Tarnish. Last Night's View. Rosalie Horner on "Holocaust" ', *Daily Express*, 4 September 1978, 21.

61. Brian Vine, 'Holocaust: The Profits of Despair?', *Daily Express*, 11 September 1978, 9.
62. Peter Fiddick, 'Holocaust: The Hollywood Solution', *Guardian*, 4 September 1978, 8.
63. Shandler, *While America Watches*, 168.
64. Last, ' "Holocaust" Proves a Dismal Failure'.
65. 'Soap opera history'.
66. 'Terrible truths with a tinsel varnish', 21.
67. Philip Purser, 'Television. The Final Insult', *Sunday Telegraph*, 10 September 1978.
68. Sean Day Lewis, ' "Holocaust" Proves Laughably Inadequate', *Daily Telegraph*, 5 September 1978.
69. Fiddick, 'Holocaust: The Hollywood Solution', 8.
70. ' "Holocaust" Clue to Woman's Death', *Guardian*, 8 September 1978, 2; ' "Holocaust" Tragedy', *Sun*, 8 September 1978; 'Jewess Killed Herself Over "Holocaust" Film', *Daily Telegraph*, 9 September 1978; 'Widow of 81 Killed Herself Over "Holocaust" ', *The Times*, 9 September 1978; 'The Tragic Jewess', *Daily Mail*, 9 September 1978; 'A Last Victim', *Daily Express*, 9 September 1978, 10.
71. Lynne Greenwood, 'Holocaust "Victim" ', *Daily Express*, 8 September 1978, 3.
72. Reuben Ainsztein, 'Where TV's Holocaust Strays from the Truth' *Sunday Times*, 3 September 1978.
73. Ibid.
74. 'Let Evil Speak for Itself', 8.
75. Geoffrey Levy in *Daily Express*, 29 August 1978, 10.
76. 'Let Evil Speak for Itself', 8.
77. Day Lewis, ' "Holocaust" Proves Laughably Inadequate'.
78. 'Your Best TV Guide to the Weekend', 13.
79. Fiddick, 'Holocaust: The Hollywood Solution', 8.
80. Banks-Smith, 'Last Night', 8.
81. William Frankel, 'Six Million Reasons', *Evening Standard*, 7 September 1978; Hugo Gryn cited in Patrick Stoddart, 'Protests Pour in Over Nazi TV Series', *Evening News*, 4 September 1978.
82. Day Lewis, ' "Holocaust" Proves Laughably Inadequate'; BBC Written Archive, T41/508 Holocaust TV Registry, Extract from the Minutes of Television Weekly Programme Review, 13 September 1978.
83. 'Soap Opera History'.
84. James Murray in *Daily Express*, 29 August 1978, 10.
85. Hilene Flanzbaum, ' "But Wasn't It Terrific?" A Defence of Liking *Life is Beautiful*', *The Yale Journal of Criticism*, 14 (1) (2001), 273–286.
86. Frankel, 'Six Million Reasons'.
87. Ibid.
88. BBC Written Archives, R78/2074/1 BBC Records Management Services – Management Registry, Extract from the Minutes of Board of Management, 11 September 1978.
89. 'The Despair of a People. Last Night's View by James Murray', *Daily Express*, 5 September 1978, 23.
90. James Murray in *Daily Express*, 29 August 1978, 10.

91. Mrs Bernice P. in Letters page, *Daily Express*, 8 September 1978, 18.
92. James Murray in *Daily Express*, 29 August 1978, 10; Ian Ball, 'Holocaust', *Sunday Telegraph*, 3 September 1978.
93. Arthur Lemberg, 'Lest We Forget Our Dark Past', 'Letters to the Editor', *Guardian*, 22 August 1978, 10.
94. James Murray in *Daily Express*, 29 August 1978, 10.
95. 'Terrible Truths with a Tinsel Varnish', p. 21.
96. William Frankel, 'Holocaust: Can the Truth Ever Be Told', *The Times*, 31 August 1978, 16.
97. Parry, 'Holocaust Meets Low-key Response', 3.
98. Herf, 'The "Holocaust" Reception', 49.
99. Paul Smith, 'Tears and Praise from Survivors', *Evening News*, 4 September 1978; cf. Paul Smith, 'Holocaust "Is Not Fair to Victims"', *Evening News*, 5 September 1978; Alex Hendry, 'A Glossy Holocaust. Verdict on BBC's TV Spectacular', *Daily Express*, 5 September 1978, 15.
100. 'Holocaust. The Facts Behind the TV Fiction', *Jewish Chronicle*, 1 September 1978.
101. Ibid.; Shandler, *While America Watches*, 163.
102. 'Holocaust Booklet for Television Series', *Jewish Chronicle*, 25 August 1978.
103. Judith Doneson, *The Holocaust in American Film*. Second Edition (Syracuse, NY, 2002), 144.
104. Ibid., 192.
105. Perra, 'Narratives of Innocence', 412.
106. On the reaction in West Germany, see also Andrei Markovits and Rebecca Hayden, '"Holocaust" Before and After the Event. Reactions in West Germany and Austria', *New German Critique* 19 (1) (1980), 53–80; Moishe Postone, 'Anti-Semitism and National Socialism. Notes on the German Reaction to "Holocaust"', *New German Critique*, 19 (1) (1980) 97–115; cf. Siegfried Zielinksi, 'History as Entertainment and Provocation: The TV Series "Holocaust" in West Germany', *New German Critique*, 19 (1) (1980), 81–96 who writes, p. 82, 'now that the nation has belched loudly and reverted to its familiar lethargy . . .'.
107. Pamela Manson, 'Lessons of "Holocaust"', *Daily Telegraph*, 15 September 1978.
108. 'A Hollow Holocaust. Last Night's View by Mary Malone', *Daily Mirror*, 4 September 1978, 16; 'Public Opinion. The Column You Write', *Daily Mirror*, 8 September 1978, 13.
109. H.L.H, in 'Public Opinon', *Daily Mirror*, 8 September 1978, 13.
110. E.L., in Ibid.
111. 'Public Opinon', *Daily Mirror*, 8 September 1978, 13.
112. 'Why Holocaust Had to Offend', 'Letters to the Editor', *Guardian*, 8 September 1978, 10.
113. 'A Readiness to Fight Is the Lesson of Holocaust', *Guardian*, 9 September 1978, 6.
114. I.D. Young, 'Smug', *Sunday Times*, 17 September 1978.
115. BBC Written Archives, T41/508 Holocaust TV Registry, G.J. Goodhardt, M.A. Collins and A.S.C. Ehrenberg, 'How Many People Watched Holocaust?' (undated research report); Martin Jackson, 'How Many People Watched Holocaust?', *Daily Mail*, 12 September 1978.

116. BBC Written Archives, R9/792/446, Viewing Report VR/78/446, 'An Audience Response Report. A Study of British Viewers' Reactions to "Holocaust"', November 1978. See also the conclusion in Andy Pearce, 'The Development of Holocaust Consciousness in Contemporary Britain, 1979–2001', (PhD Thesis, Royal Holloway College, 2010), 190.
117. Nadine Dyer and Anne Rawcliffe-King, ' "Holocaust": UK Research', *International Journal of Political Education*, 4 (1–2) (1981), 136.
118. Cole, ' "The Holocaust Industry" '.

5

'And The Trouble Is Where to Begin to Spring Surprises on You. Perhaps a Place You Might *Least* Like to Remember.' *This Is Your Life* and the BBC's Images of the Holocaust in the Twenty Years Before *Holocaust*

James Jordan

In his contribution to this volume, Tim Cole explores a number of differ-ent responses to the BBC's screening of the NBC miniseries *Holocaust* in September 1978. Building on the work of Emiliano Perra, he argues that 'the response to *Holocaust* in Britain' had more in common with 'the muted and ephemeral reception seen in Italy' than 'the more extensive and far-reaching response seen in West Germany or the United States'.[1] As he summarises, 'far from *Holocaust* stimulating deep engagement with the wartime past, both British audiences and the press responded more to *Holocaust* as TV drama'. Moreover,

> *Holocaust* was, for some critics, not necessary in Britain, where 'over the past 20 years there has been much including Thames TV's "World at War" series, which has seriously documented not only the genocide directed against the Jews but the historical context of this and other agonising events'.[2]

The question of whether documentary or drama is the more effective or appropriate way of telling the stories of the Holocaust, or a discussion of the relative merits of *Holocaust* when compared with *The World at War*, is not the aim of this chapter. Rather what follows contextualises Cole's analysis by looking at a selection of programmes shown by the

BBC in the 20 years before *Holocaust* that were partly responsible for the muted response to the miniseries. In discussing solely the BBC's output, it is not my intention to suggest that programmes on commercial television, which of course included *The World at War*, were uncommon or inferior – far from it – but rather to focus on a national broadcaster with a particular status in the British psyche. The nucleus of this discussion is five episodes of *This Is Your Life*, the light entertainment show that ran on the BBC for nine series from 1955–1964. As will be seen, these episodes constructed a life story and narrative of liberation, rescue and witness through the choice of guests and the content and manner of articulation of their on-screen memories.

BBC television and the Holocaust, 1955–1978

In the 20 years before *Holocaust*, a period that equates roughly to 1955–1978, 'the genocide directed against the Jews' was indeed a regular presence on British television.[3] Such a blanket statement, however, captures neither the content nor the diversity of those programmes. In respect of the BBC's output, for example, the Holocaust – or, rather, what later becomes understood by that term – was seldom the sole focus of the programmes in question and virtually never articulated as 'the Holocaust', a phrase and concept still in its infancy for much of the period.[4] Such a statement also fails to express just how much television, its style, reach and influence changed between the two dates. 1955 was the year that marked the tenth anniversary of the end of the war and the liberation of the concentration camps; it was also the year in which the BBC's monopoly ended with the launch of commercial television in September. Already expanding, television entered its boom years in this period, with the competition between channels, larger audiences, nationwide coverage, the introduction of BBC2 in April 1964 and longer broadcasting hours all helping to usher in a 'golden age' that defined television as an important and influential mass medium. These same years, as Jeffrey Shandler has noted in respect of American television, also witnessed the start of 'Holocaust consciousness', with the capture and trial of Adolf Eichmann considered the trigger for increased interest in the genocide.[5] It was, therefore, a time of great transition for both television and the Holocaust, one during which the Nazi genocide was depicted in many different ways.[6]

The BBC's most highly acclaimed and probably best-known programme from this period was Hugh Burnett's *Warsaw Ghetto* (BBC1, tx. 18 November 1965), the first programme to show viewers 'the entire study made by the Nazis of the race they had decided to destroy'.[7] This 50-minute documentary combined two strands of memory and representation, with a visual montage of the ghetto compiled from films and photographs shot by the SS, Gestapo and German Army, accompanied by a commentary written and narrated by survivor Alexander Bernfes. Even with its high proportion of horrific content, it was almost universally acclaimed, scoring an unusually high 81 (out of 100) on the BBC's internal Reaction Index (RI), with one viewer writing that 'One can read of these horrible happenings and often doubt their truth, but to see them is proof.'[8] It was a sentiment that reinforces the power of the image and recalls the decision taken by the Allied prosecution at the Nuremberg trial to use film as evidence.

Warsaw Ghetto, however, was not the first BBC programme to consider the murder of Europe's Jews or even the Warsaw Ghetto.[9] Rudolph Cartier, an exile from Nazi Germany who had first arrived in Britain in 1935, produced and directed a number of innovative and unusual dramas that had a clear connection to the Holocaust and his own past. *The Cold Light* (tx. 29 July 1956) and *The Joel Brand Story* (BBC1, 14 December 1965), for example, contained in different ways references to persecution, genocide, refugees, victims, perpetrators and bystanders, with his mesmeric adaptation of *Dr Korczak and the Children* (tx. 13 August 1962) pre-empting *Warsaw Ghetto* in setting and intent as it recalled 'the whole overwhelming tragedy of the Jewish people' in 'one of the most compelling and moving plays seen on television for many years'.[10] More allegorically, Cartier's production of the seminal science-fiction serial *Quatermass and the Pit* (tx. 22 December 1958–26 January 1959), written by Nigel Kneale, contained its own interpretation of genocide in the race purges of the 'Wild Hunt'.

Cartier was not alone in considering the persecution and murder of the Jews as a suitable subject for television drama. Other productions included D.G. Bridson's *The Bullet* (tx. 20 August 1958), a short play about Jewish revenge set in post-war Germany; Leo Lehman's *Thirty Pieces of Silver* (tx. 26 August 1958), a play in which Joan Miller starred as Mrs Weiss, a refugee whose husband had been killed in a Nazi concentration camp; *Echo from Afar* (tx. 13 December 1959) by Jack Pulman, the story of a Buchenwald doctor living under a new identity in post-war America; and *Address Unknown* (tx. 3 September 1962), an adaptation of Kressman Taylor's short story that was the source of one of the few Hollywood films of the 1940s to address directly the persecution of the Jews.[11] There were also plays that recognised the potential of the camp and the rubble of post-war Europe as a dramatic setting. In August 1956

Val Gielgud's *Siding 273* (tx. 19 August 1956), a version of his own 1948 play *Iron Curtain*, considered the fate of refugees caught up in the political tensions of Europe in 1946, while two years later *Uncertain Mercy* (tx. 4 September 1958) was set inside a Displaced Persons' (DP) Camp in Austria in 1956; finally *The Unplayed Part* (tx. 2 October 1960) told the story of a Jewish violinist in a concentration camp. More ambitious and significant for its recreation of Auschwitz as a set in Studio 1 of BBC Television Centre was *The Materialists* (BBC2, 17 May 1964), the third part of the trilogy *The Seekers*. A study in the nature of human belief, *The Seekers* covered 900 years of history, with this final section featuring a cast of over 100 extras, including 49 'Jewish prisoners'.

The BBC's current affairs and talks programmes also engaged with the Holocaust and its consequences, and not only with reference to the capture and trial of Adolf Eichmann. The late 1950s marked the start of Holocaust memorialisation and Auschwitz's rise to prominence in the western memory. A 1958 edition of the BBC's landmark arts series *Monitor* (tx. 9 November 1958) reflected both of these developments in a report from Paris on the recently concluded competition to design the Auschwitz Memorial. With sections written by Constantine Fitzgibbon, spoken by Robert Dougall, and additional comments by sculptor and competition judge Henry Moore, the programme was notable for being one of the first BBC productions to include film of the liberation of Auschwitz.[12] Prior to this, British television, in common with British culture more widely, presented and helped to create a view of Nazi atrocities that focused on Belsen. Judith Petersen has written of how the camp, the role of the British as liberators, Richard Dimbleby's iconic account for the BBC, and even Dimbleby himself, all helped to 'create and perpetuate Belsen's symbolic' importance, even if the coverage often failed to highlight the Jewish specificity of the prisoners.[13] In *After the Battle* (tx. 31 December 1959), Dimbleby returned to Belsen to examine the memorialisation of the camp and the overwhelming silence he encountered from those living in the neighbouring town of Bergen. He famously returned again for *Panorama* (BBC1, 12 April 1965), focusing more on the fate of those who survived the camps than contemporary German responses. But the BBC's cameras returned again one month later for *Victory in Europe: Twenty Years After* (BBC1, 8 May 1965), a joint BBC-CBS production which was broadcast as part of the celebrations to mark 20 years since the end of the war. During this live programme – made possible by the advent of the world's first commercial communication satellite a month before – former correspondents returned to familiar places of war. The 'responsibility' for Belsen fell not to Dimbleby, who was anchoring the programme in London, but his son, David, who would 'try to describe the significance of the place-name to a generation who were too young to know of war at the time these horrors were being revealed'.[14] Richard Dimbleby would be dead by the end of the year, but the 'passing of the baton' to the next generation of the dynasty had already taken place, and taken place through the intergenerational transmission of witnessing to the horrors of Belsen.

Dimbleby's reports in *After the Battle* and *Panorama* were two of several programmes that addressed German memory and guilt in different ways. An earlier edition of *Panorama* (tx. 16 March 1964) had reported from the Auschwitz trial, a significant event for European memory more generally, while *Tonight* (BBC1, 7 December 1964) featured survivor Rudolf Vrba addressing the German attitude towards Nazi war criminals in the present.[15] Looking further back into the past was *Who Raised His Voice against It?* (BBC1, 18 July 1968), a documentary that asked who in Germany had opposed Hitler.[16] Four years later an edition of *Europa* ('The Total Seduction', BBC2, 13 April 1972), a programme which brought together the best of European television, considered 'Why were the German people loyal to Hitler?' The BBC's science series *Horizon* raised similar questions in 'You Do as You Are Told' (BBC2, 28 October 1974), in which Stanley Milgram discussed his celebrated studies on obedience and authority with reference to the Holocaust: 'When six million Jews met their deaths at the hands of the Nazis, thousands of ordinary people lent a hand. How could this happen?'[17] It was a question that contained more than historical implications, raising questions of the potential for any society to marginalise and persecute a minority. This had been implicit 15 years before in an edition of *Panorama* (tx. 11 January 1960) that confronted anti-Semitism in the United Kingdom. During the course of the programme, Robert Kee interviewed a number of prominent British Jews, including the playwright Arnold Wesker. Wesker suggested that the post-war rise in anti-Semitism seen in this country might be a response to the fact that Jewish nationalism had grown stronger in the Anglo-Jewish community since the war. That in itself, he argued, was a direct consequence of the Nazi persecution:

> I think the obvious reason must be the enormous shock of what happened during the war with the six million Jews in the gas chambers, and this has had the effect of . . . making the Jewish community tighter . . . It hasn't only affected the Jewish community – I think it's affected world consciousness as well.

If Wesker's words looked outwards, referencing the Holocaust as paradigmatic event and touching on the nascent idea of a global 'Holocaust consciousness', Kee's concluding remarks were more introspective, speaking of how Jews and non-Jews in Britain were connected by a 'mutual difference' which,

> paradoxically, knits us more closely together – that's to say British culture is enriched by Jewish culture and the Jewish heritage, and the Jewish culture is enriched by the British heritage. Still at a time when simple louts who have to attack something in order to prove to themselves that they really exist at all are at work, we can never be too vigilant. The country in which the Jewish and non-Jewish strain once seemed to enrich each other most successfully – was Germany.[18]

That vigilance extended to one of the more unusual recurrent themes of the period as a number of programmes were broadcast that considered what would or could have happened to Britain should Hitler and fascism have triumphed then or in the future. 'Thirty-Minute Theatre' asked 'Could Britain go fascist?' in ... *And Was Invited to Form a Government* (BBC2, 22 May 1969), while *If Britain Had Fallen* (BBC1, 12 September 1972) was a documentary story told in three parts over the course of one evening, with a special edition of *Late Night Line-Up* (BBC2, 13 September 1972) to follow. This culminated in Philip Mackie's *An Englishman's Castle* (BBC2, 5–19 June 1978), a serial that asked 'What if Germany had won the war?', with the persecution of the Jews, now extended to Britain's shores, playing a crucial part in the plot.

Finally, in the politically charged late 1960s and early 1970s, Germany was not alone in being placed on trial by television. Uncomfortable questions were also asked in *America on Trial* (BBC1, 6 June 1971), the co-production with NET (United States) and ZDF (Germany), that saw Telford Taylor, formerly part of the American Prosecuting Counsel at the Nuremberg trials, compare the horrors of Nazi Germany with the ongoing situation in Vietnam, a subject also covered by Marcel Ophuls' *The Memory of Justice* (BBC2, 7 November 1976) five years later. That sense of justice was also evident in the first Holocaust miniseries, *QB VII* (BBC1, 24 and 25 April 1976), a dramatisation of the Dering libel trial that had made headline news as 'Auschwitz in England' ten years before.[19] *QB VII* made explicit connections between the Holocaust and the creation and continuation of Israel, links that were also made in two documentaries, *The State of the Jews* (BBC2, 2 May 1968) and *Israel: A Promised*

Land (BBC2, 11 May 1978), broadcast to mark the 20th and then 30th anniversaries of the establishment of Israel. [20]

It was within this developing context – or, more correctly, these contexts – that the BBC screened *Holocaust* three months later. This would, as Cole's article shows, provoke sustained engagement not only with what was shown but how, often focusing on the perceived superiority of British over American television. It was a familiar debate, one that had been seen 20 years before in one of the first BBC series to turn to the subject of the Holocaust.

This Is Your Life, 1955–1964

In his book on the Holocaust's relationship with American television, Jeffrey Shandler discusses an episode of the American series *This Is Your Life*. Broadcast on 27 May 1953, the life story of Hanna Bloch Kohner was 'one of the first American telecasts devoted to telling an individual's story of surviving Nazi persecution' and the first of 'at least five other broadcasts in which the series honored [sic] other Jewish survivors of Nazism, Jewish refugees, and individuals who rescued Jews from Nazi persecution'.[21] Watching that show was Ronnie Waldman, the BBC's Head of Light Entertainment, who was visiting America in search of ideas for new programmes. Rather than being impressed, he reportedly watched with a growing sense of discomfort as the cameras witnessed 'the reunion of some members of a Jewish family who had believed one another to be dead or missing through the European purges'.[22] Two years later, though, *This Is Your Life* made its British television debut and within a decade had also featured a survivor as its central figure.

One of several programme formats imported from America in the mid-1950s, *This Is Your Life* was 'one of the most popular TV programmes on British television ever, running almost 50 years, producing over 1000 editions, and, in the process, becoming a British institution'.[23] As Louis Barfe writes in his history of British light entertainment, the idea behind the show was 'simple':

> a person of note – sometimes a conventional celebrity, sometimes a worthier candidate, like a war hero – was caught unawares and presented with a potted biography. Friends, family and associates would make grand entrances in order to pay fulsome tribute to the subject of the show.[24]

At the end of the show that biography was presented to the guest in the form of the famous 'big red book', a souvenir full of photographs taken that evening.

Hosted by Eamonn Andrews, the BBC's version of *This Is Your Life* was an immediate success. The principal guests for these shows, as Barfe outlines, were drawn from the famous and the worthy, a mixture of showbusiness personalities, wartime heroes and three categories of lesser-known figures defined by the production team as 'do-gooders' (charity workers), 'dog-collars' (as above, but men or women of the cloth) and 'Pickles Cases' (people who have overcome illness or disability).[25] The first of the wartime heroes featured in the second episode (tx. 25 September 1955) when Yvonne Bailey, nee Baseden, a former member of the Special Operations Executive, relived her experiences, including her time as a prisoner in Ravensbrück.[26] Six months later, the camera returned (not for the first time) to the horrors of war with the story of Ida Cook. It was the first of at least five programmes that would feature in some way the persecution of the Jews of Europe.

Ida Cook, tx. 11 March 1956

On the evening of Sunday 11 March 1956, Mary Burchell and Nancy Spain, two popular writers of romantic fiction, were taken to the BBC's Lime Grove studios to record a talk on 'The Writing of Romantic Novels'. There the lights were rigged to fail and the talk hastily rearranged for Television Theatre. It was only then that Eamonn Andrews revealed to Burchell that she there not to give a talk, but to listen to 'a story more romantic than any fiction'. Burchell was the pseudonym of Ida Cook, who, with the help of her sister Louise, had been responsible for the rescue of Jewish refugees from Nazi Europe. The story of the Cooks was the subject of much press coverage in the early 1950s, with appearances on radio, television and the national newspapers. It is a story that has recently been the subject of a resurgence of interest thanks in part to Ida and Louise's receipt of the newly instigated 'Heroes of the Holocaust' award, to the republication of the autobiographical account of their experiences, and to a number of articles and books which have made the story familiar once again.[27] Given her contemporary profile, it seems unlikely to have been true, therefore, when Andrews told Cook that evening, that until 'a week or so ago', this was simply to have been 'the story of a writer with an unusual and intimate link with the world of Grand Opera':

> Suddenly, half way through our investigations we hit on something far more interesting and dramatic. A story that might have come straight from the case-book of a modern Scarlet Pimpernel: at great personal risk you and your sister Louise delivered from Nazi persecution a company of distraught and desperate human beings.[28]

There is no surviving copy of the programme – or indeed any of the five under discussion; however, a camera script, prepared in advance for the live broadcast, indicates that at that point there was to come from offstage a voice that belonged to a speaker whose identity was concealed from Cook and the audience. This piece of trickery would become one of the most eagerly anticipated parts of the show's routine.

> OFF-STAGE: My mother and my father and I myself owe our lives to you, Miss Cook.
> ANDREWS: A voice from those grim days of 1938. Whose is it?
> (IDA may recognise . . .)
> Yes. One of the many you saved, and one you haven't seen for many years – Walter Stiefel!
> (WALTER enters – greets IDA)
> You first met Miss Cook in Berlin, Mr Stiefel?
> STIEFEL: Yes. On a street corner and believe me, it was a very dangerous thing for her to do. It was arranged for me to meet her at the station carrying an English newspaper, but they were banned on that day, and I had a Swedish paper. Miss Cook and I were unable to recognise each other but, later, I was able to phone her and arranged the street corner meeting. It is impossible for any of us to express adequately our gratitude to Miss Cook and her sister. But for them I do not doubt that I would have ended my life in a concentration camp. I am very glad to have this opportunity of saying again – thank you, Ida and Louise Cook.
> ANDREWS: And thank you, Walter Stiefel, for coming down from Manchester.[29]

The story of Stiefel's flight was not discussed according to the remaining record.[30] Instead he took his seat on the stage, a constant silent presence, while Andrews turned to Cook, telling her, and reassuring both the studio audience and the viewers at home, that this was not to be 'a horror story', but 'the story of two girls and of how their love of opera and the people of opera led them into situations which needed tremendous courage and an unflinching faith in humanity'.[31]

Over the next 30 minutes the programme recalled how Cook had worked for the Civil Service in inter-war London, developing a love of music and then opera. It was around 1935–36, the time of 'an insidious change' in Europe, that conductor Clemens Krauss and his wife Viorica Krass-Ursuleac asked Ida and Louise to look after Frau Mayer-Lismann and her family, 'the first refugees' saved by the Cooks. At this point the script indicates that there was a change of pace, with the dialogue replaced by a montage of silent footage of Nazi persecution as the programme merged past with present through the use of the newsreels that would resonate with the audience:

> Nazis Lash Britain Again (Headline)
> Goebbels at Mic (Picture)
> Smashed Shop Window (Picture)
> Goebbels in Uniform (Picture)
> Night Orgy of Looting (Headline)
> Synagogue (Picture)
> Goebbels with Troops (Picture)

Andrews continued, recalling how in their travels the sisters saw 'the terror of Nazi persecution as the hideous, inhuman menace it is. All around you, men, women and children by the hundreds of thousands have one thought – to get out before they are engulfed by a tide of blood and torture.' 'Do we need to be reminded now of the bestiality, the misery and the murder that went on in places that you had known only as cities of light and gaiety and melody?' he asked. He did not wait for an answer to his rhetorical question: 'Early in 1938, Austria is invaded. Later in the same year Czechoslovakia. In November the fuse is touched off.' And shortly thereafter the screen then cut to a second montage, this time starting with an image of Herschel Grynszpan whose assassination of Ernst vom Rath was the trigger for *Kristallnacht*:

> Jewish Boy (Picture)
> Shot Nazi Envoy Dies (Headline)
> Jew with Placard (Picture)

As the images played Andrews provided a voiceover: 'A young Jew shoots a Nazi official and the hatred for the Jews is revealed in a crescendo of stark horror. The order goes out that every male Jew between the ages of sixteen and eighty is to be rounded up and sent to a concentration camp.' There was no further explanation, with the only pause being to allow Andrews to apologise to Cook for the subject matter, telling her 'I had no option but to recall these harrowing memories'. Andrews then continued to relay how the Cooks made regular trips to the continent, becoming 'the target for frantic appeals by men and women who knew that if they can't get out of Germany – and at once – they will die'. Their London flat becomes a 'clearing house for your refugees' until the onset of war finally makes it impossible for them to continue.

Most of the remainder of the programme focused on other aspects of Cook's life, but it returned to the rescue of Jewish refugees when she was joined onstage by Stanley Black, a tailor from whom Ida Cook had ordered a fur coat in post-war London. Black recalled for Andrews how he recognised Cook's name, 'because I had heard about all she had done for the Jewish people, and felt so tremendously grateful'. A fur coat 'was to be my way of showing a little of my appreciation'. To conclude, the last section of Cook's *Life* brought her story up-to-date with the introduction of John Slade who was working with Cook in a DP camp at Landschutt, Bavaria, home to 1200 people from 16 different countries.[32]

Cook later thanked producer Leslie Jackson 'for the perfectly wonderful evening'. 'It was', she wrote, 'just one of the most marvellous things that ever happened to me and I'm still happily dazzled.'[33] It was in some ways a fitting tribute to a remarkable woman and story, but the victim's story remained marginal to a programme that was a celebration of a British rescuer which told of the Jewish experience primarily through familiar newsreel footage. The focus on the British hero would also be true later that year when the fourth episode of the second series surprised charity worker Sue Ryder, a guest who was adamant that the story that needed to be both told and heard was that of the victim and not rescuer.

Sue Ryder, tx. 12 November 1956

The second series of *This Is Your Life* started with conservationist Peter Scott, actress Ada Reeve and Edinburgh fireman Peter Methven. Then on 12 November 1956, in a show pre-recorded in September at the King's Theatre, Hammersmith, it was the turn of Ryder, who was then working tirelessly with DPs across Europe. Like Cook, she was a person who had already featured on the BBC (although she had never heard of *This Is Your Life*) and is a person whose story has remained in the public consciousness.[34] Taking part that evening were friends and colleagues who would speak of Ryder's bravery and determination, including representatives of the Committee for Aid to Ex-Concentration Camp Survivors in Germany and former concentration camp inmates.

The programme opened with one of the most elaborate of all *Life* ruses, featuring an extended interview between Ryder and actress Edana Romney. Onstage with Ryder and Romney sat five people who spoke no English. They were all originally from Poland and all now lived in German DP camps. The first was Tadeusz Meucta, identified in the programme by his first name only. Tadeusz had been only 15 when he was deported to Mauthausen in 1940. He had been imprisoned there for five years, finally hitchhiking his way home after the war to discover his family dead. Josef Mojcik had escaped from a forced labour camp only to be sent to Auschwitz, 'where five million people were exterminated'. Next was Stefan Szypanski, a member of the Polish underground who had been in Auschwitz and Flossenbürg. The fourth person was Ludwig Jania, who 'after the most fearful interrogations [by the Nazis]' had been 'sent to a place we have all heard of – Dachau. The details of what he underwent there are too horrible to mention.' Finally came Captain Gruszynski, a Polish officer and POW who had spent seven years in different camps across Europe. These men were all homeless, all suffering from illness, physical injuries and mental scars which meant that they could not leave Germany. There were, Ryder explained to Romney, currently over 100,000 similar DPs across Europe, 'survivors of over twelve million who died or were exterminated during the war'. Unless something could be done, they were destined to remain DPs for the rest of their lives, condemned to live in the overcrowded former POW and slave labour camps, with little compensation for their treatment and no stimulation.

At that point, seven minutes into the programme according to a script annotation, the camera switched to Andrews who was seated in an offstage dressing-room. From there he explained that this elaborate opening was a subterfuge to surprise Ryder, an individual so prone to 'self-sacrifice' that it was suspected she would refuse to participate in what was planned. For that reason the announcement of the true purpose of the show was followed by the immediate presence onstage of Ryder's mother to ensure she remained. Once Ryder was safely seated in 'the chair of Honour' Andrews began the show proper, introducing it as 'a story of a young woman dedicated to helping people who were imprisoned and tortured in those infamous camps at Belsen, Buchenwald, Auschwitz and the rest'.[35]

For the next 20 minutes, the audience learned of Ryder's extraordinary efforts on behalf of the thousands of 'Forgotten Allies' trapped in camps across Europe.[36] The next day Cecil McGivern, Deputy Director of Television Broadcasting, called it 'an excellent edition, most moving and, of course, most timely', a reference to the Armistice day commemorations and the recent plight of Hungarian refugees.[37] The BBC's internal audience research gave viewing figures of 26 per cent of the adult public (55 per cent of the adult viewing public) and suggested that for many of them this had been the best *This Is Your Life* they had seen, giving it an RI of 76 (slightly above average of 72).[38] There was a minority who were critical of the fact that it had been filmed in advance, that Ryder was too young and her life 'severely limited', and that the introduction was drawn out and muddled. But the majority felt she was an 'excellent choice'. Here was 'a life that really did deserve to be told, and no more fitting day than this could have been chosen', reported one viewer.

One of the critics was Ryder herself. She 'hated the limelight' and was initially uncertain about the programme, even if the day after the recording she thanked Jackson 'so very much indeed for all your wonderful help for this Cause'. If she had appeared ungracious at the outset, she continued, 'it was only because I felt deeply embarrassed and shocked that I was the centre of a programme which I should naturally have preferred dedicated solely to these brave and unfortunate people who endured such appalling sufferings'. With that in mind, Ryder asked Jackson if, when the programme was eventually broadcast, the viewer's attention could be drawn to the importance of hospital visiting and the patients.

Ryder herself missed the broadcast as she was 'dashing from Camp to Camp in Germany', but the public response was overwhelmingly positive.[39] When donations and offers of help started coming in she realised, Andrews would later recall, that 'we [the programme makers] were trying to help, too'.[40] By 12 December 1956 approximately £2066 had been received in donations.[41] There was also a request from one viewer for contact details of the Polish workers who appeared on the programme, another from a member of the public who had adopted a Polish Displaced family, and another from a registered foster mother living in Kent who asked that Ryder be told 'we are quite willing to have 2 children, any nationality boys or girls preferably young, say under 7 or 8'.

Sue Ryder's appearance once again highlighted the heroic British response to the fate of refugees and DPs across Europe, making a neat parallel to Ida Cook's pre-war rescue efforts. It was another familiar story but unlike Cook's there was no newsreel footage involved in the retelling, as the programme considered more the aftermath and ongoing troubles rather than the historical persecution under Hitler. Furthermore, Ryder's story, rooted in the present, made reference to Auschwitz and a camp experience that went beyond Belsen, taking it into a realm of memory and memorialisation that was at that time unfamiliar for a British audience, starting to integrate both Britain and the Holocaust into a wider context. The next related episode, however, took a step backwards as it returned to the liberation of Belsen.

Hugh Llewellyn Glyn-Hughes, tx. 9 March 1959

Brigadier Hugh Llewellyn Glyn-Hughes was travelling in the same jeep with Richard Dimbleby when he first entered Belsen. As chief doctor of the Second Army, he was subsequently in charge of supervising the medical treatment in the camp. It is that role for which he is probably best remembered, but Belsen was, of course, just one part of Glyn-Hughes' life.[42] He was, Andrews said to him on the evening of 9 March 1959, a man with 'decorations too numerous to mention'.

> And the trouble is where to begin to spring surprises on you. Perhaps a place you might <u>least</u> like to remember. A place whose very name implies horror – the dreaded concentration camp at Belsen, whose very existence shocked the civilised world.

As Andrews finished speaking, footage of liberation was then shown, with a Grams track (the soundtrack accompaniment) indicating the effect as simply 'Horror'. Afterwards, Andrews continued: 'On April 15th you became the first British medical officer to set foot inside the camp. There you find only one British subject alive.' There then came a mystery voice:

> Voice (off-stage): I was that prisoner.
> (Might not recognise)
> ANDREWS: You haven't met since you both gave evidence at the Belsen Camp trials in Luneburg 1945. He's flown from Jersey where he is a headmaster, to be with you tonight. Come in Harold Le Druillenec.
> [Applause]
> Le Druillenec enters, greets.
> ANDREWS: Would you like to tell us about the liberation of Belsen.

LE DRUILLENEC: For weeks there had been rumours that the British were coming. But the remainder of my friends and I were sure they would be too late. The death roll had been enormous – over 20,000 victims, and now the guards were shooting whole batches of prisoners. We hadn't eaten for days, and I remember that morning we were pleased because we had found some grass to chew.

ANDREWS: But this time those rumours <u>were</u> true.

LE DRUILLENEC: Yes, the first thing I saw was a truck with some British soldiers in it. I thought I rushed up to them, but they told me afterwards that I crawled there on all fours.

ANDREWS: [To camera]
And no wonder, because this man's weight was down to 90 pounds.
[To Le Druillenec]
What do you remember about Brigadier Hughes?

LE DRUILLENEC: At the first interrogation nothing. You see I didn't really know who was questioning me. It was only at a later interrogation by the Brigadier that I realised it was the same man who had listened to me with such patience, kindness and understanding.

ANDREWS: For making that trip from Jersey to be with us tonight, thank you, Harold Le Druillenec.

Le Druillenec's story is yet again one that had been heard on the BBC before and has been told since. Like Cook, he is now a 'Hero of the Holocaust' and his testimony to liberation appears alongside Dimbleby's on the BBC's archive website. Here his attendance confirms the telling of a particularly British experience of the camps, one that again failed to engage with the Jewish particularity of what the liberators found. Things might, however, have been different. At the end of the surviving programme script, crossed through on p. 33, there is a section that suggests that the programme was originally intended to end where it had begun, with one final guest who would have been another silent survivor, present for symbolic purposes without any agency of his own:

ANDREWS: We began your story in Belsen, the camp of horror from which so few people came out alive. One of those survivors you have met. Our investigators found another. Unfortunately he speaks no English, but when we told him of our plans he not only left a sick bed, but insisted on paying his own expenses to fly from France to pay <u>his</u> tribute to you tonight. Come in Mr . . . Rosensaft.
(Mr Rosensaft enters, greets.)
Thank you Mr Rosensaft for making that trip to be with us tonight.
(Mr Rosensaft exits)[43]

After Cook and Ryder, two people who worked closely with refugees before and after the war, Glyn-Hughes' story took the viewer closer to the horrors by moving into the camp, but continued to describe that experience as part of a broader narrative of the war. Moreover, it focused on the familiar image of Belsen and its liberation rather than engaging with a survivor, with the Jewish specificity lost as it had been in Ryder's. The final two programmes to be discussed at least seemed to challenge this one-dimensional engagement, but how they did so is unclear. As with Cook, Ryder and Glyn-Hughes, there is no surviving copy of the programme, but in these cases the BBC Written Archives (WAC) has no script or production file either. The analysis is therefore fleeting, but the remaining records and references suggest that survivors were starting to speak for themselves and that people wanted to hear these stories. The first of these, on 24 October 1960, sandwiched between programmes on Clarence Wolfe, Warden of Aberlour Orphanage, and T. E. B. Clarke, the screenwriter at Ealing Studios, was Charles Coward, another subsequent 'Hero of the Holocaust' and 'Righteous among the Nations'.

Charles Coward, tx. 24 October 1960

There is much to say about Coward's life and his (now questioned) experiences in Auschwitz, but that fame is little in evidence from the surviving material of his appearance on *This Is Your Life*. There is virtually no surviving material in the BBC's WAC, with one of the few references coming from a review in the *Jewish Chronicle*:

> The remarkable story of how Charles Coward, a former British POW in Germany, rescued Jews from Auschwitz was told in the BBC feature 'This is Your Life' on Monday. Cecil Sklan, a fellow-prisoner with Mr Coward, paid tribute to all he had done to save Jews from almost certain death. Also brought to the studio for the occasion was a former inmate of Auschwitz [Norbert Wollheim], now living in New York, who lost his wife and three year-old son in the camp. Shots taken at Auschwitz were seen by viewers.[44]

Although only offering glimpses, it is a review that shows how the Holocaust was developing its own narrative. Coward's Britishness and heroism were still very much the focus (his guests included other former inmates), but the interview with Sklan meant an explicit connection to the Jewish victims in a way that had been missing from Glyn-Hughes' account. This was emphasised by the appearance of Norbert Wollheim at the end of the programme, his appearance as the final guest suggesting that this was in some sense the culmination of the life story:

> It was certainly the climax of the broadcast, when, at the end, Norbert Wollheim appeared. In a most dignified and impressive way Wollheim paid tribute to this unassuming Cockney, who, out of a sense of unshakeable decency and at danger to his own life, single-handedly conducted his rescue work.[45]

Once again, therefore, the surviving evidence suggests that Coward's programme was about British rescue and resolve in the face of the horrors of Nazi Germany, a celebration of one life lived fully and not a memorial for the six million lost. And yet the programme was also moving slowly closer to the survivor's story and it was no surprise therefore that in the final *This Is Your Life* under discussion the 'victim' of the show was also a victim of the Holocaust.[46]

Alice Stern, tx. 10 October 1963

Similar to the Coward episode, there is no surviving copy of the programme, no script, no production file, no audience research report and virtually no reviews. The BBC's Subject Index cards under the subject of 'Concentration Camps' record the show simply as '10.10.63. This is your life. Alice Stern. T/r. in camps for Jews. etc.'. There was a review in the *Jewish Chronicle*, but even here the coverage was surprisingly understated. Under the title of 'No Punches Pulled', a reference not to *This Is Your Life* but to a documentary series, *The Jew in the World*, which was showing on ITV, the story of Stern's life was simply one of several of 'Jewish-interest' which could be found that week 'all over the networks':

> On BBC the subject of 'This is Your Life' was a concentration camp survivor, Mrs Alice Stern, now living in London. Viewers heard how her amazing courage and will to live helped her to triumph in the face of overwhelming odds.[47]

The only additional guidance to the programme in the BBC WAC comes from the Programmes as Broadcast (a detailed record of the transmission times and content) which at least reveals the names of those featured on screen that evening. These included not only Andrews and Stern, but Mrs Gina Haurowitz, Mrs H. Libockowitz, Mrs F. Billetta, Felix Morel, Mrs A. Parnes, Mrs Hana Pravda, Doris Lilttell, with four women and two men as 'extras'. Mrs Ilsa Krause featured in a film sequence, and George Pravda in a recorded insert. Even this brief list offers further evidence of the increased presence of the Holocaust survivor. Hana Pravda, a former prisoner in Auschwitz, had recently been seen in the Studio 4 production of *Address Unknown*, and would be seen again as Emma Cohen, a concentration camp survivor (one never named as Jewish) in *Survivors* (1975–1977), Terry Nation's vision of post-apocalyptic Britain. She would later appear in *QB VII* as a Holocaust survivor alongside her husband, George Pravda, another recognisable and familiar face on British screens, including a part in *The Password Is Courage*, the film version of the life of Charles Coward, and the lead in *The Unplayed Part* (tx. 2 October 1960) one of the earliest of BBC plays to be set in a concentration camp.[48]

Stern's appearance completed the progression from rescuer to liberator to inmate to survivor that had started eight years before. In starting with Ida Cook, the 'Scarlet Pimpernel' figure, and positioning her exploits within a specifically British and literary tradition, the programme foregrounded a life story of heroic rescue rather than one curtailed by the horrors. Similarly Ryder's story was very much about heroism, and one again undertaken by a young woman in terrible circumstances. With Glyn-Hughes the pattern remained constant even as it changed, with the rescuer now also being a liberator. In each of these programmes at least one survivor had been present onstage, but they were not there to speak of their own experiences but rather to honour the actions of the principal guest. When it was Charles Coward's turn to take centrestage, the remaining documents hint at the fact that for the first time the experiences of life in the camps and Nazi-occupied Europe more generally were at least being actively remembered and sought. That was affirmed three years later when Stern became the first victim to be the focal point for the camera, telling of her life to an audience of around 10 million people.

From the vantage point of 50 years later, given the interest in *This is Your Life* and the heightened awareness of the Holocaust, these last two programmes seem the most remarkable, not because they happened but because of the lack of press coverage they were afforded and the absence of any recordings or records remaining in the BBC's archives. It is hard to imagine that they would not be preserved now, but their absence is indicative of just how far removed the present day is from the 1960s in terms of the retention of broadcast material and the Holocaust.[49] It is an absence that highlights the marketing, publicity and analysis that preceded and followed *Holocaust* 14 years later.

As an addendum, there is another interesting parallel between *This Is Your Life* and *Holocaust*. In 1955, the BBC's version of *This Is Your Life* was an immediate success, but its appeal was not universal, with many believing this type of American schmaltz to be an invasion of privacy, inferior to 'British programmes' and even vulgar in its basic premise of making entertainment from what could be embarrassing and harrowing memories. A customs officer interviewed for the BBC's audience research after the very first programme captured the kind of ambivalence it could engender: 'Although I would definitely watch another programme of this out of ghoulish curiosity, I think we'd be better off without it.'[50] Forward three years and *This Is Your Life* was regularly gaining audience figures as high as 10–12 million, meaning it was watched by around 40 per cent of the television viewing public or 25 per cent of the adult population as a whole.[51] Yet, complaints about its content and format continued to be widespread. This was a show considered by some to be 'deplorable', one that featured 'abominable victimisation' and paraded 'false enthusiasm and private emotions...[for] public curiosity'.[52] For the *Daily Mirror* it was 'the most revolting' of all television programmes, 'a non-stop exercise in embarrassment wrapped up in unbearable entertainment'.[53] But the high viewing figures meant that even the critics had to acknowledge that the show had 'come to stay'.[54] Within this dislike for the programme there was the regular suggestion that it was the show's transatlantic origin that was to blame. It was, for example, a programme containing 'un-English exhibitions' and when Anna Neagle broke down in tears on the show, the *Daily Express* condemned it as 'the most embarrassing of all the editions of the American-invented programme'.[55] In the same paper, James Thomas was more precise in his criticism, writing that 'The sober cautious BBC brought this show from American TV, where the unctuous, fulsome Mr Ralph Edwards runs it as a weekly peepshow which specialises in shock, embarrassment, and intrusion.'[56] It may have been watched by millions every week, but popularity did not equate to quality, particularly when the programme's success was gauged 'by the amount of emotion generated by its weekly victim – and that has nothing to do with decency, or with human dignity'.[57] Wilfred Altman in *Stage* offered another damning assessment of this 'mass-exploitation of morbid curiosity', one that criticised the audience as much as the programme makers: 'the more the shock, discomfort and embarrassment displayed by the victim, the more they love it...It doesn't encourage viewers to think, to enjoy, to laugh. Rather it arouses sentimentality, sympathy or snobbism.' And yet he concluded 'therein lies the programme's appeal'.[58] It is an evaluation that could have been written in response to *Holocaust* 20 years later. And yet the

similarity in responses conceals that 1958 and 1978 provided different contexts for programmes that were in many ways the antithesis of
each other. *Holocaust* offered a dramatised version of the Holocaust that
was aimed at an international market, a big budget production with
a cast of hundreds. By contrast, *This Is Your Life* was produced for a
far more geographically limited audience, with its focus being people
and events that were familiar to a British narrative of the war, a narrative that did not include the Holocaust, at least not its victims. These
programmes celebrated the British lives on display, with the destruction of the Jews of Europe being but one aspect. They were also rigidly
defined narratives which positioned the Holocaust within a process of
memorialisation. In the cases of Cook, Ryder, Glyn-Hughes and Coward, these programmes memorialised British citizens with heroic pasts,
presents and futures, with their role in the Holocaust being to rescue
others through their direct action before, during and after the war. Only
when the camera turned to Stern did the BBC's version of *This Is Your
Life* have as its victim someone who was also a victim of the Holocaust.
While that programme appears to have remained primarily a celebration of courage and resilience, describing how Stern's 'will to live' had
enabled her to survive 'in the face of overwhelming odds', the choice
of Stern was evidence that by 1964 the Holocaust had entered into the
mainstream with the victims at last being given a voice to tell their own
stories.

Acknowledgements

I thank Caroline Sharples, Tony Kushner, the incredibly generous Tony
Lee of the wonderful www.bigredbook.info, and the staff of the BBC's
Written Archives Centre (hereafter the BBC WAC), especially Els Boonen,
Katie Ankers, Jess Hogg and Jacquie Kavanagh, for their help and
comments.

Notes

1. Tim Cole, 'Marvellous Raisins in a Badly-cooked Cake', this volume;
   Emiliano Perra, 'Narratives of Innocence and Victimhood: The Reception
   of the Miniseries Holocaust in Italy', *Holocaust and Genocide Studies*, 22,
   3 (2008); Jeffrey Shandler, *While America Watches: Television the Holocaust*
   (Oxford,1999), 155–178; and the special edition of *New German Critique* 19
   (1) (1980).
2. Tim Cole, this volume.
3. The persecution and attempted extermination of the Jews of Europe had
   been present on BBC television since 1946, the year that the service returned
   after a seven-year hiatus. For a summary of the first ten years, see James

Jordan, 'Assimilated, Integrated, Other: An Introduction to Jews in British Television', in Hannah Ewence and Tony Kushner (eds), *Whatever Happened to British Jewish Studies?* (London: Vallentine Mitchell, 2012), 259–274; and James Jordan, '*The Prisoner* (1952) and the Perpetrator in Early Post-war British Television', in Jenni Adams and Sue Vice (eds), *Representing Perpetrators in Holocaust Literature and Film* (London: Vallentine Mitchell, 2012), 207–229.

4. Analysis of these early programmes is notoriously problematic. Many of them no longer exist in any form and the production files at the BBC WAC can be inconsistent and incomplete, making it impossible to speak with total certainty about what was seen on screen.

5. Shandler, *While America Watches*, xviii.

6. The BBC's relationship with the Nazi annihilation of the Jews of Europe does of course extend beyond television. The Corporation had played an important role before and during the Second World War in reporting events, broadcasting news to those living in occupied Europe, and transmitting messages on behalf of the governments in exile based in London. On a more personal level, from the 1930s onwards the BBC employed Jewish refugees from Nazi Germany in various positions, at first in areas such as monitoring and the European services, but subsequently extending more widely into the Corporation. BBC WAC R49/11/1–11 Staff Policy: Aliens: Employment of Aliens, 1937–1954. On the role of the BBC as a broadcaster of news during the war see, for example, Renee Poznanski, ' "Nobody is Protected from Deportation": The Free French in London on the Persecution of the Jews', in Jan Lanicek and James Jordan (eds), *Governments-in-Exile and the Jews during the Second World War* (London: Vallentine Mitchell, 2013), 163–188.

7. 'Studies in Racialism', *Jewish Chronicle*, 12 November 1965, 36.

8. BBC WAC Audience Research Report VR/65/654 and Joel Cang, 'Ghetto Horrors', *Jewish Chronicle*, 26 November 1965, 51.

9. Feature films were also part of this contextualisation. The 'Cinema 625' series included screenings of *Transport from Paradise* (BBC2, 19 July 1964), *Stars* (BBC2, 23 January 1965) and *Return from the Ashes* (BBC2, 15 November 1975).

10. 'Compelling Drama', *Jewish Chronicle*, 17 August 1962, 21. The Ghetto also featured in *Tonight* (tx. 16/4/1963) and *Europa* ('Testimony', BBC2, 17 July 1968), programmes that dealt respectively with the twentieth and twenty-fifth anniversaries of its destruction.

11. Patricia Erens, *The Jew in American Cinema* (Bloomington: Indiana University Press, 1988), 167.

12. 'Moving Feature on Nazi Camps', *Jewish Chronicle*, 15 January 1965, 34. In early 1965 another episode of *Monitor* (BBC1, tx. 12 January 1965) reported on the work of composer Wilfred Josephs and his *Requiem*, with footage of the 'infamous concentration camps, the bodies, the clothing, the suitcases of those done to death'. These notions of memory and memorialisation were also problematised by *Tonight* (BBC1, 3 May 1965) when Julian Pettifer reported on the tourist trade that was growing up around Dachau.

13. Judith Petersen 'Belsen and a Broadcasting Icon', *Holocaust Studies: A Journal of Culture and History*, 13 (1) (Summer 2007), 19–43. The absence has not hindered its continued status as the BBC's pre-eminent account of the

Holocaust, as if it were always used and understood in that way. This can be
seen on the BBC's online archive 'WWII: Witnessing the Holocaust' (http://
www.bbc.co.uk/archive/holocaust/). A collection of 17 (mainly radio) programmes and nine documents, this archive provides 'personal accounts of
persecution and genocide by the Nazi regime' from 70 years of broadcasting,
including, in prime position at the head of the page, placed chronologically
and conceptually first, Richard Dimbleby's picture and a link to his account
of Belsen.

14. Glyn Jones, 'Victory in Europe – Twenty Years After', *Radio Times*, 6 May
1965, 3; and DP, 'Moving Feature on Belsen', *Jewish Chronicle*, 21 May 1965,
34. The *Radio Times* feature focused on the positive and redemptive perception of liberation, with an accompanying photograph showing a face
in close-up, one that the caption felt showed 'even at Belsen, a victory
smile'. Footage of liberation was also seen in *Valiant Years*, episode 24, 'Tying
the Knot', (BBC1, 22 July 1961), and *Richard Dimbleby, 1913–1965* (BBC1,
22 December 1965); *One Pair of Eyes: 'Who Are the Cockneys, Now?'* (BBC2,
17 August 1968) and *Richard Dimbleby: A Broadcasting Life* (BBC2, 15 September 1975). There has been much written on Belsen including Jo Reilly,
Belsen: The Liberation of a Concentration Camp (London: Routledge, 1998)
and Suzanne Bardgett and David Cesarani, eds, *Belsen 1945: New Historical
Perspectives* (London: Vallentine Mitchell, 2006).

15. Other talks/current affairs programmes to address 'the perpetrator' included
Portraits of Power (tx. 9 April 1957), *Late Night Final* ('Eichmann, Law and
Grace', tx. 25 May 1960), interviews with General von Senger on *Face to Face*
(2 October 1960) and Albert Speer on *Midweek* (BBC1, 21 November 1973).
Fugitive war criminals were also the subject of *Tonight* (Pieter Menten's War,
BBC1, 16 June 1977) and *Panorama* ('Blind Eye to Murder', BBC1, 20 February
1978).

16. Lawrence Gordon Clark, 'The Germans Who Hated Hitler', *Radio Times*,
11 July 1964, 26. This issue had been addressed far earlier on the radio, in
Louis Hagen's *Follow My Leader* (Home Service, 13 and 16 May 1952), based
on the book of the same name. Hagen's book, but surprisingly not its broadcast, which brought it into the mainstream, is discussed in David Cesarani,
'How Post-war Britain Reflected on the Nazi Persecution and Mass Murder of
Europe's Jews: A Reassessment of Early Responses', in Ewence and Kushner,
eds, *Whatever Happened to British Jewish Studies*, 99–135, esp. 119–120.

17. *Horizon* also looked at the Holocaust in an edition 'What is Race?' (BBC2, 13
March 1972). The convergence of science, race and genocide were also an
important aspect of Jacob Bronowski's magisterial series *The Ascent of Man*
(1973), most notably episode 11, 'Knowledge or Certainty' (BBC2, 14 July
1973).

18. BBC WAC TV Talks, scripts 1955–1964. See also BBC WAC T32/1249
Panorama. Other programmes to discuss anti-Semitism included *Brains Trust*
(tx. 1 February 1959 and 7 January 1960), *Tonight* (tx. 4 January 1960), *View-
point* ('The Scapegoat', tx. 20 April 1960) and *European Journal* (BBC1, 20 April
1965), a report on 'Jews in Germany Today'.

19. Dering's trial had been headline news in the 1960s and had already been
the subject of the documentary *According to the Rules: A Doctor in Auschwitz*
(BBC1, 31 March 1972). That programme is previewed in Robert Ottaway,

'After Auschwitz: If I see a crust...I must pick it up', *Radio Times*, 23 March 1972, 16. For a summary of the trial see Mavis M. Hill and L. Norman Williams, *Auschwitz in England: A Record of a Libel Action* (1965; New York, Ballantine Books, 1966) or Uris' dramatised version in Leon Uris, *QB VII* (New York: Doubleday and Co., Inc, 1970).

20. Gordon Burn, 'Vietnam: A Criminal War', Radio Times, 3 June 1971, 3. Both of these were directly inspired by Telford Taylor's *Nuremberg and Vietnam: An American Tragedy* (Chicago: Quadrangle Books, 1970).

21. Shandler, *While America Watches*, 30–40.

22. Cyril Aynsley, 'Snoopers on TV? Not on Your Life!', *Daily Express*, 1 March 1955.

23. http://www.bigredbook.info/index.html, accessed 1 March 2013.

24. Louis Barfe, *Turned Out Nice Again: The Story of British Light Entertainment* (London: Atlantic Books, 2008), 272–273.

25. Philip Purser, 'Will a "Life" Man Ever Stalk Out?', *News Chronicle*, 2 February 1959.

26. Her 'life' was watched by 19 per cent of the population and gained an RI of 74, even though some felt her composure under pressure made for less than compelling television. BBC WAC Audience Research Report VR/55/477. Other stories to consider life in concentration camps included *It Happened to Me* (tx. 26/1/1960), in which Mary Lindell related to Hywel Davies her account of surviving Ravensbrück. Her story was later made into the film *One Against the Wind* (1991).

27. Five years before *This is Your Life* she and her sister Louise had appeared on television on *Designed for Women* (tx. 8 March 1951), one of the first magazine programmes, and on radio in *A Tale of Two Sisters* (Light Programme, 24 September 1951. This had been published the year before as *We Followed Our Stars* (London: Mills and Boon, 1950).

28. This and subsequent quotes are from BBC WAC TV Talks Scripts, 1955–1964. In the absence of a recording of the programme it is impossible to be certain that what played out on screen took place precisely as per the script.

29. Nigel Ward, one of the researchers, had contacted Hyman Weinberg of Weinberg's Weatherproofs, Cheetham, Manchester to assist in tracking down Stiefel, with requests made through a number of refugee organisations and the Aliens department of Manchester police.

30. Cook's appearance and Stiefel's story are briefly expanded upon in Ida Cook, *Safe Passage* and Lyn Smith, *Heroes of the Holocaust: Ordinary Britons who Risked their Lives to Make a Difference* (London: Ebury Press, 2012), 79.

31. Script. 5.

32. BBC WAC T12/503/4 This is Your Life 1956.

33. Cook to Jackson, 12 March 1956, BBC WAC T12/503/4 This is Your Life 1956.

34. Sue Ryder, *Child of My Love: An Autobiography* (London: Colllins Harvill, 1986), 242. Ryder had been on the radio the year before for *Forgotten Allies* (Home Service, 10 August 1955) and there had been documentaries that confronted the terrible plight of the refugee since television had returned. Most recently *The Great Unwanted* (tx. 3 October 1956), prepared in co-operation with Dutch World Radio and the United Nations High Commissioner for Refugees, had seen Richard Dimbleby take a journey through some of Europe's refugee camps.

35. The legacy of Belsen and the work of Sue Ryder would be seen together nearly ten years later in the *Panorama* episode from 1965 that took Richard Dimbleby back to Belsen.
36. The programme was substantially over budget, with the total cost including full overheads coming to £1825 (the normal figure was £950). Memo, LE Organiser TV to Leslie Jackson, 25 January 1957, BBC WAC T12/503/7. Although there is no surviving copy, there is footage of Ryder discussing her appearance in the subsequent review programme broadcast at the end of the series.
37. DDTelB to HLETel, 13 November 1956.
38. BBC WAC VR/56/595 Audience Research Report.
39. Other rescuers included Gertruida Wijsmuller Meijer (*Tonight*, tx. 10 April 1957) and Oscar Schindler (*Tonight*, tx. 15 December 1964), who was, like Cook, described as a 'Scarlet Pimpernel'.
40. Eamonn Andrews, 'This is Your Life', *Weekend*, 7–11 May 1958, 4–5.
41. Sue Ryder returned to the show for a 'flashback' episode and then again when her husband Leonard Cheshire was the guest on 19 September 1960.
42. Glyn-Hughes was seen again (with Dimbleby) on *Panorama* in 1965 and *24 Hours* (BBC1, 21/12/1968) when he offered a rebuttal to Russell Barton's suggestion that conditions in Belsen were not too bad in 1945. Harold le Druillenec recounted his memories of Belsen for the twentieth anniversary for local news item on *Spotlight* (BBC1, SW region, 14 April 1965).
43. It would seem likely that the illness simply prevented Rosenaft's appearance; it also seems likely that this was Josef Rosensaft. See Rainer Schulze, 'A Continual Source of Trouble': The Displaced Persons Camp Bergen-Belsen (Hohne), 1945–1950. http://www.tlemea.com/postwareurope/index.htm. Glyn-Hughes' souvenir of the evening, the big red book, is held at the Army Medical Services Museum, Ash Vale (http://www.ams-museum.org.uk/museum/). Yet again I am grateful to Tony Lee for his help in this regard.
44. DP 'Auschwitz Story', *Jewish Chronicle*, 28 October 1960, 31. The 54 seconds of silent film footage was provided by Films of Poland (*Films Polski*) and was almost certainly the liberation of Auschwitz footage which had been sourced for *Monitor* in 1958. In addition, the PasB lists Coward's guests as, in order of appearance, Norbert Wollheim, Mrs Dixon, G.A.T. Walton, R.A. Hartland, Cecil Sklan, Grigor Anderson, W.R. Kinnear, T. Reynell, C. Skeels, H.J. Powell, Herbert Rice, Wallace Clarke and T.W. Daldry. With film sequences featuring appearances from Jayne Mansfield (from Athens), Miss Line Renaud (Paris) and John Carter (North Middlesex Hospital). For more on Coward see John Castle, *The Password Is Courage* (London: Souvenir Press, 1954); Joseph Robert White, ' "Even in Auschwitz ... Humanity Could Prevail": British POWs and Jewish Concentration-Camp Inmates at IG Auschwitz, 1943–1945', *Holocaust and Genocide Studies*, 15 (2) (2001), 266–295; and Duncan Little, *Allies in Auschwitz: The Untold Story of British POWs Held Captive in the Nazis' Most Infamous Death Camp* (Forest Row: Clairview Books, 2009). The film version of *The Password Is Courage* (dir. Andrew L. Stone, 1962) contains little of Coward's experiences of the concentration camps. Joseph White's article refers to a photograph of Coward and Hartland during the show, wrongly attributed to 1962, in Hartland's personal collection of newspaper clippings.
45. 'Norbert Wollheim on TV Screen', *AJR Information*, XV (12), 3.

46. This was a pattern that would be replicated on the BBC more generally as the survivor's story came to the fore in plays including *Thirty-Minute Theatre*'s 'The Boat to Addis Ababa' (BBC2, 27 February 1969) and 'Reparation' (BBC2, 24 January 1970). 'The Boat to Addis Ababa' told the story of David Landau, 'a young Jew ... just escaped from the Warsaw ghetto', while 'Reparation' starred Sydney Tafler and Irene Prador in a play about a Jewish couple 'wait[ing] for a German Appeal Court to hear their claim for compensation for their suffering and loss of property at the hands of the Nazis'. *Radio Times*, 20 February 1969, 51 and 22 January 1970, 13. Around the same time current affairs programme *24 Hours* (2 May 1967) included an interview with Richard Glazer in a section 'Revisit to Treblinka' and then in April 1974 *Selected to Live* (BBC2, 14 April 1974) and the regional news programme *Midlands Today* (BBC1, 25 April 1974) featured Johanna-Ruth Dobschiner and Kitty Hart, respectively.
47. DP, 'No Punches Pulled', *Jewish Chronicle*, 18 October 1963, 40.
48. 'Hana-Maria, Survivor', *Radio Times*, 21 September 1972, 5. Pravda's biography and wartime experiences are recounted in her diary, now kept at the Imperial War Museum, London, and published in edited form as Hana Pravda, *I Was Writing This Diary for You, Sasha*, edited and translated by Edward Fenton (Oxford: Day Books, 2000).
49. The decisions behind the retention of scripts is a mystery and there is no suggestion of a policy behind what was or was not kept. It seems remarkable that there should be no copy in the WAC of the script to Manchester United football manager Matt Busby's first appearance on 6 January 1958, one month before the fateful Munich air crash.
50. BBC WAC Audience Research Report VR/55/369.
51. Jackson to AHLETel, 13 March 1958, BBC WAC T12/522/2 TV Light Entertainment, This is Your Life, General 1957–59; BBC WAC Audience Research Report VR/59/2 This is Your Life.
52. 'This Isn't Your Life', *Daily Mirror*, 24 April 1956; 'Tricked', *Southern Daily Echo*, 18 January 1957.
53. Unknown, 'This Isn't Your Life', *Daily Mirror*, 19 February 1958. See also 'Victims Held by Good Manners?', *Manchester Guardian*, 25 January 1957; John Blunt, 'Blunt Speaking', *Yorkshire Evening Post*, 22 January 1958; Robert Cannell, 'Anna Neagle Weeps before TV Millions', *Daily Express*, 18 February 1958; Douglas Warth, *Daily Herald*, 19 February 1958.
54. ' "This Is Your Life": Distasteful Approach', *Manchester Guardian*, 5 February 1958.
55. Jack Allwood, 'How Embarrassing ... but How Popular!', *Yorkshire Evening Post*, 3 May 1961.
56. 'The Cruel Keyhole', *Daily Express*, 19 February 1958.
57. Candidus, 'Is this Life?' *Daily Sketch*, 19 February 1958.
58. Wilfred Altman, 'Is This the Best TV Can Do? 2. "This Is Your Life" ', *Stage*, 4 December 1958.

6
The Holocaust in British Television and Film: A Look over the Fence

Olaf Jensen

The essays by Tim Cole and James Jordan in this volume confirm the impressions one regularly gets when considering public media in Britain since 1945: the Holocaust was not a topic of major concern but merely seen as an add-on to the Second World War. The war itself and the Nazis were much more interesting – and easier to make fun of. One can only admire the lightness and easiness with which British television series, from *Dad's Army* to *Allo, Allo!*; from *Fawlty Towers* to *That Mitchell and Webb Look*, deal with the Second World War and the Nazis, usually turning it into a light affair complete with a laughter track. The Germans are mainly characterised as fools, speaking English with a heavy German accent and outwitted by everyone – an exception here may be *Dad's Army* which places the irony and humiliation firmly on the caricatured members of the British Home Guard. The only German-produced equivalent that comes to mind are episodes of *Obersalzberg* within the comedy show *Switch Reloaded* that has run on channel *ProSieben* since 2007.[1] Here, the German version of *The Office* meets Hitler's headquarters: a deranged Hitler is barely in control of his office, struggling with missing swastika keys on the typewriters, bullied and controlled by Goebbels and constantly sent poisoned cookies by Graf Stauffenberg.

All these comedies have one thing in common: they make fun of the Nazi elite, the SS or Gestapo, Wehrmacht soldiers, officers and generals, the home guard or French villagers – but they do not make fun of anything to do with the Holocaust; Jews being deported, in ghettos or death camps do not make good comedy. Only a few comedians have tried to approach this topic, an example being Ricky Gervais's imaginary dialogue between Nietzsche and Hitler (where Nietzsche discovers that Hitler 'went way too far' with his writings) or when he compares *History Channel* programmes on Anne Frank with *Discovery*

115

Channel programmes on sharks, concluding that Nazis are 'rubbish' since sharks would have found Anne Frank in an instant.[2] Usually, though, the focus lies firmly on war-related issues as safe ground. It is acceptable to make fun of war and ridicule chains of command, ignorant superiors or simple-minded Germans. It is a safe ground because the war has a very specific meaning for British identity: aside from the Blitz, it was not fought on British soil, and Britain was not occupied (with the exception of the Channel Islands). Britain was victorious in fighting Nazi Germany, plain and simple. In France or Germany, the war has a completely different connotation. France was – and still is – shaken by the experience of defeat and occupation and struggles with the history and memory of the Vichy regime. Germany, obviously, is the country that launched a world war and the genocide against the European Jews.

Therefore, it is obvious that Britain has a different take on war and the Holocaust. The war, with the sacrifices made to defeat Nazi Germany, especially going it alone at the beginning, deserves unreserved respect and is a cornerstone in the history of Britain that is still very important for the collective identity of the country. However, this interpretation of the conflict has also given war itself a positive connotation, far different to the way it is seen by its European neighbours. As Tom Lawson suggests elsewhere in this volume, it also brings forth a tradition rooted in the Empire. These narratives of the Second World War have necessarily had an impact upon British popular culture. James Jordan notes that the murder of the European Jews during what we now call the Holocaust was a 'regular presence'[3] on British Television from 1955 onwards, yet one could say this was mainly as a vehicle to focus on the British experience and the heroics of non-Jewish British helpers. Of course, the memory and commemoration of some parts of the Holocaust with a specific link to Britain was always there, seen most prominently through the *Kindertransports* and the liberation of the Bergen-Belsen camp. But it seems the history of the Holocaust itself was mainly left for others to deal with. Britain chose the role of having the occasional look over the fence. The reactions to the TV series *Holocaust*, as discussed by Tim Cole, show that the emphasis was mainly on the dramatisation and the flawed representation, not the history itself. In countries like the United States and Germany, the (mis-)representation was also a major concern in the media and for the public, yet this was also followed by serious public discourses about the history, and, in Germany, about German responsibility and the responsibility of individual Germans between generations.[4]

Again, the difference between Britain and Germany is obvious. In Germany, the history and memory of war and Holocaust threatens a positive and collective identity.[5] In Britain, it seems, the war supports a positive collective identity – celebrated and renewed every year at Remembrance Day. Even the Holocaust can be used as a pillar for a unifying national spirit: the *Kindertransports* symbolise the effort made by the nation to help the European Jews and the war was won 'as quickly as possible' to end the Holocaust, signified by the liberation of the Bergen-Belsen camp by British troops. There is no tension that needs release; there seem to be no open questions or conflicts between groups or generations that need resolving. This stands in stark contrast to most of Britain's European neighbours. The narrative of war and Holocaust seems to fit neatly into the master narrative of a United Kingdom that is at ease with itself and its history. However, as shown in some of the essays in this volume and pointed out in the Introduction, this is only possible if some areas are neglected or at least downplayed. A critical awareness of Chamberlain's policy of appeasement and the (international) failure of dealing with the refugee crisis of the late 1930s could challenge some of the prevailing mythology and would, for example, move even the honourable *Kindertransports* into a rather different light, as analysed in more recent works.[6] Similarly, public awareness of the lack of sufficient reactions to early warnings and reports about mass murder of Jews in eastern Europe might be increased, along with a contextualisation with colonial genocides as pointed out by Lawson. British anti-Semitism before, during and after the war could also be contextualised as at least one reason for such restraint.

Another interesting aspect – despite the German-bashing in the tabloids, usually around football tournaments – is the surprisingly positive and almost apologetic image of the Germans and the Nazis. Recent research into how Britons remember and talk about the Second World War and the Holocaust revealed, among other things, that the image of 'the Germans' is much better than that of 'the Jews' or, even more so, that of 'the Americans', 'the Japanese' or 'the Russians'.[7] Current research into the reception of films about the Holocaust in Britain also seems to indicate that many people still think only a small number of Germans were 'real' Nazis and that the rest were reeled in through propaganda, brainwashed, and shot or put into a concentration camp if they did not obey, and therefore are not really responsible for the crimes of Nazi Germany.[8] This perception might have its roots in how the war unfolded, the Nuremberg Trials, and in the 'cold war' decades afterwards, mixed with a modern version of racism.

Culturally, this might have something to do with a circular movement between public opinion and filmic representation. The often screened and praised *Genocide* episode of *The World at War* from 1974, which is discussed in Tim Cole's essay, is an example.[9] One can't help but be surprised at how casual the interviewed Nazi perpetrators – from members of the Reich Security Main Office (RSHA) involved in early anti-Jewish legislation and forced emigration, to Himmler's Adjutant Wolff – are in talking about their actions and involvement in the Holocaust and how they got away with it. They are allowed to present themselves as if they have not made any conscious decisions and their careers developed just by fate. They appear as neutral witnesses or even Nazi opponents, almost on a par with the interviewed Holocaust survivors. We hardly get any contextual information about them such as the development of their careers within the Nazi organisations. Their motives, beliefs and level of responsibility remain unquestioned, as, for example, is the possibility of whether someone like Wolff really can become Himmler's adjutant just by 'fate'. Consequently, it is rather easy for the viewer to get the impression reinforced that there were only a handful of 'real' Nazis among the Germans, Hitler and Himmler first and foremost among them; the rest were just dragged into it by coincidence. Later documentaries such as *The Nazis: A Warning from History* (1998) are more thorough, probably due to the fact that historians such as Ian Kershaw could finally serve as advisors.[10]

Even though historical research and knowledge about the Holocaust, and Nazi perpetrators in particular, have moved on considerably, it is still surprising how media products are largely unaffected by these developments. If we look at more recent British feature films on the Holocaust, the perceptions discussed in these essays remain visible. Between September 2008 and January 2009, two Holocaust 'dramas' were released in quick succession: *The Boy in the Striped Pyjamas* (Director: Mark Herman, UK 2008) and *The Reader* (Director: Stephen Daldry, UK 2009). These were two very different feature films that would enjoy different levels of success. While *The Reader*, based on Bernhard Schlink's bestselling novel, was a box office hit and decorated with an Academy Award (Kate Winslet for Best Actress), *The Boy in the Striped Pyjamas* also won several awards, such as the British Independent Film Award for Best Actress (Vera Farmiga), and also did well at the box office.[11] Moreover, the book and the film *The Boy in the Striped Pyjamas* now have a 'second career' in education and are used in Britain in Key Stage 3 and 4 education.[12] Even though bad films can always serve as a good example to study, this is worrying. While the TV series *Holocaust* was a misrepresentation of the victims of the Holocaust, it at least sparked some debate focusing on what the suffering of Jews in Germany and Europe was like. By contrast, these new films mainly focus on the non-Jewish Germans and transmit a picture of Germans who did not or could not know what was happening, repeating dated but comforting perceptions that lack historical substance and fail to spark any debate.

The Boy in the Striped Pyjamas does not claim to be a historical movie based on facts, even though the book by John Boyne was influenced by the story of Auschwitz commander Rudolf Höß who lived near Auschwitz Stammlager with his wife and five children.[13] It aims at an audience of young children, with two eight-year old boys, Bruno and Shmuel, at the centre of the story, and tries to show their slow 'discoveries' through the eyes of Bruno. Bruno's father, a high-ranking SS man, is relocated from Berlin to 'Out-With', and made commander of the camp. Bruno, his older sister and his mother (played by Vera Farmiga) follow him to a new home near what is believed to be a 'farm'. His sister is a dedicated Nazi follower and looks as if she's modelled after *Bund Deutscher Mädel* propaganda material. The mother on the other hand, does not know what her husband is doing and what his new assignment entails, despite the fact that prisoners in 'striped pyjamas' are working in her household and Bruno is not allowed to leave the back garden through the garden gate. She also wants the window towards the camp boarded up when Bruno becomes curious as to what it is. When she eventually finds out and confronts her husband, she wants to leave.

Reviews picked up on the lack of authenticity regarding the whole setting and in particular the representation of the death camp where, for example, no guards are around, children are still alive, and Shmuel and Bruno can have a chat through the fence. Bruno later even manages to get into the camp undetected. While British reviews discussed some of the issues,[14] many were still rather positive about this 'hard-hitting kids movie', warning viewers that they might leave the screening 'feeling somewhat depressed'.[15] In the end, it is meant to be a 'fable' for children to bring home some of the issues involved in the Holocaust, not a documentary. German reviews were mixed as well. The reviewer of the *Frankfurter Allgemeine Zeitung* called the film an 'impertinence' (*Frechheit*) and 'historical blasphemy' a German director would never get away with. However, despite the many shortcomings of the film he cannot help but confess that the story and friendship of the two boys are touching. One would like to 'hate' the film in light of available knowledge about the Shoah, but by sitting in a movie theatre and not in a lecture, it works. For a brief moment and through layers of cinematic clichés, he states, the film breaks up traditional images of the Holocaust and shows the horror survivors have reported through the eyes of an eight-year old boy.[16]

The *Süddeutsche Zeitung* was less forgiving. It commented that pictures of the 'death chamber' and Zyklon B at the end of the film, combined with a thunderstorm, have something of a 'forbidden thrill' (*verbotener Rausch*) that is no longer effective since too much of what happened before was not believable: the ignorance of the mother, that Bruno remained trustful and naive for so long, and that Shmuel was so talkative as if there was indeed an element of 'adventure' possible behind the fences.[17] Even more damning was the *New York Times* reviewer Manohla Dargis: 'See the Holocaust trivialized, glossed over, kitsched up, commercially exploited and hijacked for a tragedy about a Nazi family. Better yet and in all sincerity: don't.'[18]

One could dismiss this film as just another controversial 'fable' using the history of the Holocaust as a vehicle and backdrop to stir up some emotional reactions from the audience, similar to Roberto Benigni's *La Vita e Bella* in 1997. After all, filmmaking is art and not history – and maybe some people will even go away encouraged to look further into the history and discover 'how it really was'. The images transmitted here, though, are supporting, rather than questioning, existing stereotypical perceptions of the 'Third Reich', the Germans and the Holocaust. In the 'depressing' ending, the audience most probably feels for Bruno and his parents; for the father and commandant who is responsible but loses his son 'by mistake'; for his mother, who first did not know about the camp and then was against what her husband was doing. Arguably, this detracts from the fate of Shmuel and the others in the gas chamber.

Of course, one could argue that there were cases like this; that there might have been some rare cases of young children not immediately being killed in Auschwitz. There might have been a few cases of wives of camp commanders living in close proximity to camps who did not know the *full* extent of what was going on inside the camps.[19] But these pictures tend to transmit a general notion of 'that is probably how it was' that audiences will take away with them. The portrayal of the mother, for instance, underpins an interpretation based on the myth that most Germans, and women and children in particular, 'did not know' because everything was kept a secret or they were 'brainwashed' and misled by propaganda.[20] If they had known, they would have done something about it. Despite historical research showing otherwise, this idea still seems to feature greatly in British school education, and is also visible in the number of university students wanting to work on Nazi

propaganda every year, seeking the holy grail of explaining the Holocaust. This vicious circle of repeating old myths becomes self-referential
when films like *The Boy in the Striped Pyjamas* are then used in school
education.

With the film *The Reader* things are probably more complicated. The
bestselling and award-winning novel the films is based on was written
by German author, judge and professor of law Bernhard Schlink, born
in 1944. It intends to be a parable about the challenges of coming to
terms with the Nazi past in Germany, especially for the 'second generation', those born during or soon after the Second World War and whose
parents were part of or witnesses to war and Holocaust. As with *The
Boy in the Striped Pyjamas*, what works in a book might not necessarily
work in a film. The tempo and images created do not usually encourage
awareness and critical thought but lure audiences in, aiming at emotion
rather than thought. As Raack put it 30 years ago, 'the film image strikes
the physical body on its way to the mind, it delivers a message affec-
tively reinforced'.[21] Without going into too much detail, the film *The
Reader* is more or less a romantic drama, focusing for the first hour on
the strange love affair between Hanna and Michael in the late 1950s.
Hanna is much older than Michael and 'initiates' him while Michael
has to read literature to her. The affair ends abruptly when Hanna disap-
pears without notice, leaving Michael heartbroken. They meet again by
coincidence in the 1960s: Michael is now a law student and Hanna is on
trial for crimes committed during the Holocaust. She is accused, together
with six other female guards, of having selected prisoners at Auschwitz
concentration camp for gassing and being responsible for the death of
300 Jewish prisoners who were burned alive in a locked church during a
death march. It is also revealed that she had 'favourite' female prisoners
who had to read to her, which is another heavy blow to Michael sitting
in the audience.

At the climax of the film, a written and signed report about the incident at the church becomes a crucial part of the trial and it is only
then that Michael realises that Hanna is illiterate and could not have
been responsible for the report. However, instead of confessing to being
illiterate, Hanna takes responsibility for the report and risks being sentenced as the 'leader' of the female guards. Michael is therefore faced
with a dilemma: should he inform the court of his knowledge and serve
'justice', possibly changing the outcome of the trial? But that would
mean 'helping' a Nazi criminal he despises and at the same time 'betraying' Hanna by revealing her well kept secret. He finally decides not to
pass the information on to the court and Hanna receives a life sentence.

Another ten years go by with Michael's life still heavily affected by the past. However, he can never let go of his affection to Hanna despite the way she treated him and the revelation of the crimes she committed. He starts to record readings for Hanna and sends the tapes to her in prison. Hanna teaches herself to read and write with the aid of Michael's tapes. Michael is the only person writing to Hanna and is contacted by the prison authorities to discuss arrangements for her release after 20 years. Michael agrees to take responsibility for her social reintegration and they meet again for the first time shortly before her release. The meeting turns out to be disappointing for both of them. Just before her release Hanna commits suicide in her cell.

The book, as well as the film, makes some interesting points. It might be a good reflection on the 'moral compass' of Nazi perpetrators, for example, that during the trial Hanna insists that her duties as a guard included maintaining 'order' even if it meant the prisoners would die in the fire. Similarly, by admitting to the crimes but not to her illiteracy, she gives the impression that the former are less 'shameful' than the latter. Schlink has stated that Hanna's illiteracy should not be perceived as an 'excuse' for or justification of her actions and he is aware of the fact that many Nazi perpetrators were highly educated.[22] However, at the end of the film, as with *The Boy in the Striped Pyjamas*, one cannot help but feel pity and sympathy for the perpetrators and bystanders; a subtle form of 'victimisation' of the perpetrators shines through. In the case of Hanna, it is not the myth of 'not knowing' that justifies her actions (or inactions) but her illiteracy and her supposed lack of understanding, thus reinforcing another myth of the early postwar period: Nazi perpetrators, especially camp guards, were sadistic monsters and/or uneducated simpletons.[23] Schlink's intended message regarding his own generation, symbolised by Michael and his struggles to cope with the past due to the 'abuse' by Hanna, is sidelined in the film by the focus on Hanna and can go almost unnoticed – partly due to the performance of Kate Winslet.[24] What is more, he rejects the interpretation that *The Reader* is a 'Holocaust book', claiming it is a book about his generation and their relationship to the generation of their parents and what they have done.[25]

One could discuss further whether he and his generation have become rather obsessed with German victimhood, as he appears to be in other interviews he gave.[26] However, the interesting part is that the film puts the emphasis firmly on Hanna and transmits a specific image of Nazi perpetrators and female camp guards in particular.[27] Even if, as Philip French commented in *The Guardian*, 'scene by scene, we're gripped, but the metaphor is elusive, the narrative unconvincing and the over-all effect vague and unpersuasive. The key clicks smoothly in the lock but no doors of perception open up',[28] we have to be aware that many viewers are nevertheless 'persuaded' and long-time perceptions are rein-forced. Or, to quote Manohla Dargis again and her review for the *New York Times*,

> You could argue that the film isn't really about the Holocaust, but about the generation that grew up in its shadow, which is what the book insists. But the film is neither about the Holocaust nor about those Germans who grappled with its legacy: it's about making the audience feel good about a historical catastrophe that grows fainter with each new tasteful interpolation.[29]

In the British context this means that, with films like *The Boy in the Striped Pyjamas* and *The Reader*, the audience can also feel good about *themselves* since none of these productions raises questions that are of much concern for Britain and British history, nor do they challenge dated perceptions of what it was that made people participate in the Holocaust – the view remains a distant look over the fence into the (artis-tically fabricated) horrors of Auschwitz. One could argue that television and cinema are not supposed to be history lessons and that Britain does not *need* to be overly concerned with the history of the Holocaust. However, the problem lies in the reinforcement of outdated historical knowledge by writers and filmmakers that shape and reshape public per-ceptions and, moreover, the uncritical use of feature films like these in education.

Notes

1. *Obersalzberg*, Switch Reloaded (http://www.prosieben.de, accessed 12 February 2013).
2. Ricky Gervais – *Politics* (Hitler interprets Nietzsche) (http://www.youtube. com/watch?v=JUH1H-b-N5o, accessed 12 February 2013); Ricky Gervais – *Animals* (The Difference between Sharks and Nazis) http://www.youtube. com/watch?v=IMSkwGYgqLA, accessed 12 February 2013).
3. James Jordan, in this volume, 101.
4. Peter Märtesheimer; Ivo Fenzel, eds, *Im Kreuzfeuer. Der Fensehfilm 'Holo-caust': Eine Nation ist betroffen* (Frankfurt/Main, 1979); Jeffrey Herf, 'The "Holocaust" Reception in West Germany: Right, Centre and Left', *New German Critique*, 19 (1), Special Issue: Germans and Jews (Winter, 1980), 30–52; Martina Thiele, *Publizistische Kontroversen über den Holocaust im Film* (Berlin, 2007), 297–338.

5. Mary Fulbrook, *German National Identity after the Holocaust* (Oxford, 1999).
6. Mark J. Harris; Deborah Oppenheimer, *Into the Arms of Strangers: Stories of the Kindertransport* (London, 2000); Caroline Sharples, 'Reconstructing the Past: Refugee Writings on the Kindertransport', *Holocaust Studies: A Journal of Culture and History*, 12 (3) (Winter, 2006), 40–62.
7. Thomas J. McKay, *A Multi-Generational Oral History Study Considering English Collective Memory of the Second World War and Holocaust*, unpublished PhD thesis, University of Leicester, 2012.
8. Stefanie Rauch, *The Holocaust in British Popular Culture: Interpretations of Recent Feature Films* (University of Leicester, ongoing PhD project).
9. See also Donald J. Mattheisen, 'Persuasive History: A Critical Comparison of Television's Victory at Sea and The World at War', *The History Teacher*, 25 (2) (February, 1992), 239–251; James Chapman, 'Television and History: The World at War', *Historical Journal of Film, Radio and Television*, 31 (2) (June, 2011), 247–275.
10. Regarding the demand for historians to get more involved with historical films, see for example Robert Brent Toplin, 'The Filmmaker as Historian', *The American Historical Review*, 93 (5) (December, 1988), 1210–1227.
11. About $40 million according to Box Office Mojo http://www.boxofficemojo.com/movies/?id=boyinthestripedpajamas.htm, accessed 15 February 2013.
12. Tes connect, The Boy in the Striped Pyjamas, http://www.tes.co.uk/, accessed 10 January 2013.
13. Audio commentary by Mark Herman and John Boyne, Bonus Features, *The Boy in the Striped Pyjamas* (2008), Heyday Films, Miramax, 47:53–48:16.
14. Linda Grant, 'How Can They Understand?' Film Review, *The Guardian*, 29 August 2008 (http://www.guardian.co.uk, accessed 27 November 2012); Tim Robey, Film Review: The Boy in the Striped Pyjamas, *The Telegraph*, 12 September 2008 (http://www.telegraph.co.uk); Anthony Quinn, 'The Boy in the Striped Pyjamas' Film Review', *The Independent*, 12 September 2008 (http://www.independent.co.uk, accessed 12 February 2013); Xan Brooks, Film Review, *The Guardian*, 12 September 2008 (http://www.guardian.co.uk, accessed 10 January 2013).
15. Derek Adams, Film Review, *Time Out London*, 9 September 2008 (http://www.timeout.com/london, accessed 10 January 2013).
16. Andreas Kilb, 'Auschwitz als Fiktion: Der Junge im gestreiften Pyjama', *Frankfurter Allgemeine Zeitung*, 6 May 2009 (http://www.faz.net, accessed 10 January 2013).
17. Harald Eggebrecht, 'Niedlich Naiv', *Süddeutsche Zeitung*, 17 May 2010 (http://www.sueddeutsche.de, accessed 10 January 2013).
18. Manohla Dargis, 'Horror through a Child's Eyes', *The New York Times*, 6 November 2008 (http://movies.nytimes.com, accessed 10 January 2013).
19. By the same token, we might find examples of commanders like Josef Schwammberger, who was accompanied by his wife and son when torturing inmates of 'his' ghetto in Przemyśl (Poland), see Olaf Jensen, 'Evaluating Genocidal Intent: The Inconsistent Perpetrator and the Dynamics of Killing', *Journal of Genocide Research*, 15 (1) (February, 2013), 1–19.
20. Quinn, Film Review, *The Independent*, 12 September 2008.

21. Richard C. Raack, 'Historiography as Cinematography: A Prologomenon to Film Work for Historians', *Journal of Contemporary History*, 18 (3) (1983), 411–438, here 418.
22. 'Im Gespräch: Bernhard Schlink – Herr Schlink, ist "Der Vorleser" Geschichte?' *Frankfurter Allgemeine Zeitung*, 20 February 2009 (http://www.faz.net, accessed 10 January 2013).
23. Even Theodor W. Adorno shared this opinion in his essay 'Erziehung nach Auschwitz' in *Erziehung zur Mündigkeit* (Frankfurt/Main, 1971), 93–94.
24. 'Im Gespräch: Bernhard Schlink; Peter Bradshaw, Review The Reader', *The Guardian*, 2 January 2009 (http://www.guardian.co.uk, accessed 10 January 2013).
25. Im Gespräch: Bernhard Schlink.
26. 'Bernhard Schlink: Being German is a huge Burden', *The Guardian*, 16 September 2012 (http://www.guardian.co.uk, accessed 10 January 2013).
27. For a different view on female perpetrators, see for example the essays by Irmtraut Heike and Christina Herkommer in Olaf Jensen and Claus-Christian W. Szejnmann (eds), *Ordinary People as Mass Murderers: Perpetrators in Comparative Perspective* (Basingstoke, 2008).
28. Philip French, 'Review The Reader,' *The Guardian*, 4 January 2009 (http://www.guardian.co.uk, accessed 10 January 2013).
29. Manohla Dargis, 'Innocence Is Lost in Postwar Germany', *The New York Times*, 9 December 2009 (http://movies.nytimes.com, accessed 12 January 2013).

Part III
The Holocaust in Exhibitions

7
Holocaust Art at the Imperial War Museum, 1945–2009

Antoine Capet

It can be supposed that most people interested in twentieth-century history are familiar with the Imperial War Museum (IWM) and that most will have visited its permanent Holocaust exhibition since this was formally opened in June 2000. What Suzanne Bardgett, the curator who runs the exhibition, calls its 'artifacts' cover 1,200 square metres but before 2009 it showed only one piece of 'art' indirectly derived from the discovery and liberation of Bergen-Belsen concentration camp by the British Army in April 1945: Edgar Ainsworth's drawing *Wera Berger, Aged 13, after a Year in Ravensbrück (near Belsen), April 1945*.[1] It is not always realised that the IWM has, in fact, many more drawings and paintings connected with what is now known as Holocaust Art. The museum now publishes a history of the 'hangings' from which each of these works has benefited and this indicates that, while there were many hangings immediately after the war, there was then a long period of 'purgatory' from which these works are only now re-emerging. In a revealing article of 2004, Bardgett suggested that it was the whole issue of representing the Holocaust in the Museum which was taboo until the 1980s.[2] Inevitably, the paintings and drawings suffered from this reticence, which largely explains their neglect as an iconographic source for Holocaust studies in Britain.

For the first time since 1946, these pictures were displayed in a well publicised, dedicated exhibition running from September 2008 to August 2009 – thus clearly marking the total reversal of policy which had been taking place since the 1990s.[3] This chapter discusses the previous reticence and its likely causes, but it also concentrates on the present will to 'make up for lost time' on the part of the IWM authorities, dwelling on the meaning and purposes of the 2008–2009 dedicated exhibition of Holocaust Art, and putting it in the context of what may be construed as a new awareness of the extent and meaning of the Holocaust in widely different strata of British society.

The IWM's collection of Holocaust Art includes works that pre-date 1945, such as the remarkably percipient *Lama Sabachthani* (1943) by Morris Kestelman.[4] Most of those who received a Christian education – as was 'natural' in post-war Europe – will probably remember Jesus' anguished words on the cross: 'And about the ninth hour Jesus cried with a loud voice, saying, Eli, Eli, lama sabachthani? That is to say, My God, my God, why hast thou forsaken me?' (Matthew 27, pp. 45–46). However, Jews and Christians with a deeper knowledge of their Old Testament will be aware that the Aramaic expression in fact originates in Psalm 22: 'My God, my God, why hast thou forsaken me? Why art thou so far from helping me, and from the words of my roaring?' The IWM gives large extracts from Psalm 22, usefully linking its central theme to that of the painting: 'The tension for the psalmist is in the possibility that God might not rescue, and applied to this context where intervention seemed neither feasible nor imminent, it questions the very rule and presence of God.'

Outside its forceful artistic merits, the canvas raises important historical questions. All we know is that it was painted in 1943. In its Holocaust exhibition, the IWM shows copies of the *Daily Mail* of 30 June 1942, with the title 'Greatest Pogrom: One Million Jews die – British Section of World Jewish Congress'. On 25 June 1942, the *Daily Telegraph* had 'Huns murder 700,000 Jews in Poland: Mobile Gas Chambers', with greatly increased figures on 10 November 1943: '5,000,000 Jews exterminated in Nazi Europe'. On 17 December 1942, Anthony Eden, the Foreign Secretary, made an official statement on the subject in the House of Commons following convergent revelations released by the Polish Resistance.[5] There is therefore no special premonition in Kestelman's work – he must have read all these reports – but his artistic merit is all the greater as he used his inspiration to translate the appalling, abstract news into a picture which gave a concrete impression of what this probably meant. The title ostensibly tells us that the Jews shown lamenting on Kestelman's picture are appealing to God, but for us viewers in the twenty-first century, their question inevitably raises the issue of the Allies' non-intervention.[6] One is left in doubt about Kestelman's intentions and possible subtext. Was it a denunciation of the general indifference among Gentiles – often with the explanation that they did not know enough to form an opinion (an 'excuse' which the titles in the *Daily Mail* and *Daily Telegraph* obviously demolish)? Was it an appeal to the Allies' moral conscience, founded on their Judaeo-Christian cultural background, since in 1943 most Westerners would have understood the phrase *lama sabachthani* and its allusion to the Passion of Christ? Or was it a personal cry of despair on the part of the painter, a Jew himself?

The first time this painting was hung was in Manchester, during the 'Witness II: Highlights of Second World War Art' exhibition at IWM North, 3 February–29 April 2007. The Museum's records tell us that it entered its collections in April 1999 as a gift of Sara Kestelman, but why the public then had to wait another eight years to see the painting is unclear. In theory, it would find an ideal permanent location in the Holocaust exhibition, but there must be powerful reasons of lighting and conservation which preclude such an obvious choice.

The same argument – late acquisition – cannot be adduced for the drawings and paintings made by official artists as early as 1945, since they immediately entered national collections, over half of them being given to the IWM by a committee presided over by Sir Muirhead Bone, a member of both Sir Kenneth Clarke's War Artists' Advisory Committee (WAAC) and the Board of Trustees of the IWM.[7] Three had been shown as part of the exhibition of National War Pictures at the Royal Academy in the peculiar atmosphere of the summer and autumn of 1945, when 'the Nazi camps' provided a ready-made *ex post facto* justification for the war in Britain as in the United States.[8] This exhibition included three scenes by the same WAAC artist, Leslie Cole (1910–1977): *Belsen Camp: The Compound for Women*; *One of the Death Pits, Belsen: SS Guards Collecting Bodies*; and *Sick Women and the Hooded Men of Belsen*, all of which would have to wait some 30 years before being shown again. The first two of these entered the Museum in 1947 but were not shown until they were loaned for the 1978 'The Pity War Distils' exhibition at Manchester Cathedral.[9] Thereafter, *Belsen Camp: The Compound for Women* was not publicly hung again until the 2008–2009 'Unspeakable' exhibition at the IWM. The second painting, *One of the Death Pits*, fared slightly better, appearing twice again in Manchester, in 1987 for the 'Anne Frank in the World' exhibition at the Manchester City Art Gallery, and in 2007 at the IWM North exhibition already mentioned. It was also included in the 2008–2009 'Unspeakable' exhibition in London.

The third of Cole's paintings, *Sick Women and the Hooded Men of Belsen* (1945) was shown slightly earlier than his other works, appearing at the World War II Art exhibition at the Bluecoat Gallery, Liverpool in 1974.[10] Perhaps it was deemed less likely to shock the viewing public. The 'Hooded Men' in question are members of the Medical Corps who wear special clothing protecting them against typhus. They are emptying the huts of their occupants who are either too weak to go out by themselves or already dead. The contrast with the skeletal naked survivors, how-ever, makes the picture arguably even more horribly voyeuristic than *The Compound for Women*.[11]

One of the Death Pits, meanwhile, infringes another taboo: respect for the dead. There is a double level of iconoclasm here. The human corpses are thrown like worthless puppets – and they are thrown by their for-mer tormentors who, we feel, should not be allowed to touch them any longer. Of course the men are *former* SS Guards, now used by the libera-tors to execute the gruesome task of throwing the decomposing corpses long seized by rigor mortis into the mass graves. What is it, though, that shocks us most? Is it the disrespect shown to the dead by sometimes dragging them along like bags of merchandise, or the double element of voyeurism: that of the artist and our own?

One of the Death Pits was the only one of the three Cole paintings of Belsen to be shown during the 2007 Manchester exhibition at IWM North.[12] Appearing next to it at the time were two pictures by another Gentile, Doris Zinkeisen. Publicly hanging these works, as well as the premonitory image by Morris Kestelman, together for the first time must have been difficult. Without background information on the cir-cumstances of their painting in the spring of 1945 at Bergen-Belsen concentration camp, after its liberation by British troops on 15 April, they are almost meaningless. But how much contextual information is it necessary for the curators to give? They could soon find themselves teaching a comprehensive course on the Holocaust and the relief of the camps – an impossibly complex task, for which they received no formal training. I recently discussed the problem with a Tate Britain curator, who explained that exhibition organisers are always in a quandary. Either they give full context in their wall texts and face the risk that the public will be put off by this long reading matter, or they give as little as they can, but then face accusations of negligence from the more enlight-ened amateurs. At IWM North, they chose to give the bare minimum – even less than the bare minimum in the case of *Belsen: April 1945* by Zinkeisen, one of the most powerful artistic interpretations of the Holo-caust ever given.[13] Here, the catalogue caption did not even allude to the picture – only to the biography of the author, in four short lines.[14] This is not necessarily a bad thing, however, as the force of the composi-tion is universal, that is the painting is only nominally a description of a Belsen scene; there are no background details to suggest Belsen. Even the general Nazi concept of *Nacht und Nebel* (Night and Fog) is only sug-gested by the creation of an oppressive but semi-abstract atmosphere of darkness and fumes. Were it not for the characteristic striped clothes and horribly hollow bellies, the corpses would give the viewer no clue of time and place.

The Zinkeisen painting is the first of the IWM Holocaust images I ever saw; in the (at first glance) unlikely context of a Women and War exhibition I visited in the autumn of 2003.[15] The women in question cannot be the corpses, because it is clear from the anatomical details that they were men. The painting's inclusion in the exhibition was a reference to the fact that the artist was a woman, plunged into the inferno of Belsen, with its countless victims awaiting treatment or burial when she arrived a few days after the first troops. Her experience must have been terribly traumatic – but the visitors to that Women and War exhibition were probably totally unprepared, too. The painting was hung in a darkened corner which visitors reached just before the final section, devoted mainly to Diana, Princess of Wales in Africa. Before that, there were trivial exhibits like the shoes worn by the then Princess Elizabeth when she served with the Auxiliary Territorial Service in the last months of the Second World War. I was taken aback and I did not know what to make of the picture – all I knew was that I was before probably the most powerful description of the Holocaust in British art, and that I must find out more about the painting and the painter. I cannot have been alone, and my experience points to the difficulties created for the viewer by hanging these paintings sporadically, outside a clear Holocaust context, as they were hung at the Museum in the 1980s and 1990s.

In contrast, the other picture of Belsen by Doris Zinkeisen is far more descriptive. *Human Laundry, Belsen: April 1945* is based on a well-known aspect of the relief work at Belsen where a stable was used to clean the survivors' emaciated bodies before treating them with DDT as a precautionary measure against the lice which carried typhus.[16] One aspect of the Manchester exhibition was that a wall text with the testimony of a witness amplified the theme covered by the adjoining paintings. In this case, this was particularly appropriate as a survivor explained how shocked they were to find themselves being treated by these German nurses only a few weeks after associating anything German with terror and murder. This idea is also present in the review of the 2008–2009 'Unspeakable' exhibition by Thomas Sutcliffe in *The Independent*:

> In *Human Laundry*, Doris Zinkeisen shows German orderlies washing emaciated camp inmates before they go to hospital. It is as uninflected as a travel poster, yet the transformation it depicts – brutalisers obliged to become carers, victims turned to patients – is piercingly suggestive of what you can't see.[17]

Here of course the roles of the German military are totally different from the roles ascribed to the former guards in Cole's scene of *One of the Death Pits, Belsen*. Their paramedical function has a redeeming dimension which is totally absent from the revolting task performed in the pits.

The exhibition at IWM North was therefore probably the first to try to contextualise these Holocaust paintings. Their location had obviously been carefully thought about. They were displayed near the large eye-catching composition by Barnett Freedman, *The Landing in Normandy: Arromanches, D-Day plus 20, 26th June 1944*, painted a few months after the war to glorify the triumph of Allied arms on land, sea and air and hung in the entrance section.[18] Consequently, from the start, the visitor was taken between the opposing facets of glory on one wall, and horror on the other, thereby impressing on him the inescapable duality of war. To drive the nail in further, the first room also contained the picture of *The Nuremberg Trial, 1946* by Dame Laura Knight, another warning that war can be far removed from the ideals of exciting adventure and chivalrous combat depicted in boys' comics.[19] Her composition skilfully blends an accurate depiction of the well-known dock (so accurate that specialists will easily recognise the faces) with a nightmarish suggestion of devastated landscapes. Bardgett makes the point that this was the only painting on permanent display at the IWM in the late 1970s with an 'oblique connection' with the Holocaust.[20] The connection is very oblique indeed since what the viewer immediately perceives is the destruction of cities, not the elimination of a 'race'. The commentary given on the web page today in fact does not go much further: 'the painting shows a landscape of desolation floating above the courtroom like a shared nightmare. We are invited to contemplate the dreadful consequences of totalitarian power.'

As suggested from the exhibition records kept by the IWM and alluded to earlier, it was the less gruesome pictures which were first shown in special events, in a sort of gradual progress towards the full horror of the representation of what the official artists saw in Belsen in the spring of 1945. Thus, if we take the Zinkeisen pictures, *Human Laundry* was shown 'as early as' 1974,[21] whereas *Belsen 1945* had to wait until 1987,[22] and was not shown again – this time in the IWM – until 2003, on the occasion of the Women and War exhibition.[23] It is therefore arguable that in 2007 in Manchester the combination of Arromanches, Nuremberg and Belsen provided the first real attempt on IWM premises to connect the paintings in a meaningful general narrative of the Second World War.[24]

All this saw a dramatic evolution with the 2008–2009 'Unspeakable' exhibition in a dedicated room of the Lambeth museum. Not only were all the Cole and Zinkeisen paintings prominently displayed, but the visitor was also able to see drawings which previously could only be viewed by appointment. These included Edgar Ainsworth's *Belsen 1945*, together with Jan Hartman's gouache, *Death March*, and his later *Sketch of a Survivor of Auschwitz* drawn in pencil in 1946, following his experience there. For the first time, the public was also able to see drawings which had never been shown together, especially the two outstanding series of 1945 by Mary Kessell (seven charcoal drawings all entitled *Notes from Belsen Camp*) and Eric Taylor (five watercolours: *Dying from Starvation and Torture at Belsen Concentration Camp; Human Wreckage at Belsen Concentration Camp; Liberated from Belsen Concentration Camp; A Living Skeleton at Belsen Concentration Camp*; and *A Young Boy From Belsen Concentration Camp*). The caption, of course, is all-important for *A Living Skeleton at Belsen Concentration Camp*,[25] since the viewer would never imagine that the man is still alive. The analogy with the corpses of Zinkeisen's *Belsen 1945* is striking, including the piece of striped clothing only covering the shoulders.

Also among the exhibits shown for the first time was a remarkably (and unfortunately) ambiguous table-top showcase with a recent gift of 13 drawings of Blechhammer camp by 'Bill' (as indicated by the signature). Nothing is known of the artist except that in 1944 he bartered the set in exchange for some cigarettes with a British soldier who brought it back home, his family donating it to the Museum in 2006. These images raise more questions than they solve. They are in the tradition of servicemen's mockery of military rigidity and pomposity, with superiors shown as slightly ridiculous. Even the Jewish inmates, clearly identified by their yellow stars, seem well fed and well treated, with no hint of beating, still less permanent threats to their lives – and yet we are told that this was 'a sub-camp of Auschwitz'. The visitor is confused by this light-hearted depiction of the camps (and, what is more, apparently by a Jew); his conception of the treatment of the Jews in Auschwitz and its satellite camps is blurred. If it is a case of 'sick humour', it is hard to conceive and rationalise in the middle of these harrowing Belsen images. This therefore offers a clear case of the absolute necessity of education, explanation and contextualisation when such ambiguous works are displayed.

The 2008–2009 'Unspeakable' exhibition also allayed earlier fears that another recent acquisition might have met the fate of the 1945–1946 works and remained in the stores most of the time. This is the set of five pictures painted in 1980–1982 and donated in 1983 to the IWM by Edith Birkin (née Hofmann). Birkin was sent with her family in 1941 to the Łódź ghetto, where her parents died within a year. She was deported to Auschwitz in 1944. When the camp was evacuated, she was sent on a 'death march' to Belsen and numbered among the survivors when British troops arrived. She now lives in Herefordshire, where she helped mount an exhibition on the occasion of Holocaust Memorial Day in January 2006, in which her paintings were displayed.[26] A text tells us that immediately after her liberation, she had recorded what she had experienced and witnessed and that after moving to England, she used this material to write a book but could not find a publisher as there was no interest in her story directly after the war. It was only in the early 1980s that she used her memories to paint the extraordinarily powerful gruesome acrylics on display: *A Camp of Twins – Auschwitz*; *The Death Cart – Łódź Ghetto*; *Dresden burning – Death March, Winter 1945*; *The Last Gasp – Gas Chamber*; *Liberation Day*; and *Roll Call, Belsen, 1944*. Incredibly, this extraordinary set had never been shown in the IWM until the 'Unspeakable' exhibition, nor was it put on the online catalogue until 2008.[27]

Another room within the 'Unspeakable' exhibition was devoted to the magnificently powerful works of Roman Halter, who lost his parents and his six brothers and sisters in the Holocaust. Like Birkin, he went through the Łódź ghetto, Auschwitz and Stutthof concentration camps, and the death marches, from which he escaped and survived. Seven large oils on canvas painted between 1974 and 1977 were displayed: *Man on the Electrified Barbed Wire*; *Moses the Prophet*; *Mother with Babies*; *Shlomo 1*; *Starved Faces*; *Transport* and *Woman wearing Mantilla*.

The exhibition continued with the very personal works of Alicia Melamed Adams, directly inspired by her own childhood experience in wartime Poland: *Two Frightened Children* (depicting her brother, who never returned from the camps, and herself); *The Parting* (aged 14 and parting from her imprisoned family, who would be shot the next day); and *The Refugees* (being driven out by the Russians in 1945). Each of these images was created in 1965. Other paintings show the 'work of memory' that she continues to carry out: *Looking Back* (self-portrait, 1962); *Sorrow* (self-portrait, 1965); *Forget-me-nots* (1966); *The Flower Painter* (self-portrait, 1991); and *Going Up Soon but Where?* (1998). The works are in the artist's own collection rather than that of the IWM so it was a unique opportunity to see them together in case they are dispersed some day.

Another key function of the IWM is its encouragement of younger artists like Darren Almond. His *Border* (1999) is a 'replica' of the entry and exit road signs seen when entering and leaving the town of Oświęcim, in Poland – whose German name is Auschwitz.[28] The exhibit greeted the visitor before he entered the first room. No work of art could have been more compellingly appropriate than this as an introduction (in the etymological meaning of the word), reminding the visitor that the vast majority of deportees were only able to see the entry sign.

The final, smaller room of the 'Unspeakable' exhibition was, in fact, devoted to the subsequent generations. Aviva Halter-Hurn, Roman Halter's daughter, represented the generation born of the survivors – a generation which also had to come to terms with the Holocaust. She explains that she made her four linocuts based on drawings produced in the camps, *Four Works from Auschwitz through Lino-cuts* (2001), as another sort of work of memory – on her father's family, which she never knew. Paul Ryan also offered a fascinating installation entitled *Souvenir* (2008), consisting of a rotary postcard stand as seen in all holiday resorts, filled with 'postcards' (complete with spaces for postage stamps) which the visitors were welcome to take home. Three images were available: *Concentrate* (2001), *Redrawn* (2008) and *Trace* (2008). The latter two are archetypal 'objets détournés'. *Redrawn* is the 'détournement', covering the roofs with excrement, etc., of a German architect's impression ('Generelle Bebauungsvorschlag', dated 1942) of what the market place and town hall of Oświęcim (rebaptised Auschwitz) could look like after reshaping ('Neugestaltung'). *Trace* is literally a picture on tracing paper taken from a bilingual Polish/German prewar postcard bearing the inscription 'Greetings from Oświęcim', with various local monuments in the middle. Once more, it is to be hoped that the IWM will eventually put Almond's *Border* and Ryan's *Souvenir* on permanent display, since it seems that they were commissions and that therefore it owns them.

However short and incomplete, this survey nevertheless makes it clear that there has been a considerable evolution in the approach of the IWM vis-à-vis its 'Belsen' collections inherited from the WAAC in the immediate post-war years, as well as in its policy regarding the acquisition of new works by survivors or their descendants, or simply by young British artists concerned with the Holocaust, especially the memory of Auschwitz. An interesting factor is that there has undeniably been an 'acceleration of history' in recent years. Bardgett wrote her superbly researched article in the early 2000s at a time when the Holocaust exhibition was already a strong feature of the Museum, in spite of initial denunciation.[29] But then by its own self-imposed rules, it only showed contemporary artifacts. Thus what we could call the Belsen paintings, which were made later from sketches taken back from the camp, did not entirely qualify for admission.

This evolution provides a fascinating reflection on the parallel paths followed by historiography and museography – the distance between the two taking the form of a time-gap. The general theme of the Colloquium which led to this present collection of essays referred to the 'impact' of the Holocaust on today's Britain. It is obvious that such a question would have been meaningless in, say, 1975 if only because one senses that that impact was minimal outside a narrow circle of specialised historians.[30] Now, museums are at the interface of historical research and public interest in the themes which provide the foundation of their permanent displays and special exhibitions. Arguably, a wide public interest in the Holocaust had to emerge in Britain before a national museum could hope to 'pull in the crowds' (made imperative by their remit from the various funding authorities) by offering a permanent section or mounting special events on it. It seems that the 'Anne Frank in the World' exhibition at the Manchester City Art Gallery in 1987 played a pioneering role in this respect. The name 'Anne Frank' was in itself already a crowd-puller thanks to the enormous dissemination of the *Diary*, at a time when 'the Holocaust' was not – or at least not quite on the same scale.

However, it was only when the new permanent Holocaust exhibition had proved to be an undeniable success with the visiting public that the next stage – showing these most disturbing Holocaust drawings and paintings in its collections – could be envisaged by the Museum authorities. First because interest in the Holocaust generally had to be slowly generated and sustained before some of its less 'obvious' and more 'difficult' aspects could be explored and exhibited, and secondly because art appreciation is always a minority interest. In a way one had to create a sub-minority interest (interest in Holocaust Art) within what was already a double minority interest (interest in the Holocaust itself and interest in the arts).

These things cannot be hurried, and one can only admire the way the IWM gradually transformed its 'embarrassing' collections (as they were seen in the 1970s) into 'presentable' collections for a wide public.[31] The 'Unspeakable' exhibition constituted both a culmination and a turning-point in this respect. A culmination because it was the outcome of a process which took some 30 years to come to fruition, with an exhibition which shows all the Museum's collections (and even works on

Leslie Cole, *One of the Death Pits, Belsen. SS Guards Collecting Bodies*

Doris Zinkeisen, *Human Laundry, Belsen: April 1945*

Dame Laura Knight, *The Nuremberg Trial*

Eric Wilfred Taylor, *A Living Skeleton at Belsen Concentration Camp*

loan) – and a turning-point because it is evident that now that these collections have benefited from a major 'coming-out' exhibition it will not be possible to send them back to the underground stores. What Tony Kushner so convincingly wrote as recently as the mid-2000s, 'Sixty years on from the liberation of Belsen, we have still not worked out how to deal with its imagery',[32] may after all turn out to be too pessimistic on present trends.

Notes

1. Edgar Ainsworth, *Wera Berger, Aged 13, after a Year in Ravensbrück (near Belsen), April 1945*, ink, wash, 230 mm × 357 mm, IWM ART 16629.
2. Suzanne Bardgett, 'The Depiction of the Holocaust at the Imperial War Museum since 1961', *Journal of Israeli History*, 23 (1) (2004), 146–156.
3. 'Unspeakable: The Artist as Witness to the Holocaust', Imperial War Museum, London, 5 September 2008–31 August 2009.
4. Morris Kestelman, *Lama Sabachthani* (1943), oil on canvas, 117 cm × 153 cm, IWM ART 16786.
5. *Hansard*, col. 2082, 17 December 1942.
6. The best starting point is to be found in Michael J. Neufeld and Michael Berenbaum (eds), *The Bombing of Auschwitz: Should the Allies Have Attempted It?* (New York, 2000). Important British documents are reproduced in 'The Appeal to the British', 261–270.
7. See the excellent discussion in Brian Foss, *War Paint: Art, War, State and Identity in Britain, 1939–1945* (New Haven, 2007), 189–191.
8. See Suzanne Bardgett, 'What Wireless Listeners Learned: Some Lesser Known BBC Broadcasts about Belsen', *Holocaust Studies*, 12 (1–2) (2006), 123–136. For details on American representations, particularly General Eisenhower's speech on the occasion of his visit to the Ohrdruf-Nord camp, near Gotha, on 12 April 1945, see: John Toland, *The Last 100 Days* (New York, 1966), 410.
9. Leslie Cole, *Belsen Camp: The Compound for Women* (1945), oil, 660 mm × 901 mm, IWM ART LD 5104 and *One of the Death Pits, Belsen: SS Guards Collecting Bodies* (1945), oil, 622 mm × 901 mm, IWM ART LD 5105. For more on their history, see: Antoine Capet, 'The Liberation of the Bergen-Belsen Camp as Seen by Some British Official War Artists in 1945', *Holocaust Studies*, 12 (1–2) (2006), 170–185.
10. Leslie Cole, *Sick Women and the Hooded Men of Belsen* (1945), oil, 615 mm × 863 mm, IWM ART LD 5017.
11. 'The pictures of naked women particularly were prone to exploitation as pornography, starting a trend of the female victim as a titillating sexual plaything of the Nazis which is still alive in cultural representations of the Holocaust today' – Tony Kushner, 'The Memory of Belsen', in Jo Reilly, David Cesarani, Tony Kushner and Colin Richmond (eds), *Belsen in History and Memory* (London, 1997), 181–205, 192.
12. On a related theme, the Manchester exhibition also showed Leslie Cole's *British Women and Children Interned in a Japanese Prison Camp, Syme Road, Singapore* (1945), oil on canvas, 65 cm × 91 cm.

13. Doris Clare Zinkeisen, *Belsen: April 1945* (1945), oil on canvas, 62 cm × 70 cm, IWM ART LD 5467.
14. James Campus (ed.), *Art from the Second World War* (London, 2006).
15. Women and War exhibition, Imperial War Museum, London, 15 October 2003–18 April 2004.
16. Doris Clare Zinkeisen, *Human Laundry, Belsen: April 1945* (1945), oil on canvas, 80 cm × 100 cm, IWM ART LD 5468. This relief work was also documented in a remarkably similar photograph by Sergeant Hewitt of the Army Film and Photographic Unit. For a thorough study of the AFPU photographs taken at Belsen and their use, see Hannah Caven, 'Horror in Our Time: Images of the Concentration Camps in the British Media, 1945', *Historical Journal of Film, Radio and Television*, 21 (3) (2001), 205–253.
17. 'Thomas Sutcliffe, 'Approach the Holocaust at Your Peril', *The Independent*, 12 September 2008.
18. Barnett Freedman, *The Landing in Normandy: Arromanches, D-Day plus 20, 26th June 1944* (1947), oil on canvas, 155 cm × 305 cm, IWM ART LD 5816.
19. Dame Laura Knight, *The Nuremberg Trial, 1946* (1946), oil on canvas, 183 cm × 152 cm, IWM ART LD 5798.
20. Bardgett, 'The Depiction of the Holocaust at the Imperial War Museum since 1961', 147.
21. 'World War II Art' exhibition, Bluecoat Gallery, Liverpool, 1974.
22. 'A Paradise Lost' exhibition, Barbican Art Gallery, London, 1987.
23. *Human Laundry* had also been shown earlier (and longer) at the Museum, during the 'Unofficial Flowers' exhibition, Imperial War Museum, London, September 1995–May 1998.
24. It seems that the 'Anne Frank in the World' exhibition at the Manchester City Art Gallery in 1987 was the first to show together *The Nuremberg Trial, One of the Death Pits, Belsen: SS Guards collecting Bodies* and *Sick Women and the Hooded Men of Belsen*.
25. Eric Wilfred Taylor, *A Living Skeleton at Belsen Concentration Camp, 1945* (1945), watercolour, 647 mm × 495 mm, IWM ART LD 5587.
26. 'A Hereford Woman's Story of Survival', BBC News: Hereford and Worcester, 26 January 2006 http://www.bbc.co.uk/herefordandworcester/content/articles/2006/01/26/edith_birkin_audio_feature.shtml (accessed 16 August 2012).
27. Again, the set had been shown at the 'Anne Frank in the World' exhibition at the Manchester City Art Gallery in 1987.
28. Darren Almond, *Border* (1999), sculpture, paint on aluminium, IWM ART 16762.
29. Notably from the *Evening Standard* critic Brian Sewell. See Bardgett, 'The Depiction of the Holocaust at the Imperial War Museum since 1961', 152.
30. An interesting parallel can be drawn with Germany. See Norbert Frei's address before the Stockholm Holocaust International Forum: A Conference on Education, Remembrance and Research. 26–28 January, 2000, http://www.d.dccam.org/Projects/Affinity/SIF/DATA/2000/page1172.html (accessed 16 August 2012).
31. The *Guardian* reviewer does not seem to have remotely perceived the importance of the evolution when he writes that 'The Imperial War Museum's new exhibition Unspeakable: The Artist as Witness of the Holocaust, which opens

September 5, looks like a canny attempt to lure people into its permanent collection of V2s and gas masks' – Jonathan Jones, 'Why war museums rely on the Holocaust', *Guardian*, 3 September 2008.

32. Tony Kushner, 'From "This Belsen Business" to "Shoah Business": History, Memory and Heritage, 1945–2005', *Holocaust Studies*, 12 (1–2) (2006), 189–216.

8
Holocaust Memory and Contemporary Atrocities: The Imperial War Museum's Holocaust Exhibition and Crimes Against Humanity Exhibition

Rebecca Jinks

In the last decade or so, research has begun to address the ways in which global discourses of memory, within which the Holocaust is paradigmatic, often 'borrow' Holocaust iconography and tropes of memorialisation to discuss or commemorate other tragedies.[1] This utilisation of Holocaust memory is indicative of the position that the Holocaust now generally holds throughout the Western world, and yet it also raises questions about how we represent, and respond to, the other tragedies of the twentieth century. In this vein, this chapter explores the interactions between the memory of the Holocaust and other contemporary mass atrocities in Britain, using as case studies the Imperial War Museum's (IWM) Holocaust exhibition, which opened in 2000, and its Crimes Against Humanity exhibition, which first opened in 2002 and then moved to a different part of the building in 2009. While on the face of it, the sheer difference in size and visitor numbers between the two exhibitions could easily function as a metaphor for the disparity between the status of Holocaust memory, and the memory of 'other genocides' in Britain and the West,[2] my object is to explore the symbiotic and perhaps even dependent relationship between the two exhibitions, and by extension the wider categories of 'Holocaust' and 'genocide'.

The Holocaust exhibition

Spread across two floors of the IWM's exhibition halls, the Holocaust Exhibition is an extremely detailed and engaging exhibition, which layers artefacts, films and video testimonies, documents and text panels within a carefully constructed interior architecture in an example of 'experience making' which Stephen Greenberg calls the 'vital museum';[3] the academic and media responses to the exhibition have had a generally favourable tone. A few comments were made about the slightly odd placement of the Holocaust exhibition within the IWM,[4] and other initial criticisms tended to concentrate on what is *not* there, that is the wider story of atrocity in our modern times, although of course the opening of Crimes Against Humanity went at least some way towards rectifying that.[5] As Suzanne Bardgett, project director for both exhibitions, has explained, the original concept was an exhibition centring on 'Man's Inhumanity to Man': they took this vision and 'divided it into two – deciding that a detailed account of the Holocaust should form the larger part of the space (reflecting a clear demand for a narrative exhibition on this subject) and the upper floor devoted to an examination of genocide as a general theme'.[6] There are, however, three main areas at which slightly more serious criticisms can be levelled, which centre on the museum's overall portrayal of the perpetrators, the victims and the British responses to the Holocaust.

As with so many representations of the Holocaust, whether through feature films like *Schindler's List*, literature or museum exhibitions, there is a fundamental resistance to exploring the motivations and identities of the perpetrators, presumably to ensure that clear moral lessons are drawn.[7] In the first part of the Holocaust exhibition, which covers the period before the outbreak of war and genocide, the perpetrators are known by their blaring hate propaganda, their stiff SS uniforms and the overriding impression that they herald an impending doom. Downstairs, in the section which covers the Holocaust proper, the perpetrators are portrayed only through their actions, their euphemisms, their chilling and detached accounts of the destruction process and the visible manifestations of these. The issue here, then, is not that insufficient space is given over to the perpetrators, but rather that the interpretation of them offered by the exhibition is potentially problematic.[8]

There is some attempt to answer the question 'Who Were the Killers?' with reference to the Auschwitz employees, detailing their former jobs and responses to their new occupation, but the mug shots of several of the highest or most reviled functionaries serves almost immediately to re-demonise them and set them apart. As Tony Kushner comments, the images 'tend to confirm that the perpetrators must have been monsters, sub-human, in fact animals, "the bitch and beast of Belsen", rather than ordinary men and women fully capable of such crimes'.[9] Likewise, there is little attempt to contextualise the Nazi race project within the wider European mêlée of state surveillance programmes, racial hygiene projects and population politics.[10] The perpetrators thus become faceless symbols of evil, somehow removed from the rest of humanity (and certainly the museum visitor). As most commentators note, their decided 'un-Britishness', fuelled by British anti-Germanism, only serves to preclude engagement with perpetration.[11] Kushner also notes, quite rightly, that the narrative structure of the exhibition is driven by a chronology created by the Nazis rather than their victims, and the victims are known to us *as* victims, primarily through the documentation of their destruction.[12]

I say primarily, but as Kushner is quick to point out, this overall tendency to focus on Nazi actions is 'partially countered by the use of powerful video and oral testimony of survivors'.[13] Indeed, while on the upstairs floor the vibrant klezmer music of the atrium and the survivor testimonies compete with, or are overshadowed by, the thundering of Nazi rallies and Goebbels' propaganda speeches, those sounds do not penetrate downstairs and only survivors' voices punctuate the silence. Although the video testimonies are ultimately frustratingly brief for Kushner – who argues that they are used as an illustration of Nazi actions, rather than a poignant and educative resource in their own right[14] – I myself find them well placed and long enough that visitors can gain a more individualised, humanised understanding of the process if they wish; the danger of laying too much emphasis on survivor testimony is that visitors will lose sight of the broader picture, and particularly the ideas, choices and intentions of the perpetrators. Kushner is perfectly correct to note, though, that in marked contrast to the United States Holocaust Memorial Museum or Yad Vashem, there is little exploration of Jewish life before the Holocaust, or encouragement to identify with the victims.[15] These victims are also overwhelmingly *Jewish* victims – only a few mentions are made of the millions of 'others' also killed as part of the Nazis' exterminatory social engineering project.[16]

Still, the sombre atmosphere, the atrocity photographs and the piles of personal belongings all encourage what Donald Bloxham calls the 'pathos approach', and this, combined with the representation of the perpetrators, 'prevent[s] any of the meaningful, genuinely universal but potentially divisive questions about the role of the state or of individual perpetrators being addressed'.[17] There is a general consensus amongst the critics, with which I agree, that the Holocaust exhibition does very little to question Britain's role as a bystander during the war, and certainly to provoke self-reflection in visitors. Nazism is depicted as utterly alien to Europe rather than the apotheosis of trends found throughout the continent, its crimes the work of a group of crazed fanatics rather than a project many thousands of Europeans willingly collaborated on, with its origins partly lying in modernity itself as well as in political ideologies and the chain of command. Although there is some coverage of the British and Allied responses, as Tom Lawson comments, even this helps reinforce the gap between Nazism and ourselves: 'British and American refugee policy is criticised for being less than humanitarian, but the resulting exclusion of refugees is presented as a consequence of economic self-interest and political pragmatism – normative values well within the visitor's accepted political experience.'[18] Moreover, I would argue that the exhibition precludes this sort of self-reflection by presenting the Holocaust as a discrete and *past* event – seeking immersion in an authentic historical memory, rather than implying any sort of post-Holocaust perspective which might cause self-reflection on the part of the visitors. As Andrew Hoskins observes, above the entrance hangs a sign that 'simply says "The Holocaust" above it – as if one were entering the event or the site of the event itself'.[19]

There are interactive screens, near the end of the exhibition, which invite visitors to engage with some of the issues. The screens are set into benches with a distinctly 'classroom' feel, and use text, photographs and videos to explore questions such as 'What Was the Holocaust?', 'Who Were the Victims?', or 'What Could Be Done to Help?' They are surrounded by the panels which explore issues such as 'Rescue', 'Resistance', 'Hiding' and 'Discovery' (although presided over by the infamous picture of the bulldozer at Belsen), suggesting a more active, inquiring area of the exhibition, but ultimately there are not really enough of these interactive screens, and their content extends visitors' knowledge of the events rather than asking the more fundamental but disturbing questions. Thus, while visitors are encouraged to draw strong moral lessons, the exhibition does stop short of making explicit the implications of the Holocaust for today's Britain, and the visitors themselves.

Nevertheless, the Holocaust exhibition can be placed squarely within the late twentieth century and early twenty-first century trends within Holocaust museums, barring the fact that it does not have an explicitly memorial function.[20] Its narrative is certainly typical – especially when one considers that both it and the USHMM end or begin with the Allied liberation, thus reproducing the national experience of the Holocaust and reasserting the morality of the Allies. As with many other exhibitions, whether the USHMM or the museums in former camps across Europe, there is a strong emphasis on artefacts, and very little reconstruction – the 12-metre long model of Auschwitz is the exception – but, as noted, it also embraces the recounting of survivors' memories, on screens and through listening cones.[21] Visitors will also find much of the 'Holocaust iconography' they will already be so familiar with from other museums or the History Channel, feature films or popular literature – the sights and sounds of Nazi propaganda, the ghettos in the east, the cattle car and the huge picture of the gate and railway lines at Auschwitz, the striped camp uniforms and collection of shoes of victims from Majdanek, the photographs of the victims. I want to suggest that here, and in representations of the Holocaust more generally, these familiar symbols of the Holocaust *support* the rest of the exhibition's content for the visitors, providing familiar narrative staging posts, which the more unfamiliar material is then worked into and around. This is to some degree a reflection on the prevalence (and predilections) of Holocaust consciousness in contemporary society, and the way that museum exhibitions can use this to narrate the complicated nuances of the story, but it will also become relevant when I turn to my discussion of the Crimes Against Humanity exhibition. One final respect in which the Holocaust exhibition follows the trends of other museums is with its use of an 'affective architecture', one which to some degree moulds or structures the visitor's responses without necessarily determining them. I will now discuss museum architecture as a bridge to begin to talk about the relation between the Holocaust exhibition and the Crimes against Humanity exhibition.

Architecture

As part of a wider trend within museums towards the end of the twentieth century, Holocaust museums began to actively consider the spaces within which their exhibitions would be presented. Hence the architecture of Daniel Libeskind's Jewish Museum Berlin, James Ingo Freed's US Holocaust Memorial Museum, and Yad Vashem's new Holocaust Museum, all of which employ architecture to make a symbolic statement about the nature of the material they are presenting, with a predilection for sloping walls, restrictive, dark spaces and disrupted pathways which disorientate or make the visitor feel uneasy, evoking some of the horror and dislocation of the Holocaust.[22] While the IWM's Holocaust exhibition is not a free-standing, specifically built museum, similar techniques have been used within the exhibition space; thus, the homely, wood-lined 'pre-war life' atrium gives way to the relative darkness, angles and cold grey tiles of the 1933–1939 period, which uses a visual language of spaces or displays that are either predominantly white or black, representing the experience of the victim or the perpetrator.[23] Downstairs – and the use of physical descent is classic – the walls, floor and ceiling are black and somewhat restrictive.

By contrast, in its first installation at the very top of the building, the Crimes Against Humanity exhibition was starkly white, its open hangar-like space empty of artefacts and display cases, containing only a large table with six interactive computer screens and, beyond that but partially obscured by a wall, a huge film screen. The specially commissioned film dominated the room both visually and aurally, drawing the visitor past the interactives to the seats, which were white wooden blocks arranged in clusters for one or two people, seeming to suggest that viewing this film is an individual experience. As David Dernie suggested in his analysis of the exhibition design, 'the viewing is deliberately left open to observation by other visitors, so that any associations with the comfort and anonymity of the cinema are avoided', and there is a subtle quality of unease to the area.[24] The designers, Casson Mann, wanted visitors to be immersed in the film, and took the dimensions of the screen and brought them backwards as a floor and ceiling the same width and height of the film screen, so that, as Roger Mann explains, 'the screen fills your vision... the space you exist in, in the real world, appears almost seamless with the space within the film, and the people on the screen are almost the same size as you, and you almost begin to share the same space as them'.[25] The interactives were set into a large white table of the same dimensions, which perhaps, as Suzanne Bardgett suggests, 'hints at the roles bureaucracy and diplomacy play in both perpetrating and preventing genocide'.[26]

In 2009, the exhibition closed temporarily and moved to a space immediately left of the Holocaust exhibition's exit on the second floor. Its entrance is formed by a wooden, Libeskind-esque angular passageway jutting out into the main hall, and this passageway then tunnels right through the exhibition room itself, splitting it between the interactives on the left and the film screen to the right. Inside, the room is small and quite dark, the walls, floor and ceiling formed of huge panels of either the same pine or black, also set at slightly disjunctive angles. The film space is organised along the same lines, with pine seats set apart from each other within the space created by a pine floor and ceiling running backwards from the screen. The three interactive computers – which have been updated to include recent developments – are set into a pine desk, the film still clearly audible and partly visible through windows cut into the walls of the passageway. The overall feeling, though, is rather cramped and cave-like, an effect of the low ceilings and dark colours – continuing the trajectory of the Holocaust exhibition's architecture, perhaps.

Both versions of the Crimes Against Humanity exhibition have used an affective architecture, then, although certainly the white, fairly open space of the first exhibition had a fundamentally different feel to the directed spaces of the Holocaust exhibition below. One museum specialist, Christopher Marshall, has commented on the ways in which museums have begun to utilise the more reflective spaces of art galleries in museum displays. To paraphrase his argument, museums constitute inherently projective spaces, with their visitors programmed to receive didactic messages via a range of often emphatic communication strategies, whereas the art gallery provides a more self-contained and, crucially, reflective space.[27] This, I think, is one of the fundamental differences between the Holocaust exhibition and both versions of the Crimes Against Humanity exhibition: although Marshall's comment is better suited to the airier white minimalism of the first exhibition, both installations provide a more *contemplative* environment for the visitor to engage with the issues – in Bardgett's words, one which 'sit[s] them down and make[s] them think'[28] – through physical organisation of the film space, the desk-like environment for the interactives, the avoidance of heavy text panels or labelled artefacts, and, more successfully in the first, the overall aesthetic of the space. This claim that the spatial environment stimulates contemplation and reflection also extends past the architecture, to apply to the content of the exhibition itself. I will return to that thought, but I first want to discuss how Holocaust iconography is used, particularly in the film, as a platform from which thematic issues can be explored.

The crimes against humanity exhibition

As Bardgett has described, the idea for the Crimes Against Humanity exhibition was to complement the Holocaust exhibition, and to 'amplify' the lessons learned there, as 'a kind of post-script to the Holocaust Exhibition...which would offer visitors a space in which to contemplate the wider story'.[29] It is my central contention that the Crimes Against Humanity exhibition uses the Holocaust and its iconography to do this.[30] The familiar images and events of the Holocaust which can be encountered in the Holocaust exhibition below are presented alongside those of other conflicts, which are also familiar to us, but in a slightly different way – that is to say, primarily as contemporary news reports on Rwanda and the Balkans, or perhaps the current Khmer Rouge trials, filtered through our TV and computer screens. The inclusion of these images in the Crimes Against Humanity film, within a contemplative and educational environment, then, asks the visitor to see and look at them in a new light.

It is important to note at the outset, though, that the exhibition is admirably *not* Holocaust-centric – in fact, the interactive screens list each of the Nazis' targeted groups under the more inclusive heading 'Victims of the Nazis, 1933 to 1945', which includes 'people with physical and mental disabilities, political and religious dissenters, Roma and Sinti (otherwise known as Gypsies), the small black community in Germany and homosexuals. Jews were singled out as posing a particular threat'. This is in direct contrast to the overriding focus on the Jewish victims in the Holocaust exhibition, and has, I think, the immediate and symbolic effect of legitimating this broader enquiry. The film, though, concentrates primarily on the Jewish Holocaust victims, alongside Cambodia, Bosnia and Rwanda, mentioning in passing the Soviet victims, the Armenian genocide and the destruction of indigenous populations by government-promoted schemes. The comments of eight experts, such as Fergal Keane, Michael Ignatieff and the late Alison Des Forges, are laid over a succession of already existing film sequences and still photographs. It is organised thematically into seven chapters: 'Century of Turmoil', 'Lives Threatened', 'Perpetrators', 'How the World Responds', 'Trial and Punishment', 'Aftermath' and 'Lives Destroyed', and thus integrates the case studies together as examples of a common phenomenon. Holocaust imagery is used fairly evenly, but nevertheless, that which *is* used has a proportionately greater significance to the visitor. It is used as an anchor which contextualises the other case studies, placing them on *its* spectrum, rather than marking the Holocaust out as a category all of its own.[31]

At the most basic level, much less prior knowledge is assumed for the other case studies, which are given a basic introduction. At times, the visual aesthetics of the Holocaust are appropriated to present other atrocities – for example, shots of 1990s genocides are occasionally shown in black and white. One section, which deals with the ways in which the targeted groups are separated from the wider population, first shows familiar black-and-white footage of Nazi officers tormenting Jews, the yellow star, and identity papers being searched. This is followed by similar scenes in Yugoslavia, in colour now, with soldiers entering homes, civilians being evacuated and their papers checked, and then another scene at a roadblock in Rwanda, where the bloody corpses of Tutsis are clearly visible. Or, for example, Fergal Keane argues:

> The other critical point to remember is that it was the century of mass propaganda in which radio and, in the later part of the century, television, enabled some political leaders to mesmerise populations with relentless demonisation. If you look at what happened in Nazi Germany and take a straight line through to Rwanda, where radio was again used as a means of convincing people that if they simply went out and dealt with the problem of the minority – in Nazi Germany it was the Jews, in Rwanda it was the Tutsis – then their problems would be over.[32]

At other points, generally where some ambiguity is introduced, an example from the Holocaust is immediately given as reinforcement. For instance, Des Forges recounts the tale of a college professor who saved two Tutsi lives by working at the roadblocks, and asks the visitor how one balances the morality of that situation. This is immediately followed by the example of Eichmann, who protested that he had 'saved individual Jews'. Likewise, a description of the Khmer Rouge's targeting of its own population is followed by Ignatieff paraphrasing Himmler's famous speech at Posen, calling for the *Einsatzgruppen* (mobile killing units) to steel themselves and be hard, in the service of the German nation. In this way, the newer material or more difficult issues that the exhibition introduces are supported by the central example of the Holocaust.

This thematic approach was made possible, as the film's producer Annie Dodds acknowledged, 'by the fact that the accompanying bank of interactive programmes would do what the film could not: deliver the specific historical stories, the facts, figures and points of information ... it was vital that the interactives and the film supported and complemented each other'.[33] The interactives provide the background information to the examples covered by the film and nine others over several successive on-screen pages, each with a text and photograph, and look very much like traditional museum exhibition panels. They also build upon the thematic issues encountered in the film, exploring, for example, 'terms and definitions', 'current and future flashpoints', 'how the media reports ethnic conflict' and 'the international community's response'. These last three especially encourage the visitor to consider their own reading of the issues presented to them, so to conclude my discussion of the Crimes Against Humanity exhibition, I want to return to the issue of self-reflection within the exhibition, and also the idea of the exhibition as a corrective, at least in part, to the criticisms of the Holocaust exhibition.[34]

Just as the interactives expand upon the content of the film, so the exhibition itself expands, both conceptually and in terms of content, upon the Holocaust exhibition. The aftermath of genocide is explored in this exhibition, including a heartrending testimony from a survivor of the Cambodian genocide and some very difficult questions posed by Alison Des Forges –

> One study estimated that 60 per cent of Rwandan children had seen someone killed and that, of those, a substantial majority had seen a family member killed. How can one imagine a society where 60 per cent or more than 60 per cent of the children have seen someone murdered before their eyes? What consequences does that have?

The Holocaust exhibition leaves such questions to the final small room, where a video screen shows the survivors encountered around the exhibition describing life in the aftermath and offering their thoughts on survival. The widespread occurrence of rape (especially in Rwanda and Bosnia) is also dealt with by the film, an issue which is absent from the Holocaust exhibition and is a relatively new concern within the academic historiography of the Holocaust.[35] Nevertheless, the colour film of Jadranka Cigelj's testimony of her experience of a rape camp in Bosnia is interspersed with monochrome footage of one of those camps, suggesting a reliance on the familiar representational conventions of the Holocaust to insert this distressing issue into the Holocaust's moral framework. While these and other scenes create an intense sympathy for the victims, there is nothing of the overwhelming/dominating 'pathos approach' seen in the Holocaust exhibition; instead, the exhibition's presentation of the perpetrators and example after example of human exterminatory drives creates a rather more sobering effect.

In conceptual terms, the visitor's impression – generated or confirmed by the Holocaust exhibition – of what genocide is, and who the perpetrators are, is challenged by the film. A few minutes in, and against the backdrop of forests being cut down and indigenous homes bulldozed, Jonathan Mazower, Campaigns Coordinator for Survival International, remarks:

> Most people think that genocide means state-sponsored mass killing in gas chambers or rounding thousands of people up and shooting

them – and that isn't just what it means. There are countless examples from around the world where government-promoted schemes to settle and colonise remote parts of their countries have brought people into conflict with isolated tribal peoples.

While the nuances of perpetration, such as collaboration and expropriation, are not explicitly explored, the exhibition's treatment of the perpetrators does question the notion of the killer as a faceless, impenetrable monster. Other genocidal leaders, such as Pol Pot and Milošević, are held up under the same light as Himmler and Hitler, removing the certainty of Nazism as the ultimate evil. Michael Ignatieff's simple question, 'Who doesn't want to live in a world without enemies – right?' introduces the visitor to the mindset which, along with the other factors then listed, help forge the path to genocide. But most strikingly, it is the presentation of the Rwandan perpetrators which destabilises the notion of perpetrators as people who are 'not normal': four are shown to us in total, all perfectly ordinary-looking, two of whom are barely adults. As Fergal Keane forcefully states, 'The idea that the Germans were naturally predisposed more than any other race to committing genocide, the idea that the Cambodians had some secret germ inside them or that the Rwandese did, is absolute nonsense. We are all capable of it.'

These scenes are reinforced by the inclusion of various shots of daily urban life, which begin to implicate the visitor in the same world as the filmed one (the location is London, although this is not immediately obvious). As Dodds argues,

> these impressions of a prosperous, multicultural city are there to remind people that, in some measure, our affluence and stability is connected to poverty and insecurity elsewhere, that our own political and economic policies have far-reaching effects – be it the supply of arms to repressive regimes or trade practices which cause the collapse of poorer economies – that can help make the conditions for genocide more likely.[36]

The faces of multicultural, bustling crowds fade into a mound of skulls which are the remains of Cambodian victims of the Khmer Rouge, and, following an audio montage of statements by the recognisable voices of those such as Tony Blair and Bill Clinton, the film's experts stress that 'we are often not innocent in the genocides of others', that 'for genocide to happen it requires the indifference that lets it happen as well as the evil that makes it happen', and discuss the UN and the 'failure of the international community'. Ignatieff comments:

We supply arms, we engage in foreign policy decisions that tend to produce the collapse of other countries. It's not an accident that genocide happened in Cambodia after the pulverisation of the society by American bombing during the Vietnam war. This is not to say that the Americans are responsible for the genocide in Cambodia. It is to say that a society that has been pulverised by war is a society that is very susceptible to genocide.

Or, as Des Forges argues:

We pay very little attention to the consequences of our actions – the question of how much we pay for coffee, how much we pay for sugar – and yet all of these things can have very immediate and direct impact on people's lives. Changes in world commodity prices, which for us represent a small variation in what we have to pay, represent for the producer of that good, sometimes the difference between surviving and famine.

All this provokes the sort of self-reflection that the Holocaust exhibition below does not, but with one final caveat: it provokes self-reflection as a *human being*, as a member of the international community, rather than as a *Briton*. I would suggest, then, that while Crimes Against Humanity makes explicit the contemporary relevance of the Holocaust today, it stops short of questioning specifically British responses to atrocities.[37] A growing body of research is exploring the linkages between colonialism and genocide,[38] but at the IWM there is no mention of the role that imperialism or colonialism can play in the roots of genocide – indeed, the word 'colonial' appears only once during the film – or the legacies of Britain's imperial past, and in this respect both the Holocaust exhibition and the Crimes Against Humanity exhibition marginalise the role of Britain throughout these tragedies. An exploration of, say, the atrocities accompanying the British suppression of the Mau Mau uprising in Kenya in the 1950s, or the role of British imperialism in the famines devastating India in the late nineteenth century,[39] would be far more effective in jarring visitors from any deep-seated complacency to consider Britain's responsibility for past and indeed present atrocities.

Both of these concerns – the self-reflection the exhibition encourages, and its marginalisation of a British perspective – are reflected in the visitor comments. Interestingly, although many fewer are received in comparison to the Holocaust exhibition (not least because the cards are not very prominently placed or plentiful), many more show a higher degree of engagement with the issues, in direct contrast to those received for the Holocaust exhibition, where visitors overwhelmingly but simply respond that they were 'very moved' and 'learnt a lot', along with the clichés of 'never again' and 'never forget'. A recurrent request is that the film be shown more widely to the public, even children: one visitor commented, 'A film that needs viewing by young people – the ones who will be responsible for the world in the 21st century.'[40] Another echoes my earlier observations about the media images which saturate our news: 'News on telly [sic] just washes over us. This is now not the past.'[41] Many displayed a personalised engagement with the exhibition's content, calling for the inclusion of other atrocities which had occurred in their own countries – Australia, the United States, Argentina and, frequently but controversially, Palestine, as well as Britain. As one visitor remarked, 'There is a disturbing lack of portrayals of crimes against humanity committed by Britain itself during colonial times. Britain should perhaps learn from Germany in exposing and admitting their [sic] own crimes.'[42]

Conclusion

I have argued that the familiar staples of Holocaust representation found in the Holocaust exhibition reappear in the Crimes Against Humanity exhibition, providing a platform from which that exhibition may provoke a deeper self-reflection, albeit not a specifically British one, and this comes across even in something as subtle as the architecture and spatial environment of the exhibition (although far more successfully in its first installation). This anchoring permits a greater conceptual and factual exploration of the issues at hand than can be found in the Holocaust exhibition. Indeed, in its consideration of 'Man's Inhumanity to Man', its fuller exploration of the perpetrators and international responses to atrocities, this contemplative environment also goes some way towards correcting the Holocaust exhibition's presentation of the same. There is an interdependent and symbiotic relationship between the two exhibitions. The Crimes Against Humanity exhibition is clearly dependent upon the Holocaust, and the Holocaust exhibition, for its representational strategies, but the Holocaust, and Holocaust exhibition, are almost dependent upon explorations of other genocides as in the Crimes Against Humanity exhibition for their continuing significance. Nevertheless it is, literally and figuratively, how the 'Holocaust lens' is used to insert other atrocities into a moral framework that is the strongest indicator of the central role of the Holocaust in determining how Britain and the West respond to contemporary atrocities today.

Notes

1. For example, David B. MacDonald, *Identity Politics in the Age of Genocide: The Holocaust and Historical Representation* (Abingdon, 2008); Alan E. Steinweis, 'The Auschwitz Analogy: Holocaust Memory and American Debates over Intervention in Bosnia and Kosovo in the 1990s', *Holocaust and Genocide Studies*, 19 (2) (2005), 276–289.
2. The Holocaust exhibition covers c. 1,200 m² and two floors; the first Crimes Against Humanity exhibition a single level of 280 m² at the very top of the building (the second installation is somewhat smaller but more central on the second floor). Both are permanent exhibitions. Visitor numbers are not recorded for the Crimes Against Humanity exhibition, although they are for the Holocaust exhibition by the attendant at its entrance. (This is despite the higher recommended age for the Crimes Against Humanity exhibition, 16, whereas it is 14 for the Holocaust exhibition). The Holocaust exhibition is also more prominently advertised, both within the museum, on the website, and through external advertising.
3. Stephen Greenberg, 'The Vital Museum', in Suzanne MacLeod (ed.), *Reshaping Museum Space: Architecture, Design, Exhibition, Museum Meanings* (London, 2005), 226–237, especially 230–232.
4. The sobering content of the Holocaust exhibition occupies a slightly odd position above the great atrium, which Anne Karpf describes as 'the biggest boys' bedroom in London', where the tanks and other military hardware point towards, as she says, 'the obsession with technology which, along with triumphalism and the much mythologised spirit of defiant optimism, for so long characterised the war in British popular imagination'. Anne Karpf, 'Bearing Witness', *Guardian*, 2 June 2000 [cited 1 November 2012], available from http://www.guardian.co.uk/theguardian/2000/jun/02/features11. g21. See also: Isabel Wollaston, 'Negotiating the Marketplace: The Role(s) of Holocaust Museums Today', *Journal of Modern Jewish Studies*, 4 (1) (2005), 63–80, 64. Suzanne Bardgett writes that the large introductory and end spaces within the exhibition were conceived as transitional points, which would settle visitors and give them a sense of the gravity of the exhibition, and which would allow them time to reflect before leaving. Suzanne Bardgett, 'The Depiction of the Holocaust at the Imperial War Museum since 1961', in David Cesarani (ed.), *After Eichmann: Collective Memory and the Holocaust since 1961* (Abington, 2005), 146–156, 155.
5. A typical example is Jay Rayner, 'Don't Isolate the Holocaust', *Observer*, 4 June 2000 [cited 1 November 2012], available from http://www.guardian.co.uk/lifeandstyle/2000/jun/04/foodanddrink2, or Tony Kushner, 'The Holocaust and the Museum World in Britain: A Study of Ethnography', in Sue Vice (ed.), *Representing the Holocaust* (London, 2003), 22 and n. 52 on p. 38.
6. Suzanne Bardgett and Annie Dodds, 'Exploring the Common Threads of Genocide: The Crimes Against Humanity Exhibition at the Imperial War Museum', in Toby Haggith and Joanna Newman (eds), *Holocaust and the Moving Image: Representations in Film and Television since 1933* (London and New York, 2005), 281.
7. A clear exception to this is Jonathan Littell's recent novel *The Kindly Ones* (London, 2009).

8. It is important to note here the major arguments of reception studies, which stress that museum visitors are not passive receptors of exhibition narratives but rather construct and take away their own meanings, variable by age, sex, ethnicity, politics, social upbringing, personality and so on. Some visitors may well, therefore, actively contest the proffered interpretation, but it is also important to bear in mind that this interpretation strongly maps onto wider cultural attitudes towards and conceptions about 'evil' perpetrators, within which the Holocaust certainly is paradigmatic. See Rhiannon Mason, 'Cultural Theory and Museum Studies', pp. 17–32; and Gordon Fyfe, 'Sociology and the Social Aspects of Museums', in Sharon Macdonald (ed.), *A Companion to Museum Studies* (Oxford, 2006); Eilean Hooper-Greenhill, *Museums and the Interpretation of Visual Culture* (London, 2000), 33–49; and Sharon Macdonald, *Difficult Heritage: Negotiating the Nazi Past in Nuremberg and Beyond* (London, 2009).

9. Kushner, 'Holocaust and the Museum World', 21.

10. Despite the room in the downstairs section whose walls are entirely covered with a diagram of the Nazi bureaucratic command, the ideas conveyed here do not inform the entire exhibition. Likewise, the European-wide programmes of population politics are not noted in the text panels or the European eugenics movement by the rather gruesome medical experiment table.

11. Kushner, 'Holocaust and the Museum World', p. 24.

12. Ibid., 24–25. See also K. Hannah Holtschneider, 'Are Holocaust Victims Jewish? Looking at Photographs in the Imperial War Museum Holocaust Exhibition', in Daniel R. Langton and Philip S. Alexander (eds), *Normative Judaism: Jews, Judaism and Jewish Identity*, Proceedings of the British Association for Jewish Studies 2008, Melilah Supplement (2008).

13. Ibid., 22. See also Tony Kushner, 'Oral History at the Extremes of Human Experience: Holocaust Testimony in a Museum Setting', *Oral History*, 29 (2) (2001), 83–94; Suzanne Bardgett, 'Witness Statements: Testimonies at the Holocaust Exhibition', *Museum Practice*, 1 (1) (2004), 54–56.

14. Kushner, 'Oral History at the Extremes of Human Experience', 92. Kushner has equally expressed frustration that the Manchester Shoah Centre, which was to have based its Holocaust exhibition around testimonies of the life story of survivors, was abandoned as a project 'partly through a lack of financial will and partly through its radical vision', and saw this project as something of a contrast to the IWM's Holocaust exhibition. Kushner, 'The Victims: Dealing with Testimony', in Donald Bloxham and Tony Kushner (eds), *The Holocaust: Critical Historical Approaches* (Manchester, 2005), 48–50, 48.

15. Kushner, 'Oral History at the Extremes of Human Experience', 24–25.

16. There are, of course, competing definitions of 'Holocaust' – some see it as merely referring to the murder of the six million Jews, while others include the murders of the Roma, homosexuals, 'handicapped', Jehovah's Witnesses and political opponents of the regime. The problem with excluding the latter categories is that one may not be able to fully understand the Nazis' exterminatory drives.

17. Donald Bloxham, 'Britain's Holocaust Memorial Days: Reshaping the Past in the Service of the Present', in *Representing the Holocaust*, 59.

18. Tom Lawson, 'Ideology in a Museum of Memory: A Review of the Holocaust Exhibition at the Imperial War Museum', *Totalitarian Movements and Political Religions*, 4 (2) (2003), 173–83, 182.
19. Andrew Hoskins, 'Signs of the Holocaust: Exhibiting Memory in a Mediated Age', *Media, Culture & Society*, 25 (1) (2003), 11. As he remarks (p. 14), the 'artefact-driven (over diorama-driven) representation of the past is a purist venture which helps to forge a restricted perspective of the Holocaust as an historical event'.
20. See Wollaston, 'Negotiating the Marketplace', 66–67. Nevertheless it can be argued that, within the context (or tone) of our contemporary Holocaust consciousness, museum exhibitions *implicitly* take on a memorialisation function, spatially suffusing the exhibition environment (and at certain points the Holocaust exhibition comes even closer to implying a memorial function – such as with its collection of shoes from Majdanek, a replication of the Auschwitz Museum). As Dan Stone argues, 'Holocaust museums have increasingly acquired a commemorative as well as an educational function. And this commemorative function is inseparable from their entertainment function.' Dan Stone, 'Memory, Museums, Memorials', in Dan Stone (ed.), *The Historiography of the Holocaust* (Basingstoke, 2004), 521.
21. See Hoskins, 'Signs of the Holocaust', esp. p. 10 for a discussion of the interaction between artefactual and the more mediated audiovisual representation in the Holocaust exhibition.
22. On these museums, see (for example) Bernhard Schneider, *Daniel Libeskind: Jewish Museum Berlin* (Munich and London, 1999); Edward Linenthal, *Preserving Memory: The Struggle To Create America's Holocaust Memorial Museum* (New York, 2001); Joan Ockman et al., *Moshe Safdie: Yad Vashem – The Architecture of Memory* (Baden, 2006); and more generally on museum architecture within the field of museum studies, MacLeod, *Reshaping Museum Space*.
23. For the designer's own discussion of the visual languages deployed in the exhibition, see Greenberg, 'The Vital Museum'.
24. David Dernie, 'The Crimes Against Humanity Exhibition', in his *Exhibition Design* (London, 2006), 124.
25. Ross Parry and Andrew Sawyer, 'Space and the Machine: Adaptive Museums, Pervasive Technology and the New Gallery Environment', in *Reshaping Museum Space*, 47.
26. Bardgett and Dodds, 'Exploring the Common Threads of Genocide', 283.
27. Christopher R. Marshall, 'When Worlds Collide: The Contemporary Museum as Art Gallery', in *Reshaping Museum Space*, 170.
28. Bardgett and Dodds, 'Exploring the Common Threads of Genocide', 283.
29. Ibid., 281–282. Likewise, Antoine Capet describes it as a 'sequel': Capet, 'Crimes Against Humanity: An Exploration of Genocide and Ethnic Violence', *H-Museum Review*, February 2003 [cited 29 September 2011], available from: http://www.h-net.org/reviews/showrev.php?id=15054
30. On 'Holocaust Iconography', see Barbie Zelizer, *Remembering to Forget: Holocaust Memory Through the Camera's Eye* (Chicago, 1998), and Oren Baruch Stier, *Committed to Memory: Cultural Mediations of the Holocaust* (Amherst, 2003), Chapter 1, for example.
31. This is not to argue that the imagery and expert comments are used to *equate* these other atrocities with the Holocaust. (Concerns about 'equation'

and/or denying 'Holocaust uniqueness' were, of course, the main staples of a debate that raged in the 1990s and early 2000s over comparative studies. For excellent overviews and critical comments, see Dan Stone, *Histories of the Holocaust* (Oxford, 2010), Chapter 5, and A. Dirk Moses, 'Conceptual Blockages and Definitional Dilemmas in the "Racial Century": Genocides of Indigenous Peoples and the Holocaust', *Patterns of Prejudice*, 36 (4) (2002), 7–36, esp. 9–19; see also Alan S. Rosenbaum, ed., *Is The Holocaust Unique? Perspectives on Comparative Genocide*, 3rd ed. (Boulder, 2009). Rather, the thematic exploration means that similar elements across cases are placed alongside each other in a genuinely comparative manner. There is no sense of a hierarchy of suffering, or that the other atrocities must be the same as the Holocaust in order to be defined as genocide, and the Holocaust does not have a significantly disproportionate amount of time devoted to it.

32. Keane does, however, overestimate the influence of radio in the Rwandan genocide, like many others. See Scott Straus, 'What Is the Relationship between Hate Radio and Violence? Rethinking Rwanda's "Radio Machete" ', *Politics & Society*, 35 (4) (2007), 609–637.

33. Bardgett and Dodds, 'Exploring the Common Threads', 285.

34. This is not to argue that the Crimes Against Humanity exhibition is a deliberate and conscious rejoinder to these criticisms, especially since some of them were made after its opening. The differences can perhaps be put down to the way that public discourses and official representations of the Holocaust have, by the end of the twentieth century, become really quite cohesive and also circumscribed, with 'acceptable' narratives which some may be wary of circumventing. The same cannot really be said about representations of other genocides or atrocities, although see my comments on 'Holocaust uniqueness' below and at n. 32. I also want to stress that for the most part these criticisms of the Holocaust exhibition are not fundamentally serious, and it remains on the whole an excellent exhibition. It is very easy for historians to pick holes in exhibitions without remaining sensitive to the limits of curatorial time, space and money, and for my part I have tried to direct my criticisms towards the exhibition's preference of one narrative over another, choice between the acquisition and display of one photograph and another, and so on, rather than expecting 'a book on a wall'.

35. See Zoë Waxman, 'Unheard Testimony, Untold Stories: The Representation of Women's Holocaust Experiences', *Women's History Review*, 12 (4) (2003), 661–677; Lisa Pine, 'Gender and the Family', in *The Historiography of the Holocaust*.

36. Bardgett and Dodds, 'Exploring the Common Threads', 286.

37. Certainly, the IWM attracts a large number of international as well as British visitors, and exhibitions need not be explicitly aimed at the British. However, since this is the Imperial War Museum, primarily dedicated to portraying British involvement in war, an exploration of British colonial rule and atrocities would hardly be out of place.

38. See Dan Stone's overview in his *Histories of the Holocaust*, Chapter 5, and, for example, A. Dirk Moses, ed., *Empire, Colony, Genocide: Conquest, Occupation, and Subaltern Resistance in World History* (New York and Oxford, 2008); Dan Stone and Dirk Moses (eds), *Colonialism and Genocide* (London, 2006); Caroline Elkins and Susan Pedersen (eds), *Settler Colonialism in the*

Twentieth Century: Projects, Practices, Legacies (New York and London, 2005); Patrick Wolfe, *Settler Colonialism and the Transformation of Anthropology: The Politics and Poetics of an Ethnographic Event* (London, 1999). For a consideration of this in relation to the IWM and the Holocaust Exhibition, see Donald Bloxham and Tony Kushner, 'Exhibiting Racism: Cultural Imperialism, Genocide and Representation', *Rethinking History*, 2 (3) (1998), 349–358.

39. Caroline Elkins, *Britain's Gulag: The Brutal End of Empire in Kenya* (London, 2005); Mike Davis, *Late Victorian Holocausts: El Niño Famines and the Making of the Third World* (London and New York, 2001).
40. Visitor comment, February 2008.
41. Visitor comment, May 2004.
42. Visitor comment, April 2004 (original underlining).

9
The Holocaust and Colonial Genocide at the Imperial War Museum

Tom Lawson

Relatively little comment has been passed on the role of the Holocaust at the Imperial War Museum (IWM). There is a critical discourse about the role of the exhibition in the museum of course, and Rebecca Jinks's and Antoine Capet's essays contribute admirably to that discourse, yet the specific question of the relationship between thinking about the Holocaust and thinking about Empire and imperial genocide has seldom been asked. Yet as Jinks's essay makes clear, Britain has an imperial past and as such it is not possible for the Holocaust exhibition to just avoid that context. It would be very difficult anywhere in Britain, but in the IWM, the official repository of the nation's war memories, it is impossible. What is more, the IWM specifically tasks itself, in its Crimes Against Humanity exhibition, to engage with genocide in a wider context and as such to place the Holocaust in that context. And the British Empire *was* a site of genocide. One might expect then to find that the IWM grapples with the problem of genocide in the British Empire (in Australia, in Ireland, in India for example). It does not. As such, I want to use this commentary to think more about the relationship between the galloping British memory of the Holocaust that Capet identifies, and Britain's memory of genocide in its Empire that Jinks highlights, using the IWM as a case study.

As Capet makes clear in his essay on Holocaust art in the IWM, there has been, at the very least, an acceleration in Holocaust memory since the later 1980s. Of course, the Holocaust exhibition is both indicative of that acceleration and has contributed to it. It is notable also that the Holocaust memory boom has been accompanied by a growth in interest in, and reflection on, Empire and its implications. One need only think of books and television programmes by Niall Ferguson and recently Jeremy Paxman,[1] and the commemorations of the bicentenary of the abolition of the slave trade.[2] Although hardly in a critical mode, this turn to Empire does acknowledge the occurrence of genocide in the British world. Of course, that these two things, the turn to Empire and the upsurge in memorial reflection on the Holocaust, have occurred at the same time may be the result simply of a turn to the past more generally, the development of a more historically aware public discourse, the idea that history is the 'new Rock and Roll'.[3] But I would like to suggest that there are links between these two memory cultures – in that both use genocide to underpin positive visions of the ethical and moral basis of British identity. As such, the turn to Holocaust memory actually fulfils the same function as the recent return to Empire. In both cases, genocide is cited as an example of an atrocity that Britain sought to prevent. What is more, the memory of the Holocaust actually represents a continuity in British memories of genocide from the nineteenth century, and the Holocaust exhibition at the IWM particularly so.

As I have argued elsewhere, fundamentally the Holocaust emerges from the IWM as a good news story for Britain, and certainly early responses from visitors suggested that it was read that way too.[4] This is not really the result of the narrative on offer, which is rich and detailed and deliberately eschews triumphalism, but because of its context. Although there is some limited reflection on the iniquities of British refugee policy during the lifetime of the Third Reich in the exhibition, at root Britain is presented in the IWM as a whole as the liberal alternative to Nazism – as refuge, as liberator. In that context the Holocaust exhibition acts as a large scale, fully worked through example of 'why we fight'. There are, it seems to me, few other ways to interpret the museum visitor's literal journey in the exhibition from the darkness of Auschwitz to the light of British victory and the ephemera of war in the main atrium. Of course, this fits into a more widespread culture of Holocaust memory in Britain, which emphasises that the Holocaust is a story in which Britain played a role as refuge and liberator, and in which Britons can feel good about their past and their present.[5]

On the face of it, the idea of genocide within the British Empire would not have a positive tale to tell about Britain, and as such its absence from the IWM could, one might imagine, be easily explained as simply a form of evasion. And as Jinks points out, this is an absence despite a very specific site in which the history of British genocide of indigenous peoples could, and it is difficult not to suggest, *should* have been explored. The Crimes Against Humanity exhibition makes specific reference to genocide as being as much about the destruction of indigenous communities and culture, and particularly the indigenous relationship to the land, as it is about the gas chambers of Auschwitz. This claim is made in the central film in the exhibit and then can be explored in more detail on the interactive computers which accompany the film. That the British were responsible for a series of demographic disasters in their Empire, perhaps most notably in North America and Australia, is not mentioned once.[6]

A simple explanation for this might be that the IWM's remit is to explore conflict from the First World War to the present day. Yet other pre-1914 incidences of genocide are mentioned in the Crimes Against Humanity display. Certainly the exhibition concentrates on the twentieth century. But in doing so, it rather undermines its own ambitions to place genocide in its full historical context. There might have been a dubious case to be made that genocide only occurs after the genocide convention established a definition for it, but that is not the approach taken here and several incidences of genocide are explored – including the Armenian case and of course the Holocaust – that occurred prior to the codification of the crime. This, and the inclusion of genocide of indigenous peoples, suggests a conceptual approach to genocide has been adopted and as such it would seem appropriate if pre-1900 occurrences of genocide in the British world had been considered. After all, what better way to demonstrate that genocide was and is part of the world of the visitors themselves? To ignore genocide in the British Empire is also to ignore the fact that the author of the convention and of the concept of genocide, Raphael Lemkin, specifically understood that it had occurred in the British Empire, for example in Tasmania.[7]

This is not to say that the IWM avoids Empire entirely. Especially in its post-1945 conflicts section, the museum confronts the history of decolonisation. Whilst the claim that Britain simply accepted the break-up of its Empire, and that since 1945 it has fought wars that were either 'in its interests or to uphold international law' might come as a surprise to the Mau Mau rebels, there is an investigation of Britain's emergence into the post-colonial world.[8] But there is no place in the IWM for Imperial wars, either during or before the twentieth century.

As such you might argue that the Holocaust acts here as a 'screen memory', as others have alleged, particularly, for example, with regard to the function of Holocaust memory in the United States.[9] That is to say that the memory of the Holocaust obscures confrontation with the horrors of the British past, in part because it dwarfs the scale of the suffering unleashed by Empire and in part because the Holocaust establishes such a positive sense about the British past that no further exploration of its darker recesses can be allowed.

Whilst such an analysis might be justified if one simply considered the IWM alone, the IWM of course exists within a wider context, and within that context I think we can see an interaction between memories of the Holocaust and imperial genocide that suggests the screen memory thesis is too simplistic. The IWM, for example, exists within a tradition of museum display in Britain which has, since the mid-nineteenth century, used an understanding of what we would call genocide to underpin a construction of Britishness, which highlighted Britain's moral and ethical superiority. As such, the Holocaust exhibition is part of a *colonial* discourse which has traditionally used and referenced genocide in its making of British identity. After all, the Holocaust exhibition implicitly points to that superiority by identifying the barbarity of Britain's enemies. I shall briefly explore this further through the example of genocide in Tasmania, the case of genocide in the British world that is referenced most regularly.[10]

During the mid- to late nineteenth century, genocide in Tasmania (or 'extirpation' to use the contemporary parlance) underpinned competing visions of British superiority.[11] For both those that embraced the idea of racial hierarchy and those that regretted the passing of an entire people, that the Tasmanian population had been swept aside by the British Empire simply demonstrated that the British were pre-ordained to cover the globe.[12] The British were the men of the future; indigenous peoples were the past.[13] For liberal humanitarians who were concerned about the impact of British settlement on indigenous peoples, the destruction wrought in settler colonies like Tasmania was simply an example of the settlers ignoring their British heritage and their responsibility to protect (and transform) indigenous peoples.[14] From the 1830s onwards, groups like the liberal 'Aborigines Protection Society', made up of survivors from the evangelical abolition campaign, argued that the extension of imperial authority over these settlers was the only solution to the demographic disaster of British settlement for indigenous groups. Whilst this was an alternative vision of the worth of indigenous peoples, it articulated a similar faith in British supremacy. Indigenous peoples were to be transformed into Englishmen, civilised and their culture forgotten and destroyed.[15] Other discourse did the same – the nineteenth-century debate on human origins saw, because of the fate of indigenous Tasmanians, indigenous peoples as the victims of the march of biological, historical and cultural progress – and as such used their apparent decline in the face of settler societies as examples of British superiority.[16] Such a vision was also represented in England to a wider public – for example in museums like the Natural History Museum, which displayed the remains of indigenous Tasmanians in an account of the races of man.[17]

The point here is that we can, through the example of Tasmania, see the construction of a sense of Britishness that relied to some extent on the memory of genocide. For the most part the narrative that emerged was that Britain sought to prevent genocide, that it preached a civilisation that might have saved indigenous peoples had it not been for their barbaric treatment by the settlers. Ironically, that was of course an understanding of the world that embraced cultural genocide too; it certainly recognised no value in indigenous communities. This idea of the British as an alternative to genocide is not confined to Tasmania of course. Gladstone's famous call for humanitarianism in Bulgaria in the 1870s drew on and helped shape a powerful Victorian sense that the British Empire represented liberality as opposed to the barbarism of other imperial powers.[18] Campaigners against Belgian actions in the Congo did likewise at the beginning of the twentieth century, continuing in the tradition established by the Aborigines Protection Society to campaign on behalf of indigenous peoples. Indeed members of the Congo Reform Association lamented the passing of the days when England was the conscience of Europe.[19] All of this was suffused with a sense of British moral and ethical superiority, and a vision that indigenous peoples could be saved both from their enemies and themselves.

In the twentieth century, British museum culture essentially continued to represent a nineteenth-century story of British power and might to visitors, with regard to Tasmanians and other indigenous peoples. Again, this constructed a sense of identity that relied on genocide to imply that the British represented, in essence, the apex of human progress. To return to the Tasmanian example, as well as human remains, the ephemera of an apparently disappeared people was strewn across the British regions. A necklace belonging to Trugannini, believed in Britain at least to be the last living Tasmanian, was displayed in Exeter's Royal Albert Memorial Museum until 1997 labelled as the 'pathetic relic of a vanished people' of whom it was 'not hard to see why' they had become 'the province of history'.[20]

In the post-war period, and in the context of decolonisation, the Tasmanian genocide was then adopted by radical critics of Empire as a motif representing the suffering unleashed by the British Empire. It might be suggested that this acknowledgement of imperial genocide came at a time before the dominance of Holocaust memory. But this ignores the simple fact that memories of colonial genocide were often filtered through an understanding of suffering at Nazi hands. Take V.G. Kiernan's labelling British policy in Australia as an abortive Final Solution for example.[21] That such commentators accepted without question the idea that the indigenous population had been entirely wiped out is itself indicative of the enduring colonial attitudes of some post-colonial thinking. Not only did such a construct ignore the enduring indigenous population of Tasmania, it assumed that the indigenous population were the passive victims of the colonial strong-men.[22] Although it was offered as radical critique, such thinking was not far away from the colonial mindset that assumed indigenous peoples were some kind of Stone Age hangover simply waiting to exit history.

In the twenty-first century, the British Empire has struck back against this kind of radical critique, and attempts have been made to reassert the worth of the Empire as the grand civilising project. Such a discourse, typified by Niall Ferguson, does not as one might expect evade or deny the genocidal consequences of the British Imperial project. Instead, genocide is used as evidence of an absence rather than an excess of imperial power. Consequently, Ferguson is content to label the disappearance of the indigenous population of Tasmania as a genocide, but argues that it occurred *because* the British settlers deviated from the imperial intentions to protect and succour indigenous populations. The British government acted to try and restrain them, according to Ferguson. They failed in Tasmania, but, he suggests, succeeded in preventing genocide in continental Australia. As such, genocide becomes just another example of the success rather than the failure of Empire.[23]

All of these discourses – from the 1830s to the present day – suggest that in various ways the memory of genocide has been employed to sustain a vision of British ethical, moral (and at times racial) superiority. Whether or not such discourses revel in genocide, or despair at it, they invariably use genocide to tell a positive story about the nature of Britain – overwhelmingly since the end of the nineteenth century a story of liberal humanitarian Britain that sought to prevent genocide and bring the gift of civilisation to the world.

Seen within that context, the memory of the Holocaust and its portrayal at the IWM is another example of a colonial discourse of genocide – albeit one writ extremely large. Liberal humanitarian Britain fought the Nazi devil, and this museum for the Nazis victims is as much a tribute to that as it is memorial for those and that which was destroyed. As such, you might argue that the Holocaust is acting as a 'screen memory' in the IWM. After all, there is no reflection on genocide in the British Empire at all. But it is not the mere presence of the Holocaust in the museum, and the absence of colonial or imperial genocide which is important here. What is crucial is what the presence of the Holocaust in the IWM says about Britain, what it demands that its visitors think about Britain. In that sense, the memory of the Holocaust as written in the IWM has rather a lot in common with the memory of the colonial genocide it avoids. Indeed, the IWM could simply import any one of the ways in which genocide in the British Empire has been remembered, and it would not disrupt or challenge their Holocaust narrative. Nor would it challenge the British visitors, or the story about Britain that it seeks to tell. As such, in order to actually escape the confines of a colonial mindset, the Museum would not just have to tell the story of imperial genocide (in a manner that avoided triumphalism), it would have to tell a different story about the Holocaust too. Without that, the memory of colonial genocide is, if only in functional terms, present in Britain's *imperial* war museum.

Notes

1. See for example Niall Ferguson, *Empire: How Britain Made the Modern World* (London, 2003) and Jeremy Paxman, *Empire: What Ruling the World Did to the British* (London, 2011).
2. For a critical examination of those celebrations see Diana Paton, 'Interpreting the Bicentenary in Britain', *Slavery and Abolition*, 30 (2) (2009), 277–289.
3. Matthew Dodd, 'The New Rock "n" Roll', *The New Statesman*, 10 December 2001.
4. See Tom Lawson, 'Ideology in a Museum of Memory: A Review of the Holocaust Exhibition at the Imperial War Museum', *Totalitarian Movements and Political Religions*, 4 (2) (2003), 173–183.
5. See for example David Cesarani, 'Britain, the Holocaust and Its Legacy: The Theme for Holocaust Memorial Day, 2002', Theme Paper for Holocaust Memorial Day 2002, available to download at http://hmd.org.uk/assets/downloads/1149797162-22.pdf. Cesarani stated that the Holocaust is part of British history, in part because 'Britain fought Nazi Germany for six years and, thanks to their courage and sacrifice, British service personnel helped to save the remnant of European Jewry from annihilation. British troops liberated the Bergen-Belsen concentration camp and rescued tens of thousands of Jews from death.' Whilst he also argued that a more critical approach could be taken, the paper makes clear how the Holocaust could be instrumentalised by and for Britain.
6. See Rick Halpern and Martin Daunton (eds), *Empire and Others: British Encounters with Indigenous Peoples 1600–1850* (Philadelphia, 1999) for a series of case studies.

7. Ann Curthoys, 'Rapheal Lemkin's Tasmania: An Introduction' and Rapheal Lemkin, 'Tasmania', both in *Patterns of Prejudice*, 39 (2) (2005), 162–196.
8. Quotation from the Imperial War Museum's 'Post 1945 Conflict' display. On the Mau Mau rebellion and the British Empire see John Newsinger, *The Blood Never Dried: A People's History of the British Empire* (London, 2010), 182–198.
9. See for example Peter Novick, *The Holocaust in American Life* (Boston, 1999), 15.
10. Henry Reynolds indeed argues that the Tasmanian case is often referenced thoughtlessly and without much understanding. See Henry Reynolds, *An Indelible Stain? The Question of Genocide in Australia's History* (Ringwood, AU, 2001), 50.
11. See for example Mrs Charles Meredith, *My Home in Tasmania: During a Residence of Nine Years* (London, 1852).
12. See for example *The Times*, 30 December 1864, 6, which contains an editorial entitled 'We have exterminated the race in Tasmania' which displays in equal measure pride and regret at this apparent feat. In actual fact the indigenous Tasmanian population was not wiped out and there is a substantial indigenous Tasmanian community today.
13. Indeed the indigenous Tasmanian population was quite literally represented as a hangover from the Stone Age. See for example John Lubbock, *The Origin of Civilisation and the Primitive Condition of Man: Mental and Social Condition of Savages* (London, 1870).
14. The classic statement of the liberal humanitarian position with regard to the indigenes of Empire is contained within the *Report of the Parliamentary Select Committee on Aboriginal Tribes (British Settlements)* (London, 1837).
15. For an excellent history of the Aborigines Protection Society that makes clear their commitment both to the transformation of indigenous peoples and their understanding of the need to extend, rather than draw back from the colonial project see James Heartfield, *The Aborigines' Protection Society: Humanitarian Imperialism in Australia, New Zealand, Fiji, Canada, South Africa and the Congo, 1836–1909* (New York, 2011), 18–20, 43.
16. See for example Robert Knox, *The Races of Men: A Philosophical Enquiry into the Influence of Races over the Destinies of Nations* (London, 1862), 229.
17. See for example *Guide to the Specimens Illustrating the Races of Mankind* (London, 1908), 33. The museum received its first human remains from Tasmania in 1899.
18. For an interesting discussion of that call within the tradition of humanitarian intervention see Michael R. Marrus, 'Holocaust Bystanders and Humanitarian Intervention', *Holocaust Studies: A Journal of Culture and History*, 13 (1) (2007), 1–18.
19. Hunt Hawkins, 'Joseph Conrad, Roger Casement, and the Congo Reform Movement', *Journal of Modern Literature*, 9 (1) (1981–1982), 65–80, particularly 70.
20. This is taken from the text accompanying Trugannini's necklace in the Royal Albert Memorial Museum in Exeter. A photograph of the display, from 1997, was given to the author by Tony Eccles, Curator at the Museum.

21. V.G. Kiernan, *Lords of Human Kind: European Attitudes to the Outside World in the Imperial Age* (London, 1969), 276.
22. For a discussion of the manner in which sympathetic historians have belittled and patronised the indigenous Tasmanian community as the ultimate victims see Henry Reynolds, *Fate of a Free People* (Camberwell VIC., 2004).
23. Ferguson, *Empire*, 108.

Part IV
Commemorating the Holocaust

10
'We Should Do Something for the Fiftieth': Remembering Auschwitz, Belsen and the Holocaust in Britain in 1995

Mark Donnelly

Six years before Britain's first annual Holocaust Memorial Day was observed in 2001, the 50th anniversaries of the liberation of Auschwitz and Bergen-Belsen were remembered as part of a wider public calendar of war-related commemorative activities.[1] Holocaust Memorial Day has (rightly) been the subject of much scholarly attention, some of it critical of the day's 'pathos' approach to commemoration.[2] In contrast, there has been markedly less discussion of how the anniversaries in 1995 of the liberation of the camps were remembered in Britain. This chapter attempts to supplement previous studies that *have* focused on aspects of Holocaust commemoration in Britain in 1995, notably those by Judith Petersen and Joanne Reilly *et al*.[3] The aim is to question whether the ways in which Holocaust commemoration was performed and articulated in 1995 helps us to think about how subsequent commemorations have been organised and understood. The approach that this discussion takes is both empirical (setting out salient features of the public discourse of Holocaust memory in 1995 under various genre headings) and critical (commenting on some of the implications of these discursive features for thinking about Holocaust memory in Britain). Part of the justification for this study is that the imbalances between scholarly interest in the commemorations of 1995 and 2001 could be usefully readjusted, if only because of the ways in which they relate to certain methodological possibilities for analysing 'Holocaust memory' in a British context. After all, as Jeffrey Olick has argued, commemorations should not be conceptualised as isolated, discrete occurrences.

They themselves stand in relation to an 'accumulated succession of commemorations', and thus we might usefully think in terms of a 'memory
of commemoration' and indeed a 'memory of memory' (original emphasis).[4] Memory is understood here not as a 'thing' that exists somewhere,
but always as acts of remembering or the performance of 'mnemonic
practices'. Moreover, these acts or performances of memory have their
own discursive historicity – they are, as Olick argues, part of an ongoing process of mnemonic practices in operation rather than a product
of, or somehow a reflection of, some other processes (political, social,
cultural).[5] On this reading, the various ways in which the Holocaust
has been remembered in Britain (including Memorial Days since 2001)
were not straightforwardly determined by the context in which they
occurred, nor were they simply tools to meet sociopolitical exigencies
in the present. Instead, they can be thought of as practices that were in
a dialogue with – and which bore traces of – earlier mnemonic practices,
and whose relationship with the context in which they were performed
was mutually constitutive rather than reflective.

Public acts of Holocaust remembrance in Britain in 1995 were largely
directed towards the anniversaries of the liberation of two camps:
Auschwitz and Bergen-Belsen. The anniversary of the liberation of
Auschwitz was the central event of European Holocaust remembrance in
1995, and it was marked by major international ceremonies in Poland
on 26 and 27 January 1995. Bergen-Belsen (henceforth Belsen) meanwhile had a particular place in Britain's war remembrance because it
was the only main camp that was liberated by British (and Canadian)
troops.[6] Moreover, as many commentaries pointed out in 1995, it was
the camp in which the sisters Anne and Margot Frank had died in
March 1945.[7] Ceremonies were held at Belsen on 27 April 1995 (delayed
from the actual anniversary of liberation on 15 April because that date
coincided with Passover).

Before discussing some of the discursive features of the ways these
anniversaries were marked in Britain, we should of course acknowledge
that the anniversaries themselves were part of a wider programme of
war-related commemorations that year. As experience has taught us,
some anniversaries of events have more symbolic significance than others (1st, 10th, 25th, 50th, centenary and so on). Thus it was that 1995
became a 'banner year' for war-related commemorations, in part because
of the 'roundness' of the 50 years that had passed since 1945.[8] In Britain,
these commemorations climaxed in May with a three-day festival to
remember VE Day in London's Hyde Park (attended by 1.5 million people),[9] the staging of state ceremonies at Westminster Hall, Buckingham

Palace and St Paul's Cathedral, and a public holiday on the anniversary of VE Day itself. Millions of Britons over the VE Day anniversary weekend attended street parties and/or watched and listened to media coverage. According to Judith Petersen, for example, ITV screened seven hours and ten minutes of VE Day programming between 16 April and 9 May. Meanwhile BBC1 broadcast 23 hours and 20 minutes of coverage in May-June 1995.[10] Much of this BBC1 output consisted of live coverage of state ceremonies, but it also contained feature programmes about Britain's war effort and a peak-time screening of the film *The Battle of Britain* (1969).[11] Throughout the various commemorative activities, a well-rehearsed discourse was invoked by politicians, journalists and media commentators about how and why Britain had fought the war, and about what 'lessons' could be drawn from the British contribution to Allied victory. This discourse had become familiar through its regular articulation at previous ceremonies – for example, the annual Remembrance Sunday commemorations, the 50th anniversaries that marked the declaration of war (September 1989) and the D-Day landings (June 1994) – and via its representation in various media texts, in institutions such as the Imperial War Museum, and within school curricula. This discourse traced the limits of Britain's war memory in relation to what is often called the 'good war' paradigm – marking out what could be said about Britain's war effort within the boundaries of what was regarded as legitimate or reasonable speech. The 'good war' paradigm is commonly seen as a predominately self-serving and self-congratulatory socio-historical resource, particularly with regards to those symbolic wartime events that could be narrated and interpreted through a (more or less) exclusively 'national' frame of reference.[12] It was a paradigm which, as Angus Calder wrote in relation to the 'myth' of the Blitz, has had the power to 'condition a great deal of "common-sense" thinking' about Britain at war.[13] Its cultural power derived from the ways in which it produced narratives about Britain's war effort that invoked only a small (and iconic) repertoire of symbolic resources, all of which could be made congruent with a particular type of story architecture.

The story architecture in question was important because, as Eviatar Zerubavel has argued, the types of narratives commonly constructed about historically symbolic subjects should not be thought of as representations of the past-in-itself, but rather as manifestations of what he terms 'sociomnemonic structures' – particular archetypal plotlines or schematic formats that people use to narrate the past, and which can be seen as being prevalent in certain cultural and sociopolitical contexts.[14] Furthermore, as Alon Confino and Peter Fritzsche have argued, while it is true that collective memories can be 'potentially integrated into any number of narratives', once they become 'embedded in a narrative stream they turn out to be remarkably strong and they thus deflect counternarratives and counterarguments'.[15] One of the striking features of the 1995 commemorations was the way they highlighted how the 'good war narrative' had retained enough of its cultural legitimacy to push counterarguments about, or alternative readings of, Britain's war effort to the margins (but not, we should acknowledge, to deny them entirely).[16] Therefore, as well as relating Holocaust commemoration in Britain in 1995 to a 'memory of commemoration', there is also some value in relating it to the 'good war' paradigm, and questioning how this relationship might inform our thinking about some of the philosophical problems that scholars have raised about Holocaust commemoration more generally. In order to discuss these issues, I have organised the discursive constructions of Holocaust remembrance in 1995 under three genre headings: 'the Holocaust as someone else's problem', 'remembering for the future', and 'the Holocaust and the case for humanitarian intervention'.

The Holocaust as someone else's problem

The events that came to be known as the Holocaust were always marginal to Britain's good war paradigm, functioning primarily as a justification of all that the British military did in pursuit of victory. Raphael Samuel summed it up thus: 'Britain won. They don't regard the Holocaust as their problem.'[17] This marginalisation was both symptomatic and constitutive of a political discourse in Britain that rarely addressed the Holocaust. To be sure, there were times when issues around the Holocaust did become a focus of political discussion. We might mention here, for example, the discussions that took place between the Board of Deputies of British Jews and the Department of the Environment from 1979 to 1983 about the siting and installation of a Holocaust memorial. Another example would be the work of the All-Party Parliamentary War Crimes Group from 1986 onwards. But the point being made here is that by 1995 there was no tradition of senior British politicians making speeches about the Holocaust, and thus there were no strong precedents that might persuade politicians (and their advisers) at that time that the Holocaust was a matter for their attention. It was not a subject that politicians were expected to be able to speak about as a focal point of ethico-political discourse. This also meant that when a British political leader did make a major speech about the Holocaust – for example,

Tony Blair during Holocaust Memorial Day 2001 – there was no existing stock of symbols, tropes, gestures and vocabulary from previous commemorative speeches about this subject that could be referenced. We might contrast this absence of symbols with John Major's speech at the VE Day commemorations in Hyde Park on 6 May 1995, which was full of references back to various tropes of the good war paradigm that had become familiar in public discourse (St Paul's cathedral as a symbol of resilience, David Low's cartoon of the wounded British soldier handing the laurel of peace back to Europe, the people's war – but no references to the Holocaust).[18]

John Major had previously attended a ceremony in Poland in 1993 to mark the 50th anniversary of the Warsaw uprising. But when some 300 West European parliamentarians – along with Polish and Israeli politicians – assembled at Auschwitz to commemorate the 49th anniversary of its liberation in 1994, Britain (together with Spain, Ireland and Denmark) did not send a political representative.[19] This ceremony at Auschwitz was the first such meeting of its kind, organised by the European Jewish Congress. Those present included Egon Klepsch, President of the European Parliament, and parliamentary heads from Belgium, Germany, Italy, Greece, Luxembourg, Holland and Portugal. Also attending was Simone Veil, the former French health minister who was returning to Auschwitz-Birkenau for the first time since being an inmate there in 1945. The absence of British representation at the ceremony was a clear signal that Britain's political classes regarded Auschwitz as something for other nations to remember. This signal was amplified in 1995 when 20 heads of state attended the ceremonies to mark the 50th anniversary of the camp's liberation. Again, there was no senior representative of the British state among them. Backbench Labour MPs Alice Mahon and David Winnick anticipated this absence and drew attention to it in the House of Commons on 25 January 1995 – two days before the main ceremonies in Poland. Winnick suggested that the Speaker of the House of Commons might be authorised to attend at Auschwitz on behalf of the British parliament. The Speaker of the House, Betty Boothroyd, replied that she was unaware of any government plans to commemorate the anniversary.[20] The following day Greville Janner (Labour MP and former President of the Board of Deputies of British Jews) asked the Leader of the House, Tony Newton, whether there would be time set aside on the anniversary itself for the Commons to 'to join in mourning the victims of Nazism' who died in Auschwitz.[21] Newton said that this would not be possible, but pointed out that Lord Jakobovits, the former Chief Rabbi, would represent the Queen at the official Polish ceremony and later Jewish ceremony at Auschwitz. This choice of delegate was another way of stating that the meaning of the liberation of the camp within Britain's public sphere was regarded as a matter of interest only for the country's Jewish communities.

There was a similar lack of British political participation in ceremonies to mark the anniversary of the liberation of Belsen on 27 April 1995. The main 90-minute ceremony at Belsen had been attended by German Chancellor Helmut Kohl, President Roman Herzog, Rita Süssmuth (President of the German Parliament), Ignatz Bubis (President of the Central Council of Jews in Germany), Chaim Herzog (former President of Israel) and more than 5000 people from the local community.[22] But as the roles of victims and perpetrators were remembered at Belsen, the main focus for British commemorative activity was elsewhere (spatially and ethically). The British military base at Belsen hosted a private ceremony, attended by camp survivors and veterans of the liberation, at which prayers were said over the graves of 250 prisoners who had died in the British military field hospital after the camp was liberated.[23] This was followed by a lunch at which survivors from Belsen met with some of those who had helped to liberate the camp. British media interest in this anniversary was slight, and was directed largely towards the story of the camp's (British) liberators rather than its (predominately Jewish) victims. *The Guardian*, for example, published a feature article that reproduced British army chaplain Tom Stretch's eyewitness account of entering Belsen.[24] Several newspapers found a way of integrating the experiences of liberator and victim, recounting a story about the marriage between a British soldier and a former Belsen inmate. The couple were Norman Turgel, a Jewish British soldier serving in the Intelligence Corps, and Gena Goldfinger, an inmate who had worked as a nurse in Belsen. The couple married in October 1945 in a Lübeck synagogue, and for decades after the war they travelled and spoke to students around the world about their wartime experiences. As an *Evening Standard* headline for the story read in 1995, '50 years on, love still triumphs over Belsen evil'.[25] In fact British newspapers had been interested in this story since the marriage ceremony itself in 1945, when Gena Goldfinger had been proclaimed by the press as 'the Bride of Belsen'.[26] The articles about Tom Stretch, Norman Turgel and Gena Goldfinger exemplify the way in which stories about the camp's liberation were framed in 1995 in much the same terms as they had been in the original British press coverage of 1945. Moreover, a similar discursive positioning of Bergen-Belsen was at work in the Imperial War Museum's 'Belsen Fifty Years On' exhibition in 1995. As Jo Reilly *et al.* observed,

In general, the Holocaust occupied only a minor place in British war commemorations in 1994 and 1995. But reference to the British army's liberation of Belsen enabled attention to be drawn to Nazi atrocities without in any way confusing matters by considering Jewish death and suffering during the war. Indeed, as in 1945, the liberation of Belsen could be used to concentrate further on the moral righteousness of the British war effort. The tendency to view the liberation of Belsen as *British* rather than Jewish/victim-centred was dominant in Britain during April 1995 ... The Imperial War Museum's commemoration on 12 April 1995 in no way corrected past imbalances and in fact reconfirmed its use of Belsen as part of the British war story.[27]

One further point can be made here about the positioning of Auschwitz, Belsen and the Holocaust as 'someone else's problem'. In 1995, the anniversaries of the camps' liberation were a matter of interest only for 'quality' national newspapers (including the *Jewish Chronicle*) and BBC2. In contrast, the country's most popular 'red top' daily newspapers – *The Sun* and *Daily Mirror* – provided almost no coverage of the 50th anniversaries.[28] Moreover, Judith Petersen has argued that in British television's coverage of the cycle of war-related 50th anniversaries, only one programme on BBC2 in January 1995 challenged the marginalisation of the Holocaust within Britain's national and official discourses of war commemoration (see below). But overall, she reasons, television's treatment of the Holocaust did nothing to disturb the sense of moral integrity and self-congratulation that was ingrained in Britain's memory of the 'good war'. 'Britain's war memory', Petersen concluded, 'appeared to be too precious to grant the wartime experience of Europe's Jews a prominent place in it'.[29]

The linguistic distancing of the Holocaust as 'someone else's problem' in 1995 was part of a British tradition that reached back across the post-war decades. As Susanna Schrafstetter has argued, for example, there was far more media interest in the campaign to secure compensation payments for former British POWs in the 1960s than there was in an equivalent campaign for Holocaust survivors.[30] To be sure, there were exceptions to this marginalisation of Holocaust memory in synagogues and private homes, and in the small annual ceremony at the Hyde Park Holocaust memorial from 1983 onwards. But in the wider public spheres of politics, media and state ceremonials, Britain's war memory continued to be conceptualised and performed as a national (rather than a cosmopolitan) story. As such, while political leaders and media commentators were able to rework long-established narratives about the country's 'good war' in 1995, there were no equivalent voices articulating why the Holocaust should be commemorated at all in Britain. In Confino and Fritzsche's terms, the Holocaust 50 years on had not yet become embedded in the 'narrative stream' of Britain's war memory.[31] Indeed, we might illustrate this point further by noting here that a recent monograph on Britain's Second World War memory by a British academic made no reference to the Holocaust.[32] Even when Britain took the lead on Holocaust commemoration at the Stockholm Forum in 2000, the distancing of the genocide from the good war paradigm that was evident in 1995 continued. As Sharon Macdonald argued, the choice of the date for Britain's first Holocaust Memorial Day in 2001 – the date of the liberation of Auschwitz – did not evoke any obvious 'British' connections, and reinforced the idea that Britain had no direct association with the events of the Holocaust.[33] Thus the Holocaust was framed as an event in which victims and perpetrators were always both distinct and unmistakably 'other', which meant in turn that there were no obvious reasons to ask critical questions about Britain's relationship to it (for example, concerning British refugee policies at that time, British colonial practices of subjugation against the colonised, British policies on allowing former Nazi war criminals into the UK shortly after the Second World War). But as Daniel Levy and Natan Sznaider's analysis of memory politics suggests, perhaps we can avoid seeing Holocaust memory and British war memory as being necessarily and forever antithetical. According to these writers, the nation state as the main 'container' of collective memory is 'in the process of slowly being cracked' – if this is so, then old assumptions about the Holocaust being 'someone else's problem' will cease to matter so much.[34] This is because on Levy's and Sznaider's reading, Holocaust memory will increasingly become 'de-territorialised' and 'future-oriented'. Instead of being positioned in relation to histories of any given nation state, Holocaust memory will become 'cosmopolitan' – formed in the interaction between the global and the local, not rooted in a singular political or geographic space, and functioning as a focal point for the recognition of universal 'moral-political obligations'.[35]

Remembering for the future

The model of ascribing meaning to the Holocaust as something that would happen again unless it was remembered can be traced back to the earliest reports from the liberated Bergen-Belsen in April 1945.

'Remembering for the Future' was also the title chosen for Britain's first major international conference on the Holocaust in July 1988, organised by Elizabeth and Robert Maxwell. More recently still, in the publicity that surrounded the UK release of *Schindler's List* in February 1994, the moral and political imperative to 'remember' was taken for granted. A *Guardian* leading article on the weekend of the film's release, for example, stated: 'Spielberg's film is needed. Only through constant vigilance and remembrance can we hope to curb the anti-Semitic reflex embedded in European culture which spun so horrifically out of control in the second world war.'[36]

'Liberal' newspapers such as *The Guardian*, *The Observer* and *The Independent* adopted this injunction to remember in their editorials and feature articles about the ceremonies at Auschwitz and Bergen-Belsen in 1995.[37] The *Daily Telegraph* similarly sought to instrumentalise Holocaust memory, arguing that '[i]f we are to give political expression to what Auschwitz means for us 50 years after its liberation, it must be to support those in Israel and its neighbours who are struggling against extremists on either side to bring peace to the Middle East'.[38] From a different perspective, Beatrix Campbell in *The Independent* argued that there was an ethical imperative for people to commit themselves to remembering the Holocaust via the 'hazards of listening' to survivor testimony. In this way, she argued, the Holocaust had become 'a test of our commitment to the victims of history'.[39] Indeed, the injunction to remember provided an important discursive context for feature interviews in newspapers with camp survivors like Leon Greenman and Gena Turgel (nee Goldfinger) in 1995. In both cases, their continued commitment to educating schoolchildren and the wider community about the Holocaust was highlighted.[40] We should also place under this discursive heading of 'remembering for the future' David Cesarani's *Bringing the Holocaust Home*, a programme that was screened on BBC2 as part of its *Open Space* strand – where programme makers could operate free from any BBC editorial control. It was shown on BBC2 on 14 January 1995, and took the form of a personal call by Cesarani for the establishment of an official Holocaust museum in Britain – an equivalent of the United States Holocaust Memorial Museum in Washington. The programme juxtaposed footage of the annual Remembrance Sunday ceremony at London's Cenotaph with the much smaller commemoration that was held each May at the Holocaust memorial in Hyde Park. The small stone memorial that was established in 1983, argued Cesarani, was 'no longer an adequate memorial, and cannot transmit the truth of what occurred in the Holocaust'.[41] Cesarani went on to ask of the

Holocaust in the programme: 'Can we afford not to teach this story to our children, and their children, so that they may never have to go through it again?' He argued that Britain had a 'unique relationship' with the fate of Jews in the Nazi era, but that this was usually left out of Britain's war memory. A Holocaust museum, he believed, would 'set the record straight' and 'stand as a warning to future generations'. He also referred to the rise of far-right political groups in Britain and elsewhere in Europe, some of whom were Holocaust deniers. Cesarani concluded: 'If ever there was a time for a museum to educate people about the dangers of racial intolerance, that time is now.'[42]

The various injunctions for people to 'remember for the future' in 1995 could be understood in two different ways. At one level, they could be seen as a call to ensure that the Holocaust was remembered in the future. This owed much to the fact that by the late twentieth century, Holocaust memory had reached a moment of transition. As the numbers of people with personal memories of the Holocaust decreased, so the importance of memorials, museums and commemorative ceremonies as realms or sites of memory (*lieux de mémoire*) increased. Understood this way, 'remembering for the future' functioned as a moral imperative – the Holocaust should continue to be commemorated as a mark of respect for those who were murdered. Understandably, this imperative was open to criticism. Why should there be a particular commemorative focus on victims of the Holocaust, and not other victims of war and genocide in the modern era? Also, as James Young pointed out in a widely influential study of memory, sometimes monuments and ceremonies can work in unintended and negative ways. Instead of functioning as sites and occasions that promote reflection and thought, they are assumed to have taken over the responsibility for remembering that was formerly ours.[43] Thus they facilitate a process that allows people to pay lip-service to the event that is being commemorated on annual days or occasional visits, but then to move on and forget.

These criticisms notwithstanding, 'remembering for the future' could be understood in another way. The term implied a kind of civic economy of memory. Remembering the Holocaust, the argument ran, would produce positive outcomes for the nation's social and civic health, because it would act as a barrier against various forms of discrimination and persecution, and ultimately help to prevent the emergence of conditions in which a future genocide might be possible. This meaning of the term anticipated (at least in some respects) what we referred to earlier as the development of 'cosmopolitan, future-oriented' Holocaust memory in the twenty-first century. But whereas Levy and Sznaider attempted to articulate how such a memory politics could contribute to a global discourse of universal human rights, none of the advocates of 'remembering for the future' in 1995 explained how commemorative acts might act as moral or ethical barriers. What *were* the lessons of the Holocaust that could be used for such purposes? Who were these lessons primarily directed towards – people with access to forms of political and military power, or everybody equally? And was something as violently extreme as the Holocaust an appropriate event to use as the basis for civic education? These questions were unanswered in 1995. Partly as a consequence, when 'remembering for the future' was re-adopted as an important organising theme in Britain's inaugural Holocaust Memorial Day (one of the sections of the ceremonies was titled 'Post 1945 – "Never Again"') uncertainties remained about what this slogan meant in practice. In 1995 the most concrete implication of the term was to confer a form of 'historical legitimacy' for state action to be used against 'ethnic cleansing' in former Yugoslavia.

The Holocaust and the case for humanitarian intervention

One of the 'lessons' of the Holocaust that was sometimes cited in 1995 was the duty of outside powers to intervene to prevent genocide in places such as Bosnia, Rwanda and Chechnya. This line of argument, for example, was implicit in the way that some British Jews in 1995 criticised Churchill's wartime government (along with its main allies) for its failure to save more victims of the Holocaust when they had the chance. At a meeting organised by the Yad Vashem Charitable Trust as part of the liberation of Auschwitz commemorations, Churchill's coalition was accused of 'indifference' to the plight of Europe's Jews. This indifference extended to the government's failure to act on a chance to rescue 1000 orphans from Vichy-controlled France in late 1942.[44] The question of whether Britain (and others) could have done more to prevent the Holocaust was more than a matter of historical interest at this time. In the year that Auschwitz and Belsen were commemorated, intervening to prevent genocide was once again an issue of urgent contemporary political debate. In his widely reported speech at the main ceremony at Auschwitz on 27 January 1995, Holocaust survivor Elie Wiesel made a direct connection between past and present, referring to the 'bloodshed' that was happening in Bosnia, Rwanda and Chechnya. Tedeusz Szymanscy, a Polish survivor of Auschwitz who had helped to keep the camp as a memorial since 1946, drew a similar parallel in an interview with *The Observer*. He explained to his interviewer that although he was

Polish, he had been born near Gorazde in Bosnia: 'I want to say to the people there, "What are you doing? Are you mad?" Just look at this place. You achieve nothing through war. You only achieve death.'[45]

This kind of linkage featured regularly in British political discourse concerning the Bosnian war in particular in the mid-1990s. It served two immediate purposes. The first was to affirm the status of atrocities in Bosnia as genocide. The second was to underwrite the case for military intervention in Bosnia by outside powers to stop the killings. The context for linking Bosnia and the Nazi genocide had been set on 5 August 1992, when journalists (principally from *The Guardian* and *Channel 4 News*) filmed pictures of Bosnian Serb-run detention camps in northern Bosnia (at Omarska and Trnopolje). These pictures were screened on British television the next day. On 7 August 1992 they made the front pages of newspapers, including the *Daily Mirror* (whose headline was 'Belsen 92') and the *Daily Mail*. Both publications likened Omarska and Trnopolje to Nazi 'concentration' camps; the *Mirror* in fact juxtaposed pictures from the Bosnian camps with photos of an unnamed Nazi camp from 1945 to stress the point.[46]

In 1995, *The Independent* made these parallels the central theme of their editorial on the Auschwitz anniversary:

> All the moral components of the Auschwitz story are present today. Last year, in five short weeks, half a million Tutsis were slaughtered in Rwanda. In the early stages of the massacre the small UN force was pulled out and the world agonised. The Bosnian tragedy also caught us unawares, despite constant warnings about what would happen if Yugoslavia imploded. It took the pictures of emaciated Muslims in a Serb camp, reminiscent of Auschwitz, to cause real pressure to be brought to bear. Our recognition of these horrors owes a great deal to the memory we have of the Holocaust. We know we cannot just sit by.... We can assert the right of the international community to intervene in the internal affairs of other countries to prevent genocide.[47]

When events in the former Yugoslavia were debated in the House of Commons on 9 May 1995 (the day after the VE Day commemorations in Hyde Park) several speakers used references to the Holocaust as a device to strengthen their argument. Indeed, the Holocaust was summoned in support of claims made by opposing sides in the debate. Bob Wareing (Labour), for example, likened the actions in Croatia to those of the Nazi perpetrators of genocide. He referred to atrocities committed by

Croat forces in northern Bosnia in September 1991, the consequences of which he had witnessed personally. When he visited a mass grave there in 1993, he said, the 'stench was indescribable; I felt like a British soldier arriving at Belsen'.[48] He went on to deplore the fact that Croat President Franjo Tudjman, who Wareing described as being 'defensive on the question of Nazi genocide' had been invited to the Hyde Park commemorations that weekend.[49] Other speakers accused Serbia of bringing genocide back to Europe. Sir Patrick Cormack (Conservative) called on the government to adopt a 'resolute approach' against Serbia, stating that 'some of the things that have happened in Bosnia rank in fearfulness and horror with what happened in the holocaust'.[50] Malcolm Wicks (Labour) spoke of how in 'the face of genocide [against Bosnians] more than 50 years after the holocaust, our Foreign Office policy has never dared speak its name'.[51] He urged the government to 'relearn the lessons of 1945 in a more complex post-war period' and to abandon what he saw as the appeasement of Serbia.[52]

Massacres of Bosnian Muslims had an obvious impact on Britain's various Muslim organisations and communities. Writing in *Muslim News* in August 1992 (when the camps at Omarska and Trnopolje were discovered by the British media), Shabbir Akhtar reminded readers of his previously stated prediction that 'next time there are gas chambers in Europe, there is no doubt concerning who'll be inside them' (i.e. Muslims).[53] Kalim Siddiqui, founder of the Muslim Parliament in Britain in 1992, interpreted the government's failure to act in Bosnia as a signal of its unwillingness to save Muslim lives. To underscore the point, the words of the vice-president of Bosnia-Herzegovina were prominently displayed at the Muslim Parliament's Bosnia conference in 1993: 'You all know that the West would do something for Bosnia if the Bosnians were not Muslims.'[54] This line of thought was reinforced in July 1995 when John Major refused to meet with a delegation from the UK Action Committee on Islamic Affairs (UKACIA) to discuss help for Bosnia. In response to this refusal, the UKACIA's Joint Convenor accused the government of 'giving the Serbs clear signals to attack and ethnically cleanse the rest of the so-called safe areas'.[55]

In popular publications for British Muslims like *Muslim News* and *Q News,* the important political issues in the mid-1990s were the continuing ramifications of *The Satanic Verses* crisis, the first Gulf War (1991) and the war in Bosnia. There was no comment on events to commemorate the Holocaust in 1995 – no entry, in other words, of Muslim voices into the public discourse about the Holocaust. There were no obvious forewarnings of British Muslims' objections to the specificity of Holocaust Memorial Day that were made in 2001, and with renewed force by Iqbal Sacranie, general secretary of the Muslim Council of Britain, in 2005.[56] Of course, by 2005 the political context in which such objections were raised had changed. Whereas the notion of disinterested military intervention for humanitarian purposes that was alluded to in 1995 seemed credible when applied to the cases of Kosovo (1999), East Timor (1999) and Sierra Leone (2000), subsequent US- and UK-led invasions of Afghanistan (2001) and Iraq (2003) have compromised the term to a point that was probably unimaginable at the beginning of 2001.[57]

Conclusion

Holocaust commemoration in Britain in 1995 was constituted by practices that we might usefully regard as having their own historicity. These mnemonic practices were not simply reflective of the context in which they were performed, nor were they an expression of a particular state of Holocaust consciousness in Britain at the time. Instead, they helped to form the culture in which memory work was carried out, in ways that simultaneously bore traces of previous memory work in relation to the Holocaust, and which also had a bearing on subsequent commemorations of the event in Britain. In retrospect, one of the striking features of the 50th anniversaries of the liberation of the camps in 1995 commemorations was the relative absence of attempts by politicians, media commentators or public intellectuals to develop a vocabulary that explained why it was right or necessary to commemorate the Holocaust in Britain. The principal focus of political and media attention in 1995 was on the VE Day commemorations, and the ways in which these were choreographed and articulated showed the extent to which Britain's good war paradigm retained its discursive shaping power 50 years after the war. Holocaust memory functioned largely as a supplement to this paradigm – the Holocaust from this perspective reinforced the moral justification of Britain's war against the perpetrators of genocide. Thus it was that when the focus of war-related commemorative activity switched in 2001 to the inaugural Holocaust Memorial Day, there was no comparable ceremonial tradition or well rehearsed discourse available to be invoked or reworked, no collection of symbols or tropes whose meanings were recognisable from previous commemorations that could be used by organisers or participants to set the tone for the occasion. Perhaps in turn this helps to explain why in its earliest years Holocaust Memorial Day was criticised for being victim-centred, over-sentimentalised and with an undue emphasis on the redemptive features of survivor testimony. But this is not to argue that the 1995 anniversaries offered no discursive potential for future Holocaust commemoration in Britain. Perhaps, as Levy and Sznaider have argued, Holocaust memory will continue to become de-territorialised and cosmopolitan. In such circumstances the marked tendency in Britain in 1995 to regard the Holocaust as 'someone else's problem' could be adapted to the point where the event becomes regarded as a universal focus of politico-moral reflection – everyone's problem, rather than someone else's in particular. Similarly, the injunction to 'remember for the future' could serve as a mark of respect for the dead rather than an instrumental starting point for a certain type of national civic pedagogy. Finally, the doctrine of humanitarian or liberal interventionism to prevent genocide, ethnic cleansing and crimes against humanity – spurred in part by Holocaust memory – would be understood as a multilateral obligation of the type that was articulated in 2001 in the common 'Responsibility to Protect' international norm, and which was subsequently endorsed in the UN World Summit Outcome Document of 2005.[58]

Notes

1. My thanks to Dan Stone for his comments on an early draft of this chapter.
2. Donald Bloxham, 'Britain's Holocaust Memorial Days: Reshaping the Past in the Service of the Present', *Immigrants and Minorities*, Special Issue on Representing the Holocaust, 21 (1–2) (2002), 41–62, 47. See also, for example, David Cesarani, 'Seizing the Day: Why Britain Will Benefit From Holocaust Memorial Day', *Patterns of Prejudice*, 34 (4) (2000), 61–66; Mark Levene, 'Britain's Holocaust Memorial Day: A Case of Post-Cold War Wish Fulfilment or Brazen Hypocrisy?', *Human Rights Review*, 7 (3) (2006), 26–59; Sharon Macdonald, 'Commemorating the Holocaust: Reconfiguring National Identity in the Twenty-first Century', in Jo Littler and Roshi Naidoo (eds), *The Politics of Heritage: The Legacies of 'Race'* (London, 2005), 49–68; Tony Kushner, 'Too Little, Too Late? Reflections on Britain's Holocaust Memorial Day', in David Cesarani (ed.), *After Eichmann: Collective Memory and the Holocaust since 1961* (London, 2005), 116–129; Andy Pearce, 'The Development of Holocaust Consciousness in Contemporary Britain, 1979–2001' (unpublished PhD thesis, Royal Holloway, University of London, 2010), 158–182; Dan Stone, 'Day of Remembering or Day of Forgetting? Or, Why Britain Does Not Need a Holocaust Memorial Day', *Patterns of Prejudice*, 34 (4) (2000), 53–59.
3. Joanne Reilly, David Cesarani, Tony Kushner and Colin Richmond (eds), *Belsen in History and Memory* (London, 1997); Judith Petersen, 'How British Television Inserted the Holocaust into Britain's War Memory in 1995', *Historical Journal of Film, Radio and Television*, 21 (3) (2001), 255–272.

188 'We Should Do Something for the Fiftieth'

4. Jeffrey K. Olick, *The Politics of Regret: On Collective Memory and Historical Responsibility* (London, 2007), 58.
5. Ibid., 107.
6. See, for example, Suzanne Bardgett and David Cesarani (eds), *Belsen 1945: New Historical Perspectives* (London, 2006); Ben Flanagan and Donald Bloxham (eds), *Remembering Belsen* (London, 2005); Tony Kushner, 'Belsen for Beginners: The Holocaust in British Heritage', in Monica Riera and Gavin Schaffer (eds), *The Lasting War: Society and Identity in Britain, France and Germany after 1945* (Basingstoke, 2008), 226–247; Joanne Reilly, *Belsen: The Liberation of a Concentration Camp* (London, 1998); Reilly *et al.*, *Belsen in History and Memory*; Ben Shephard, *After Daybreak: The Liberation of Belsen, 1945* (London, 2005); Ulf Zander, 'To Rescue or Be Rescued: The Liberation of Bergen-Belsen and the White Buses in British and Swedish Historical Cultures', in Klas-Göran Karlsson and Ulf Zander (eds), *The Holocaust on Post-War Battlefields: Genocide as Historical Culture* (Malmö, 2006), 343–383.
7. See, for example, *Jewish Chronicle*, 14 April 1995, interview with Belsen survivor Esther Brunstein; *The Times*, 28 April 1995; *The Guardian*, 15 April 1995. Tony Kushner has pointed out that interest in Anne Frank was growing in the 1990s. In 1993 *The Diary of Anne Frank* was the most popular non-fiction work in terms of library borrowing; see Tony Kushner, ' "I Want to Go On Living after My Death", The Memory of Anne Frank', in Martin Evans and Ken Lunn (eds), *War and Memory in the Twentieth Century* (Oxford, 1997), 3.
8. Olick, *Politics of Regret*, 175.
9. Martin Evans and Ken Lunn, 'Preface', in Evans and Lunn (eds), *War and Memory*, xv.
10. Petersen, 'How British Television Inserted the Holocaust into Britain's War Memory', 260, 267. Channel 4, in line with its remit to provide alternative programming from the other channels, broadcast 3 hours and 20 minutes of VE Day programming between 1 and 6 May 1995. This comprised a series of ten-minute programmes called *Loved Ones*, which were personal tributes to lost relatives. There was also a reference to VE Day celebrations written into the episode of *Brookside* on 3 May 1995. See Petersen, 266.
11. *The Battle of Britain* (United Artists, 1969) originated from the desire of an independent film producer and former RAF fighter pilot, Ben Fisz, to increase awareness about the Battle among 1960s British youth. In May 1995, it functioned as a signifier of the defensive (and hence un-troubling) nature of Britain's war effort in 1940. For a discussion of the film see S.P. MacKenzie, *The Battle of Britain on Screen: 'The Few' in British Film and Television Drama* (Edinburgh, 2007).
12. For example: Angus Calder, *The Myth of the Blitz* (London, 1991); Mark Connelly, *We Can Take It! Britain and the Memory of the Second World War* (Harlow, 2004), Graham Dawson and Bob West, 'Our Finest Hour? The Popular Memory of World War II and the Struggle Over National Identity', in Geoff Hurd (ed.), *National Fictions: World War Two in British Films and Television* (London, 1984), 8–13; Malcolm Smith, *Britain and 1940: History, Myth and Popular Memory* (London, 2000).
13. Calder, *Myth of the Blitz*, xiv.
14. Eviatar Zerubavel, *Time Maps: Collective Memory and the Social Shape of the Past* (Chicago, 2003), 13–14. Zerubavel acknowledges Hayden White's influence

on his thinking here, particularly White's 'The Historical Text as Literary Artifact', in *Tropics of Discourse: Essays in Cultural Criticism* (Baltimore, 1978), 81–100.

15. Alon Confino and Peter Fritzsche (eds), *The Work of Memory: New Directions in the Study of German Society and Culture* (Chicago, 2002), 8.

16. The 1990s saw publication of several revisionist histories about Britain in the Second World War. For example: Calder, *Myth of the Blitz*; John Charmley, *Churchill: The End of Glory: A Political Biography* (London, 1993); Steven Fielding, Peter Thompson and Nick Tiratsoo, *England Arise! The Labour Party and Popular Politics in 1940s Britain* (Manchester, 1995); Kevin Jefferys, *The Churchill Coalition and Wartime Politics, 1940–45* (Manchester, 1991); Clive Ponting, *1940: Myth and Reality* (London, 1990). See also Alan Clarke's review of John Charmley's Churchill biography in *The Times*, 2 January 1993, 'A reputation ripe for revision', and Neal Ascherson's response to Alan Clarke's review, 'What if Churchill Had Sued for Peace in 1941?', *The Independent on Sunday*, 10 January 1993. See also the three-part television series on BBC2 in 1995, 'Myths and Memories of World War Two' – in particular, Part One (featuring a film by Alan Clarke), first broadcast 20 June 1995, and Part Three (featuring a film by Nick Tiratsoo), first broadcast 2 July 1995.

17. Cited in Steven Cooke, ' "Your Story Too?" The New Holocaust Exhibition at the Imperial War Museum', in John K. Roth and Elisabeth Maxwell (eds), *Remembering for the Future: The Holocaust in an Age of Genocide*, 3: Memory (New York, 2000), 591.

18. Prime Minister John Major's speech on 6 May 1995, full text at http://www.johnmajor.co.uk/page1068.html.

19. *Jewish Chronicle*, 4 February 1994.

20. Hansard, House of Commons Parliamentary Debates, Vol. 253, Col. 339, 25 January 1995.

21. Ibid., Vol. 253, Col. 478, 26 January 1995.

22. *The Times* (28 April 1995); *Daily Telegraph*, 28 April 1995.

23. *Daily Telegraph*, 28 April 1995.

24. *The Guardian*, 13 April 1995.

25. *Evening Standard*, 7 December 1995.

26. See, *The Independent*, 'From Out of the Horror, A Love Story', 13 April 1995; *Sunday Telegraph*, 'A Good Marriage – Made in Hell', 15 January 1995; and the same story ten years before in *The Times*, 'The 40-year Love of a Bride from Belsen', 15 April 1985.

27. Reilly *et al.*, 'Approaching Belsen: An Introduction', in Reilly *et al.* (eds) *Belsen in History and Memory*, 12–13. See also, Hannah Caven, 'Horror in Our Time: Images of the Concentration Camps in the British Media, 1945', *Historical Journal of Film, Radio and Television*, 21 (3) (2001), 205–253.

28. The *Daily Mirror*, for example, simply printed a version of Trevor Fishlock's article on Auschwitz from the *Daily Telegraph* in its edition of 28 January 1995. The *Mirror* also contained just two references to Belsen in 1995. One was a tiny paragraph about the death of a photographer who had taken pictures of the camp in 1945, see edition 26 July 1995, 11. The other was a quote from TV interviewer Gloria Hunniford talking about her diet and weight: 'I was 6st 10lbs when Caron [her daughter] was born and looked like something out of Belsen', see edition 22 May 1995, 20.

29. Petersen, 'How British Television Inserted the Holocaust into Britain's War Memory', 270.
30. Susanna Schrafstetter, ' "Gentlemen, the Cheese Is All Gone!" ' British POWs, the "Great Escape" and the Anglo-German Agreement for Compensation to Victims of Nazism', *Contemporary European History*, 17 (1) (2008), 23–43, here 42–43.
31. Confino and Fritzsche (eds), *The Work of Memory*, 8.
32. Connelly, *We Can Take It!*
33. Macdonald, 'Commemorating the Holocaust', 58.
34. Daniel Levy and Natan Sznaider, 'Memory Unbound: The Holocaust and the Formation of Cosmopolitan Memory', *European Journal of Social Theory*, 5 (1) (2002), 87–106, here 88.
35. Ibid., 103.
36. *The Guardian*, 19 February 1994. For similar interpretations of the importance of *Schindler's List* see: *Daily Telegraph*, 5 January 1994; *Telegraph Magazine*, 15 January 1994; *The Times Magazine*, 15 January 1994; *The Independent*, 9 and 16 February 1994; *The Guardian*, 17 February 1994.
37. See, for example, Mark Frankland, *The Observer*, 29 January 1995; *The Guardian*, leading article, 27 January 1995; *The Independent* leading article, 27 January 1995.
38. *Daily Telegraph* leading article, 28 January 1995.
39. *The Independent*, 27 January 1995.
40. Leon Greenman was interviewed along with other former inmates of Auschwitz in *Telegraph Magazine*, 21 January 1995; Gena Turgel was profiled in *The Sunday Telegraph*, 15 January 1995, *The Independent*, 13 April 1995, and *Evening Standard*, 7 December 1995.
41. *Bringing the Holocaust Home – Open Space Special*, BBC2, 14 January 1995.
42. *Bringing the Holocaust Home*. Nine days after the programme was screened, Prime Minister John Major confirmed in a written answer in parliament that the Imperial War Museum (IWM) was considering the creation of a new museum 'which would cover the Holocaust and other 20th century acts of genocide'. Hansard, House of Commons Parliamentary Debates, vol. 253, col. 23, 23-1-95. The IWM announced its plans to build a permanent Holocaust Exhibition as part of its Millennium project, using National Lottery funding, in April 1996; see *The Guardian*, 24 April 1996. The exhibition itself was opened on 6 June 2000.
43. James Young, *The Texture of Memory: Holocaust Memorials and Meaning* (New Haven, 1993).
44. See, for example, the report of a meeting organised by the Yad Vashem Charitable Trust to discuss the British government's 'indifference' and failure to rescue 1,000 Jewish orphans from Vichy in late 1942/early 1943, *The Times*, 23 January 1995.
45. *The Observer*, 22 January 1995.
46. See David Campbell, 'Atrocity, Memory, Photography: Imaging the Concentration Camps of Bosnia – The Case of ITN Versus *Living Marxism*, Part 1', *Journal of Human Rights*, 1 (1) (2002), 1–33.
47. *The Independent*, 27 January 1995.
48. Ibid., vol. 259, col. 615, 9 May 1995.
49. Ibid., vol. 259, col. 617.

50. Hansard, HoC debates, vol. 259, col. 606, 9 May 1995.
51. Ibid., vol. 259, col. 637.
52. Ibid.
53. 'Palestine within Europe?', *Muslim News,* 42, August 1992, cited in Anthony McRoy, *From Rushdie to 7/7: The Radicalisation of Islam in Britain* (London, 2006), 23.
54. McRoy, *From Rushdie to 7/7,* 24.
55. Ibid., p.25. See 'PM Rebuffs Muslims on Bosnia', *Muslim News,* 75, July 1995.
56. Iqbal Sacranie had encouraged British Muslims to boycott Holocaust Memorial Day in January 2005. After the London bombings of 7 July 2005, he was appointed as a government adviser on questions of 'Muslim Extremists'. In this capacity, he suggested that Holocaust Memorial Day be altered to EU Genocide Memorial Day. See Zander, 'To Rescue Or Be Rescued', 355–356.
57. Despite these considerations, the international community adopted the collective norm of the 'Responsibility to Protect' in the early twenty-first century. This norm holds states responsible for preventing and/or halting genocide, war crimes, crimes against humanity and ethnic cleansing. If they fail to do so, the international community has a responsibility to offer support to the state in question, and in the final analysis to use military coercion (under the auspices of the United Nations Security Council and the General Assembly) to uphold this collective norm. The Responsibility to Protect was enshrined in the UN World Summit Outcome Document of 2005. See http://www.responsibilitytoprotect.org/
58. Ibid.

11
Britain's Holocaust Memorial Day: Inculcating 'British' or 'European' Holocaust Consciousness?

Andy Pearce

At the time of writing, two major landmarks have occurred in what might be called the history of the 'afterlife of Holocaust memory' in Britain.[1] Most recently, the beginning of a new academic year in schools and colleges in England and Wales brought the occasion of the 20th anniversary of the National Curriculum – an event of immense significance in relation to Holocaust education in the United Kingdom. Whereas previously the presence of the Holocaust in educational curricula varied considerably, the incorporation of the genocide into the statutory content for the first National Curriculum for History in 1991 ensured that school history would become a core conduit in the expansion of knowledge and awareness among a new generation of young people. Beyond the chalkface, the other noteworthy anniversary of 2011 took place on 27 January when Britain held its tenth annual Holocaust Memorial Day (HMD). A day which 'provides an opportunity for everyone to learn the lessons from the Holocaust, Nazi persecution and subsequent genocides and apply them to the present day to create a safer, better future', HMD speaks to and of a process of heightened institutionalisation which began in earnest at the turn of the millennium and has continued unabated since.[2] HMD thus provides an illuminating window onto the preconceptions, priorities and politics which currently envelop and influence the shape of memorialisation in Britain, but it also does much more than this: as one of the first such days to be created in Western Europe following the Stockholm Declaration of 2000, Britain's HMD also gestures to a gamut of issues related to memorialisation in general and Holocaust memory in the contemporary world in particular. Amongst others, these include the practices and procedures of collective remembrance, the forces behind a 'turning' to memory in the postmodern epoch, and the rationale for (and consequences of) the emergence of the Holocaust as a global phenomena in the past quarter of a century.

It is towards this cluster of themes that this essay positions itself, as it seeks to contextualise the recent history of British Holocaust-related activities within a wider framework of transnational trends. My focus will be on the circumstances around the creation of Britain's HMD, and the extent to which this cannot be understood without reference to external developments; principally, the 'globalisation' of Holocaust memory and moves within the European Union aimed at making the Holocaust its 'negative foundation myth'.[3] However, it will also be argued that the establishment of HMD cannot be understood without reference either to long-term or short-term domestic developments, and that in actually instigating a day of remembrance Britain demonstrated the influential role that it has come to play in international Holocaust politics. Far from representing the manifestation of some external memory from abroad then, HMD stands as a British initiative serving and reflecting British interests; inculcating in the process the formation of a national rather than a supranational historical consciousness of the Holocaust.

The mnemohistory of the Holocaust in Britain and beyond

The recent intensification of Holocaust-related activities in Britain over the past 15 years is remarkable for a number of reasons, not least because it marks a sharp departure from the longstanding marginalisation of the genocide of European Jewry within British historical culture for much of the post-war period.[4] On the surface, Britain is therefore on a similar trajectory of Holocaust memorialisation to that seen in other nations and its own 'turn' to the Holocaust can be narrated through the longstanding 'mnemohistory' of the Holocaust in the post-war period.[5] According to this grand narrative, there have been discernible 'milestones on Holocaust history's road towards the centre of European historical culture' which have functioned as waypoints demarcating the shift from silence and forgetting, to speech and memorialisation.[6] However, appearances can be deceptive, and whilst it is clear that the status of the Holocaust has undergone profound transformation in the post-45 epoch, the reality is naturally far more complex. Thanks to ground-breaking research, the accepted notion of conscious forgetting and intentional effacement of the Holocaust is being challenged and problematised; scholars are now beginning to highlight the multifarious and often subterranean ways in which memories and representations of the genocide found form and expression in the immediate decades after the war, as well as drawing attention to the multidirectionality of Holocaust memory and its relation to the experience of decolonisation.[7] Consequently, a renewed emphasis must now be placed on examining precisely how individual nation states have approached the legacies of what we call the Holocaust in the aftermath of the Second World War. Since it is no longer sufficient to speak of some wholesale gear change occurring across the Western world from the 1960s, it is all the more imperative that the stages through which change occurred, and the agents which brought about shifts in thought and action, are identified and subjected to due scrutiny.

In the case of Britain, it has long been established that the circumstances surrounding the 'last phase' of the war were a cause of much misunderstanding, to the extent that the processes of victory and liberation had 'a lasting effect upon popular perceptions of why it had been fought and what it had been about', particularly in terms of the fate of European Jewry.[8] By the same token, it has also been shown that the 'necessity of forging a manageable collective memory' – particularly during the period 1945–46 – led in its turn to a 'domestication' of Nazism's anti-Semitic violence[9]; one that was in keeping with the ingrained sociocultural 'liberal imagination' which specifically conditioned British attitudes to and conceptualisations of the Holocaust – both during its enactment and in the subsequent post-war decades.[10] Finally, we know that events in Palestine between 1945 and 1948 'cut directly across sympathy for the Jewish victims of Nazism', leading in the short term to an immediate spike in domestic anti-Semitism and in the longer term ensuring that some sections of the population remained ambivalent to the Israeli state.[11] What has been added to this body of knowledge in recent years is a greater layer of sophistication: we now have, for example, a better understanding of 'the guilty secret of British liberal historiography of the Third Reich' and the factors which conditioned the relative disengagement with the Holocaust on the part of the British historical academy. At the same time, new findings about the presence of the Holocaust in culture and society have prompted David Cesarani to contend that 'rather than a spasm of attention followed by silence, there was in fact a persistent drum-beat about the fate of the Jews'.[12] How audible these noises were amidst the sounds of post-war reconstruction and the creaking of waning great-power status is, however, a different matter. The question of will also becomes of paramount importance – particularly given the challenge of bridging geographical, experiential and imaginative gaps between Britain and the genocide. More research is certainly needed in this area, as it is in relation to the applicability of Michael Rothberg's thesis regarding the emergence of Western Holocaust memory in the 1950s and 1960s in 'punctual dialogue with on-going processes of decolonization and…modes of coming to terms with colonialism, slavery and racism'.[13] A provisional response would be that in Britain at least, this was certainly not the case.

A key period within the dominant post-war metanarrative of the Holocaust is commonly seen to fall between the Eichmann Trial of 1961 and the international broadcasting of the NBC mini-series *Holocaust* in 1978. Up until now, orthodoxy has commonly held that it is between these years that the world began to progressively 'turn' towards remembering the destruction of Europe's Jews, ensuring in the process that the events which we today know as 'the Holocaust' came rapidly into prominence throughout the Western nations. Although aspects of this narrative require some amendment in the wake of challenges to the 'myth of silence', there is nevertheless no doubt that this period *did* see considerable changes in political, social and cultural approaches in a number of nation states. This was not, however, true of the United Kingdom, for here the Holocaust was not a 'self-contained issue' but instead still 'a slightly murky, problematic subject'.[14] Whereas in North America, Israel and other parts of Western Europe the presence of the Holocaust could be measured in terms of a growing body of published historiographical works or cultural 'products', very much the opposite was true of Britain; indeed, it was not until the end of the 1970s that scholarship examining British responses to the Holocaust appeared, and at a cultural level there appeared some uncertainty as to the meaning and relevancy of the events for the United Kingdom. In this vein it was telling that within the Imperial War Museum (IWM) the annihilation of Jewry was spoken of through the term 'concentration camps' – just as it was equally revealing that the acclaimed *World at War* documentary series broadcast in 1974 entitled its episode examining the Holocaust 'Genocide'. In both instances, it was clear 'the Holocaust' as an idea and referent was yet to take root, but it was also evident that impassivity towards the fate of the Jews was beginning to give way to intrigue. This development was not as spectacular or immediate as, say, the impact of *Holocaust* in the United States or West Germany, but change was occurring nonetheless; in British culture if not within the political establishment.[15]

The formation of British Holocaust consciousness

A conceptual tool which can help us to identify the shifts that were to occur in Britain from the 1970s onwards is historical consciousness. A term which has yet to enjoy great popularity within the English-speaking world, historical consciousness refers principally to 'the interrelation between interpretation of the past, an understanding of the present, and a future perspective'.[16] More than merely an account of 'what happened', historical consciousness is concerned with the construction of meaning for the purpose of spatial, temporal and even moral orientation. As such it subjects the past as memory to processes of purposeful sense-making, and in so doing performs 'specific cultural activities' such as the formulation of identity.[17] Historical consciousness can offer a theoretical structure through which we can begin to approach the ways in which thinking about and thinking with the Holocaust in Britain began to change from the second half of the 1970s. In this manner, when we speak of Holocaust consciousness we are talking less of actual substantive knowledge (although this is indispensible for the formation of memory) and more of the use of such information for particular ends. This is not to deny our new understandings about the amount of 'noise' that was in fact present in Britain and elsewhere in the years directly after 1945, but rather it is to suggest that Holocaust consciousness delineates the organisation of awareness about the destruction of the Jews into a cognitive and cultural framework, through which 'the Holocaust' becomes objectified and articulated. Whereas elsewhere – particularly North America, for example – we observe the emergence of such a consciousness during the 1960s, in Britain this took far longer to occur, suggesting that from an early stage the United Kingdom has followed an incongruous path in its development of Holocaust consciousness.[18]

We can trace the tentative formation of a British Holocaust consciousness to the later 1970s and early 1980s by virtue of advances that were beginning to occur in culture and society. A keystone was the appearance of a British historiography of the Holocaust which, in the 1980s, increasingly scrutinised issues of how much was known about the events during the war and what was done in response. This gradual epistemology was all the more timely in light of the explosion in 1986 of the War Crimes Affair – a controversy which, in addition to a constitutional crisis, engendered a heightening of public interest in the Holocaust that would prove to be the catalyst in organised attempts to formalise Holocaust education.[19] Various educational initiatives aimed at bringing the Holocaust into the lives of schoolchildren were made throughout the decade – both within institutions like the IWM and through bodies such as the Inner London Educational Authority (ILEA) – but with differing success; a main challenge remained how to make the Holocaust accessible and relevant to young people with no personal or cultural links to the events. Where attempts were made to throw a spotlight on potential contemporary parallels – as in the instance of the ILEA – government opposition was made abundantly, and very publicly, clear.[20]

This was all the more interesting given the convoluted process by which the first official Holocaust memorial was created in 1983. Although the then Conservative government considered the site in Hyde Park to be the responsibility of the Jewish community, state involvement in realising the memorial was indispensible.[21] There was therefore symbolic significance both in the memorial's creation and in the mnemonic discourse which it proffered, with the ambiguity of the site in both literal and figurative terms reflective of the concerns and preoccupations of the Anglo-Jewish community and the government of the day. This aside, it is noteworthy that for the political elite the idea of establishing a memorial to the Holocaust was more palatable than endorsing educational initiatives aimed at exploring the present-day relevance of the genocide. Beyond gesturing to the important differences between memorials and education systems in the formation of collective memories, it is here that the concept of Holocaust consciousness encourages us to reflect on the political considerations in operation in Britain during the 1980s. Put simply, Holocaust memory served only limited purposes for those in power at this time; for them, the Holocaust was to be understood in a 'traditional' way: it was fact, it had happened, and beyond its sentimental meaning it bore little relevance to the present. Attempts such as those by the ILEA to push memory in a different direction, to make this past more 'exemplary' in terms of teaching us eternal truths or 'lessons', was antithetical and unwelcome and subsequently firmly resisted.[22] Seen from this perspective (and bearing in mind that cultural engagements with the Holocaust were also on the increase) it becomes apparent that far from being some monolithic or immutable entity, Holocaust consciousness in 1980s Britain was a nebulous and multifaceted phenomenon; one which saw the genocide perceived, understood and used in quite different ways at 'elite' and 'grassroots' levels.[23]

Europeanisation and institutionalisation

It has become axiomatic that the cessation of the Cold War marked a major threshold in post-war history of the Holocaust, and a central dynamo in this regard was the acceleration of the European project. Following the foundation of the European Union (EU) and the subsequent intrusion into member states' areas of governance, questions of commonality and what unified its members other than treaty obligations heightened in salience.[24] To some extent this underlying issue of fashioning a collective identity for continental Europe predated the creation of the EU, although the Maastricht Treaty did mark a notable departure in providing 'a new set of terms around which the politics of cultural policy would be organized'. Underscoring this provision was the attempt to ensure the legitimacy of EU institutions by cultivating 'shared identification with a common core of "European" values' throughout its member states[25]; a notion which in theory went directly against the idea of the nation as the primary agent in the 'structuring of consciousness'.[26]

The ongoing search for a European identity was one which was to bring about a so-called 'Europeanisation' of the Holocaust.[27] Opinion remains divided as to whether this process was attributable to a German policy of 'centring' and 'decentring' the Holocaust, or rather explicable by way of a Europeanisation of the German *politics* of memory,[28] but in either case the outcome is seen to be the same: namely, the Holocaust became identified as the 'core', foundational, 'inaugural event' of the EU – the 'paradigmatic "lieu de mémoire" of Europe' from which 'any cultural construction of European identity has to start'.[29] Such an interpretation is not without contention, not least regarding its very viability, not to mention whether this aspiration has actually been realised, but we shall return to this below.[30] For our purposes it is important to note the manner in which 'Europeanisation' occurred and its relation to Britain.

At the time of European 'unification' British Holocaust consciousness was exhibiting signs of moving out of its infancy. A significant indicator was an increase in interest within non-Jewish society, thanks in no small part to the exposés of the War Crimes Affair. The success of this campaign (symbolised in the passage of the War Crimes Bill in 1991) seemed to suggest a more open attitude on the part of government to confronting the legacies of the Holocaust; indeed, this appeared to be confirmed by the unexpected decision to include the Holocaust within its mandatory stipulations for the National Curriculum – particularly given that this inclusion inevitably came at the expense of other, more 'British' historical events. However, as important as these advances were, their symbolic value did not necessarily translate into instant positive outcomes: the pursuit of war criminals ran into a growing lack of conviction, in every sense of the word, whilst in schools there was a lack of clarity on the purpose of Holocaust education and no small degree of hostility towards the subject on the part of teachers.[31] In the shadow of Maastricht and growing scepticism towards all things European, a massive spur to widening Holocaust consciousness in society came with the release of *Schindler's List* – initially through its immense box-office success, and then later through the distribution of an edited version of the film to all UK schools.[32] The film's core tenets were propagated and further reinforced pre-existing tendencies within British culture towards the Holocaust, such as the universalisation of its victims and demonisation of its perpetrators.

In the first half of the 1990s, Holocaust consciousness in Britain was thus undergoing some elemental shifts. Just as thinking *about* the Holocaust at a cultural level was being intensified by visual stimuli coming from Bosnia, Rwanda and Hollywood, so attitudes towards thinking *with* the Holocaust were changing – particularly at an 'official', statist level. Although the idea of Holocaust 'lessons' had not as yet been popularised, there was nonetheless an increasing willingness in various realms to instrumentalise the Holocaust – if only, at the most pernicious level, to buttress anti-German sentiment following reunification. More generally, the emergence of the EU and movement towards the 50th anniversary of the Second World War served only to reinforce self-congratulatory British war memory; so much so that the prospect of any interrogative Holocaust consciousness developing, let alone one that would highlight the shortcomings of Britain's response to genocide and disturb idealised patterns of remembrance, was hampered from the start.[33]

By the mid-1990s 'Europeanisation' of the Holocaust in any sweeping, normative sense was yet to materialise, but increasing references to the genocide were particularly being made in educational forums established under the auspices of the Council of Europe. British educators were especially vociferous in this regard, and were notably advancing the moral and didactic potential that could be harnessed from Holocaust education.[34] In certain respects this was all well and good, though in view of the relative absence of any embedded critical historical consciousness in Britain it is perhaps unsurprising that the *type* of learning being promoted was more akin to a 'banking' conceptualisation of education rather than one aimed at 'problem-posing'.[35] Such pedagogical strategies would befit the lessons-centric approach to Holocaust education which would gain popularity in Britain and beyond from the turn of the millennium, but the general activism of Britons in European dialogues at this time was soon given greater political weight after the electoral success of 'New' Labour in 1997.

Labour's interest in Holocaust-related activities was made clear almost immediately through the convening of the London Conference on Nazi Gold. The Nazi Gold Affair and the broader issue of restitution proved to be a decisive phase in the movement of the Holocaust to the centre of European thinking, in no small part because the various historical commissions spawned by the controversy forced the member states of the EU to accept degrees of culpability and responsibility in the looting and plunder of the property of Europe's Jews. Naturally, this could not be foreseen, and by the time the conference proceedings opened in December 1997, Britain itself had been implicated in the scandal, but in a sense this made the event all the more symbolic; from the outside, the Labour government had demonstrated leadership on a highly topical issue of national and international importance and was duly congratulated.[36] Undoubtedly there was an extent to which this was warranted, for on paper the conference offered a glimpse of what might be achieved with the right amount of political will. Furthermore, beyond initiating a transnational movement towards restitution, the London event piqued domestic interest and signified an apparent preparedness to confront Britain's less glorious links to the Holocaust – but this should not obscure the uses that Holocaust consciousness was being put to by the Labour administration.

The sense in which the London Conference put Britain 'on the map' of Holocaust remembrance was substantiated by the Swedish invitation to Britain to become a founding member of the international Task Force in 1998, although the history of Holocaust education in the United Kingdom was also cited as a key reason for British involvement.[37] The importance of the Task Force – and Britain's role in it – became clearly apparent at the Washington Conference on Holocaust-Era Assets in December of the same year, when amidst a series of proposed initiatives for expanding education, remembrance and research the British delegation submitted the 'Proposal for International Commemoration of the Holocaust' to warm endorsements.[38] Whilst not obliged in any legal sense, Britain had in effect committed itself to the institutionalisation of a national day of Holocaust remembrance – despite the fact that seven months later in June 1999, Prime Minister Blair confirmed that government were merely considering 'a proposal'.[39]

HMD 2001

The creation of Britain's HMD was formally announced on 26 January 2000 by Tony Blair in London and Foreign Secretary Robin Cook in Stockholm. In the case of Cook, his announcement during the course of his opening speech to the Stockholm Forum served a dual purpose: on the one hand, it publicly confirmed to the international community Britain's commitment to taking the lead in contemporary Holocaust politics, and on the other, it illustrated to those at home that there was a continental rationale for the introduction of such a day. This presentation of HMD as an initiative which chimed with other developments in Europe was only reinforced as the conference proceeded and the 'essential message' that 'through the Holocaust, Europe could imagine itself as a community of shared values' was repeated.[40] The historic Stockholm Declaration gave legislative endorsement to such a notion, and would later be adapted into the 'Statement of Commitment' which functioned as the centrepiece of Britain's HMD.[41]

What then of the day itself? As a holistic commemoration, Britain's first HMD was to represent a fusion of educational, symbolic and interactional communicative forms that would reflect the conception of the day as a socially inclusive event centred on remembering and learning.[42] The intended inclusiveness of the day was to be achieved through a three-pronged strategy of promoting initiatives in educational institutions, encouraging participation within the wider community, and holding a national ceremony – each of which were to be mutually reinforcing. Aside from how this revealed both particular understandings of the practice of social remembrance and assumptions as to how the Holocaust could (and should) be remembered, these organisational principles were designed to achieve wide participation at a grassroots level and make HMD appear 'less state-orchestrated and more part of local communities'.[43] In effect, responsibility for HMD at a local level was therefore devolved to the relevant authorities, although events were to conform with provided guidelines; including, for example, the recommendation that any ceremonial activity incorporate HMD's 'Statement of Commitment' in its entirety.

As important as these communal events were, however, the intention for HMD to be 'about learning the lessons of the Holocaust' meant that schools were identified as a focal point for activity.[44] In order to support this, public funds were committed to the production of an educational pack which although intended primarily for use in schools also contained provisions for other institutions.[45] This high level of public investment was to be expected, for it reflected how the Labour government intended HMD 'above all, to be an educational event' that was particularly concerned with advancing awareness among the younger generation.[46] According to this approach, the 'future' of remembrance would be underwritten by expanding knowledge and understanding through education which would in turn be used to focus on and reinforce the 'building blocks of a civilised society'.[47] In moral, ethical and theoretical terms there was little that was wrong with these objectives. What was problematic, however, was the explicit reduction of the complex issues of the Holocaust into 'lessons'; a move which displayed a number of revealing underlying assumptions about the role of education in general, as well as particular understandings of what the Holocaust was (and is). It is interesting to highlight that the debate over the efficacy and possibility of Holocaust 'lessons' also had a significant history in Britain, emerging in the context of original discussions around the National Curriculum and then reappearing in the 2000s.[48]

The centrality of Holocaust 'lessons' to Britain's HMD was further reinforced during the course of the national ceremony. Although not intended to be 'the measure of the day's success', the ceremony at Westminster Hall was undoubtedly the centrepiece of the day's commemorative activities and made manifest publicly the Labour government's 'state validation' of British Holocaust memory.[49] Describing the ceremony as 'A curious cross between a state funeral ... and a royal variety performance', Sharon Macdonald contends that it 'was not a single ritual but a show – a sequential set of pieces, some performed on stage and others relayed on screen – culminating in a ritualised participation from the audience'. Reflecting on this format, Macdonald has presented a four-part model for approaching the ceremony as it moved 'from past, into present and towards a preferred future'. The first of these ('Anchoring: the Holocaust in Europe') constructed 'a vision of a horrific society against which to define our own', with a 'revisiting of "national values" ' conveyed 'subtly, but nevertheless surely' through the screening of the British liberation of Belsen, references to the *Kindertransports* and readings by Auschwitz survivors who found their way to Britain.[50] The universality of the Holocaust was also reinforced, partly by invoking the 'contemporary cultural icon' Anne Frank, through the choral work 'In Memoriam', and with the acknowledgement of other victims of Nazism through the renowned thespian Sir Ian McKellen's speech on

'The Forgotten Holocaust' of homosexual persecution.[51] A final feature of this section was a celebration of the virtuosity of rescuers in the 'Righteous Among the Nations' segment led by the musician-activist Bob Geldof; a celebrity selected, according to BBC producer Gaby Koppel, because he 'symbolises so powerfully our responsibility to act on behalf of others'.[52]

The second 'stage' identified by Macdonald ('Extension: Continuing Atrocities') developed many of these themes and was characterised by the repetition of now staple Holocaust mantras and maxims. Having opened with Sir Anthony Sher's presentation 'Post 1945 Never Again', this section combined footage and recollections from Cambodia with testimony of survivors from Bosnia. Accompanying these were the reflections of journalist Fergal Keane on his unintended coverage of the Rwandan genocide, followed by a song from a Rwandan-born musician about an orphan who survived the killings, included because it apparently conveyed the message 'to save, preserve, and to keep alive ... African heritage with music, poetry and dance'.[53] Crucially Macdonald notes that 'there were no references to Britain' within any of these presentations, save the circumstances of the final survivor to speak who had escaped Bosnia to live in the UK and so served to again depict 'Britain as a haven' whilst 'continuing the contrast of Britain with other, terrible regimes'.[54]

The penultimate segment of the ceremony ('Making Explicit: Spelling out the Messages') saw a reinsertion of the Holocaust as the focal point of attention, symbolically in the form of a speech by the Chief Rabbi and a rendition of the Jewish Memorial Prayer 'El Male Rachamim'. Yet if these two components motioned towards the Jewish specificity of the Nazi genocide they were countered by the subsequent screening of HMD's 'Statements of Commitment', fronted by the broadcaster Sir Trevor McDonald. As seen in the cases of the education pack and guidelines for local authorities, these 'Statements' not only created a direct link to the Declaration of Stockholm, blueprint for policy and general polestar for HMD but also explicitly framed the Holocaust as being of ecumenical significance and the spread of its memory a global aspiration.[55] Their inclusion within a ceremonial occasion therefore bestowed upon them ersatz liturgical proportions by elevating them, de facto, to the status of a system of rites to be observed and upheld.[56]

As pronouncements addressed to all humanity, the 'Statements' clearly (if implicitly) had significance for the British audience attending and watching the ceremony, but their specific meaning for Britain was only explicitly laid out in a speech delivered by Blair. Bridging the

Jewish prayer and the screening of the 'Statements', the prime minister described the Holocaust as 'the most heinous act of collective evil in our history', before proceeding to detail various 'lessons' to be learnt from it and 'other racial genocides'. Concluding his statement, Blair laid bare the political reward to be reaped from Holocaust remembrance by asserting that

> in remembering the Holocaust and its victims, we recommit ourselves to the kind of society we believe in: A democratic, a just and a tolerant society, a society where everyone's worth is respected ... A society where each of us demonstrates by our words and actions, our commitment to the best, most decent values of humanity and compassion. A society that has the courage to confront prejudice ... This is indeed our hope. And that is why the Holocaust deserves this permanent place in our collective memory.[57]

As a commemorative address Blair's speech had a special importance, for it sought to establish a broad 'consensus regarding [the] norms and values' of Holocaust memory, and endow the discursive framework erected at the ceremony with political legitimacy and authority.[58] Yet what was also revealed by his speech was the type of historical consciousness HMD was to create. Because of this constructive process it becomes immensely significant that the word 'Jew' was used by Blair only once and that the terms 'Britain' and the 'United Kingdom' were not employed at all. The implication was thus that the 'Holocaust' did not specifically refer to Jews as victims, nor in terms of a historical event did it involve Britain. Instead, the 'Holocaust' acquired the appearance of being but a set of memories whose invocation and remembrance had the distinct animus of providing 'a powerful way of writing its lessons into our national conscience'.[59] This was a clear indication that as much as British Holocaust consciousness was to be exemplary under New Labour, this exemplification had all of the authoritarian characteristics of 'traditional' forms.

This inscription of the Holocaust into British collective memory was performed in the final 'stage' of the ceremony, identified by Macdonald as 'Symbolic Enactment: Ritual Performance of the Multicultural Nation'. 'The crescendo to which all of the earlier parts of the event led',[60] the segment began with the Prince of Wales lighting 'a candle on behalf of the nation'.[61] In Macdonald's eyes, the use of the Prince and not the Queen to light the candle was related to the event's aim to 'not ... be a national event in the same way as other national days' such as Remembrance Sunday, but instead present Britain 'as made up of numerous different communities'. This was in turn enacted by the Prince following numerous other representatives of various community and religious groups, and by how their collective lighting of the candles symbolised 'a form of unity, based not on allegiance to a monarch or the idea of a nation that should be fought for, but against a generalised enemy of racial purity-seeking evil'.[62]

When the ritualism of the candle-lighting ceremony is considered as an 'incorporating' and 'inscribing practice', Macdonald's argument becomes persuasive; particularly if it is the case that 'bodily practices of a culturally specific kind entail a combination of cognitive and habit-memory' such as seen in ceremonial commemoration.[63] Equally, Macdonald's interpretation of the candle ceremony as a mode of discourse also has substance when it is recalled that from conception HMD was not merely limited to the realm of 'gesture politics' but rather explicitly bound 'to questions of multiculturalism and civil society'.[64] An alternative, though not altogether contradictory, analysis of the candle-lighting has been forwarded by Donald Bloxham, for whom this culmination was testament to a 'pathos approach' towards the Holocaust and its memory that was embedded in HMD. Perceptively observing that 'if "lessons" of the Holocaust are to be found at all, they are to be found on the side of the perpetrators, not in the lighting of candles of remembrance', Bloxham asserts that this final 'act' of HMD demonstrated 'decency in the desire to remember and may show the conviction of "never again"', but did 'nothing concrete about ensuring "never again"'. The fundamental problem was that 'in this pathos approach, 'the Holocaust' is left hanging in the air as an ill-defined metaphor of terrible evil', as the task of explaining the Holocaust – which could draw upon a 'large body of historical scholarship' – is avoided out of a refusal to 'turn the mirror around'.[65] This absence of 'self-reflexivity' and aversion to consideration of 'our' relation to the perpetrators may well expose a reticence about examining our own moral shortcomings and conducting the unpalatable task of determining commonalities between 'us' and 'them'.[66]

This resistance to what James Young has termed an 'anti-redemptory narrative' of the Holocaust was, generally speaking, a prominent feature of HMD in toto, and was given melodic expression through the specially composed 'Holocaust anthem' which accompanied the 'Candle-lighting Finale'.[67] Arranged by Howard Goodall, the composer best known for penning the theme tunes to the British television comedy series *Mr. Bean* and *The Vicar of Dibley*, the anthem 'I Believe in the Sun' met what event producer Koppel described as the need for 'something moving and uplifting' on which to conclude the ceremony, and therefore the entire HMD. Koppel has even stated that 'I didn't want the audience to leave the auditorium feeling overwhelmingly depressed by the solemn subject matter. I needed a gleam of hope to finish with' – ideally one which would resonate with an opening theme 'and some linking phrases to bind the event together'. Goodall was charged with creating 'a musical identity for the event': a quite bizarre notion if one recalls Adorno's perturbing reflection on thought, 'musical accompaniment' and the Holocaust. Leaving to one side both this considerable complication and the unnerving notion of effectively ending Holocaust remembrance on a redemptive 'note', Koppel saw the anthem as reflecting how HMD 'wasn't to be an event just for Jews. It was a national occasion, relevant to all British citizens.' According to Koppel, Goodall's anthem did just that, since 'afterwards we were besieged with requests for CDs of his wonderful anthem'.[68]

Ignoring the somewhat abstract logic that equates the popularity of a piece of music with collective remembrance, Goodall's composition clearly made a profound impact on a large number of people; but to assume that this could be used as a barometer for measuring the successful absorption of its message was facile, and even bordering on the ridiculous. Entitled and inspired by the inscription 'I Believe in the Sun' made on the wall of a cave by Jews hiding in Köln, the anthem's popularity did not necessarily indicate an interest in its subject matter and it could just as easily be countered that the production of a 'Holocaust anthem' for mass consumption represented the nadir of Holocaust 'kitsch and death' and the zenith of a 'Holocaust Industry'.[69] Obviously this was not its intention, but the presumption that HMD's laudable aim of increasing Holocaust awareness could be gauged as a success or failure through CD sales alone exposed an intrinsic naivety at the same time as illustrating the deeper challenge of empirically 'showing that learning about Nazi genocide actually affects current behaviour' – as the fundamental principles of HMD maintained.[70]

Summary

Britain's inaugural HMD in January 2001 can be put forward as a case study par excellence of how the transnationalisation of Holocaust memory must still be analysed in the contextual framework of individual nation states, for whilst it was part – and in some respects, the quintessential example – of the first wave of Holocaust Europeanisation, it was inseparable from post-war historical, sociocultural and political developments within the UK and reflected how Holocaust consciousness in Britain expanded from the late 1970s in an unusual and particular manner. Whilst the incorporation of the Holocaust into the National Curriculum is (quite rightly) regarded as a key point of transition, advances in education were paralleled by a movement from memorialisation towards musealisation and ultimately commemoration. Just as all of these changes were closely interlinked with each other and cumulatively helped to broaden awareness, so they were also responses to and beneficiaries of increased interest, knowledge and understanding, especially within the non-Jewish population. They were also all political in their own right – none more so than HMD.

Although any state-orchestrated collective remembrance will court controversy, the primacy placed on Holocaust 'lessons' throughout the conception, formulation and planning of HMD was one of the main reasons for its high level of politicisation. Through HMD, the Holocaust was to become *so* 'exemplary' as to be 'traditional': the assumption that Holocaust consciousness needed to be nurtured through 'education, remembrance and research' translated into a day informed by specific understandings of commemoration and particular understandings of the Holocaust, but one underpinned by a presumed general 'consensus that the world would be a more humane and safer place if only there was more Holocaust education, more children visited Holocaust museums, saw films such as *Schindler's List* and so on'.[71] This did not and could not neutralise how 'a political process' was driving the day and erecting in the process a veritable wall of silence around it, for as Laurence Rees observed during the brief consultation period for the proposed day, 'anyone who enters into the debate and does not wholeheartedly support the idea is liable to be attacked as an anti-Semite or historically ignorant or probably both'.[72] In terms of reception this highly charged and almost accusatory atmosphere antagonised many commentators and only invited further criticism of the level of politicisation Holocaust memory had appeared to reach. This had direct consequences for the day's effectiveness, for the degree of political involvement in HMD's construction impacted upon what was selected and intended for remembrance, how and why. As it happened, HMD was aligned to longstanding British strategies for (dis)engaging with the Holocaust, with the end product being the formation of an 'institutional' memory which not only diluted Britain's historical relation to the Holocaust but also entailed the effacement of Britain's own national history of imperialism, discrimination and persecution, both against Jews and other minorities.[73] It is worth considering whether the passage of subsequent HMD's since 2001 together with 20 years of Holocaust education has managed to rectify this, or whether a widespread 'critical' Holocaust consciousness in Britain remains elusive.

Notes

1. The phrase is respectfully borrowed from the title of Richard Crownshaw, *The Afterlife of Holocaust Memory in Contemporary Literature and Culture* (Basingstoke, 2009).
2. 'About HMDT', Holocaust Memorial Day Trust, http://hmd.org.uk/about.
3. Jan-Werner Müller, 'On "European Memory"', in Malgorzata Pakier and Bo Stråth (eds), *A European Memory? Contested Histories and Politics of Remembrance* (New York, 2010), 36.
4. The term 'historical culture' is, as Klas-Göran Karlsson notes, to some extent ambiguous and open to contrasting interpretations. Here I align myself to Karlsson's definition of historical culture as both structure and process; 'a concept denoting the artefacts, the social and institutional contexts and the arenas, scholarly, educational, political and others, in which history is represented and operated in society, as well as an activity to communicate and use history for various individual and societal purposes' – Klas-Göran Karlsson, 'The Holocaust as a Problem of Historical Culture: Theoretical and Analytical Challenges', in Klas-Göran Karlsson and Ulf Zander (eds), *Echoes of the Holocaust: Historical Cultures in Contemporary Europe* (Lund, 2003), 32.
5. Aleida Assmann, 'The Holocaust – a Global Memory? Extensions and Limits of a New Memory Community', in Aleida Assmann and Sebastian Conrad (eds), *Memory in a Global Age: Discourses, Practices and Trajectories* (Basingstoke, 2010), 98.
6. Klas-Göran Karlsson, 'The Holocaust as a History-Cultural Phenomenon', in Martin L. Davies and Claus-Christian W. Szejnmann (eds), *How the Holocaust Looks Now: International Perspectives* (Basingstoke, 2007), 90.
7. Especially David Cesarani and Eric J. Sundquist (eds), *After the Holocaust: Challenging the Myth of Silence* (London, 2011); Michael Rothberg, *Multidirectional Memory: Remembering the Holocaust in the Age of Decolonization* (Stanford, 2009); David Bankier and Dan Michmann (eds), *Holocaust Historiography in Context: Emergence, Challenges, Polemics and Achievements* (Yad Vashem, 2008); Lawrence Baron, *Projecting the Holocaust into the Present: The Changing Focus of Contemporary Holocaust Cinema* (Lanham, 2005); Hasia R. Diner, *We Remember with Reverence and Love: American Jews and the Myth of Silence after the Holocaust, 1945–1962* (New York, 2009).
8. David Cesarani, 'Great Britain', in David S. Wyman (ed.), *The World Reacts to the Holocaust* (Baltimore and London, 1996), 609. See also Donald Bloxham, *Genocide on Trial: War Crimes Trials and the Formation of Holocaust History and Memory* (Oxford, 2001); Tom Lawson, 'Constructing a Christian History of Nazism: Anglicanism and the Memory of the Holocaust, 1945–1949', *History and Memory*, 16 (1) (2004), 146–176.
9. Dan Stone, 'The Domestication of Violence: Forging a Collective Memory of the Holocaust in Britain, 1945–46', *Patterns of Prejudice*, 3 (2) (1999), 15.

10. Tony Kushner, *The Holocaust and the Liberal Imagination: A Social and Cultural History* (Oxford, 1994).
11. David Cesarani, *Justice Delayed: How Britain Became a Refuge for Nazi War Criminals* (London, 2001), 168.
12. David Cesarani, 'From Bullock to Kershaw: Some Peculiarities of British Historical Writing about the Nazi Persecution and Mass Murder of the Jews', in *Holocaust Historiography in Context*, 354; Idem., 'Challenging the "Myth of Silence": Post-war Responses to the Destruction of European Jewry', The J.B. and Maurice C. Shapiro Annual Lecture, 2 April 2009, United States Holocaust Memorial Museum, available via: http://www.ushmm.org/research/center/presentations/lectures/lecture.php?content=2-shapiro. The reluctance of British historians to directly engage with the Holocaust must not obscure the fact that one of the earliest historiographical works on the subject was Gerald Reitlinger's *The Final Solution*.
13. Rothberg, *Multidirectional Memory*, 22.
14. Kushner, *The Holocaust and the Liberal Imagination*, 259; Suzanne Bardgett, Interview, 25 September 2007.
15. On the reception of *Holocaust* in the United Kingdom, see Tim Cole's chapter in this volume. For evidence of an increasing prominence of the Holocaust we need to look into the cultural hinterland of Britain, taking note of not only significant 'mainstream' events such as the 1979 ITV broadcast *Kitty: Return to Auschwitz* – a landmark exploration into one survivor's experience of the Holocaust – but also references to the fate of the Jews in 'popular' realms, such as infamously popularised in the Sex Pistols song 'Belsen Was a Gas'.
16. Karl-Ernst Jeismann, cited in Elfriede Billmann-Mahecha and Monika Hausen, 'Empirical Psychological Approaches to the Historical Consciousness of Children', in Jürgen Straub (ed.), *Narration, Identity and Historical Consciousness* (New York, 2005), 164.
17. Jörn Rüsen, 'Some Theoretical Approaches to Intercultural Comparative Historiography', *History & Theory*, 35 (4) (1996), 12; Idem., 'Introduction: Historical Thinking as Intercultural Discourse', in Jörn Rüsen (ed.), *Western Historical Thinking: An Intercultural Debate* (New York, 2005), 1; Idem., 'Sense of History: What Does it Mean? With an Outlook onto Reason and Senselessness', in Jörn Rüsen (ed.) *Meaning and Representation in History* (New York, 2008), 40–64.
18. On America, see Peter Novick, *The Holocaust and Collective Memory: The American Experience* (London, 2001). There are a host of reasons for why British Holocaust consciousness has pursued a different course of development compared to its wartime ally, and a notable consideration may well be differences in the position and attitudes of American Jewry compared to Anglo-Jewry.
19. Cesarani, *Justice Delayed*, 190–224; Lucy Russell, *Teaching the Holocaust in School History* (London, 2004), 71–72.
20. Russell, *Teaching the Holocaust in School History*, 64–66; Barrie Stead, 'Holocaust Lessons for Britain', *The Jewish Chronicle*, 28 March 1986, 26.
21. Steven Cooke, 'Negotiating Memory and Identity: The Hyde Park Holocaust Memorial, London', *Journal of Historical Geography*, 26 (3) (2000), 449–465.

22. The categorisation of 'traditional' and 'exemplary' is drawn from Jörn Rüsen's typology of historical consciousness, which puts forward a schema of four different 'types' of orientation: traditional, exemplary, critical and genetic – each of which is characterised by a particular approach to understanding history and exercising historical thought. For extended explanation see Jörn Rüsen, *History: Narration, Interpretation, Orientation* (New York, 2005).

23. Whilst at an official, 'institutional' level Holocaust consciousness exhibited distinctly 'traditional' characteristics and was hostile to attempts to use the Holocaust in an 'exemplary' manner, close examination of British culture from the 1970s into the late 1980s reveals evidence of more 'critical' ways of thinking about and with the Holocaust. This much is indicated by the spate of Holocaust-related documentaries to appear at this time, in addition to literary works and cultural criticism. Beyond illustrating the dynamism of historical consciousness, this divergence clearly has much broader significance for our understanding of the role played by 'elite' agents and 'organic' forces in the formation of collective memory.

24. Cathleen Kantner, 'Collective Identity as Shared Ethical Understanding: The Case of the Emerging European Identity', *European Journal of Social Theory*, 9 (4) (2006), 501.

25. Clive Barnett, 'Culture, Policy and Subsidarity in the European Union: From Symbolic Identity to the Governmentalisation of Culture', *Political Geography*, 20 (2001) 411.

26. Patrick Wright, *On Living in an Old Country: The National Past in Contemporary Britain*, (London, 1985) 142.

27. Daniel Levy and Natan Sznaider, 'Memories of Europe: Cosmopolitanism and Its Others', in Chris Rumford (ed.), *Cosmopolitanism and Europe* (Liverpool, 2007), 168.

28. Daniel Levy and Natan Sznaider, 'Memory Unbound: The Holocaust and the Formation of Cosmopolitan Memory', *European Journal of Social Theory*, 5 (1) (2002), 97; Jenny Wüstenberg and David Art, 'Using the Past in the Nazi Successor States from 1945 to Present', *The Annals of the American Academy of Political and Social Science*, 617 (May 2008), 82; Claus Leggewie, 'A Tour of the Battleground: The Seven Circles of Pan-European Memory', *Social Research*, 75 (1) (Spring 2008), 219.

29. Dan Diner, 'Restitution and Memory: The Holocaust in European Political Cultures', *New German Critique*, No. 90: Taboo, Trauma, Holocaust (Autumn 2003), 38–40; Assmann, 'The Holocaust', 100.

30. Jan-Werner Müller, 'On "European Memory"', in Pakier and Stråth (eds), *A European Memory?*, 25.

31. Cesarani, *Justice Delayed*, 268–283; Reva Klein, 'Facing up to the Final Solution', *Times Educational Supplement*, 17 April 1992, 31; Carrie Supple, *From Prejudice to Genocide: Learning about the Holocaust* (Revised third edition, Stoke-on-Trent, 2006), xi–xiv.

32. Trudy Gold, 'An Overview of Hollywood Cinema's Treatment of the Holocaust', in Toby Haggith and Joanna Newman (eds), *Holocaust and the Moving Image: Representations in Film and Television since 1933* (London, 2005), 196; Ian Wall, 'The Holocaust, Film and Education', in Haggith and Newman

(eds), *Holocaust and the Moving Image*, 203–210. The film was seen by over a quarter of the population whilst on cinema release.

33. This is not to say that the advances made in Holocaust memory were effaced or reversed; rather, as Judith Petersen has shown in her examination of Britain's VE Day programming in 1995, the Holocaust was still used to 'reinforce' rather than challenge 'the moral integrity of Britain's war memory' – Judith Petersen, 'How British Television Inserted the Holocaust into Britain's War Memory in 1995', *Historical Journal of Film, Radio and Television*, 21 (3) (2001), 264–265.

34. Robert Stradling, *The European Content of the School Curriculum Report* (Strasbourg, 1995), 19; Carmel Gallagher, *History Teaching and the Promotion of Democratic Values and Tolerance* (Strasbourg, 1996), 28.

35. On 'banking' and 'problem-posing' approaches to education see Paulo Friere, *The Pedagogy of the Oppressed* (London, 1996), 52–67. At issue are distinct understandings of knowledge and the capacity of students to engage in critical thinking.

36. See 'Opening Plenary Statement by Stuart Eizenstat', in *Nazi Gold: The London Conference* (London, 1998), 9.

37. Stuart E. Eizenstat, 'Overview of the Task Force for International Cooperation on Holocaust Education, Remembrance, and Research', in J.D. Bindenagel (ed.), *Proceedings of the Washington Conference on Holocaust-Era Assets* (Washington, 1999), 976–977.

38. Stephen Smith, 'Proposal for International Commemoration of the Holocaust', in *Proceedings of the Washington Conference*, 998.

39. *Hansard*, 11 June 1999, Column 408. The 'official' narrative of how HMD came about usually takes as origin the visit of Andrew Dismore MP to Auschwitz as part of the Holocaust Educational Trust's *Lessons from Auschwitz* programme. It is said that Dismore was so moved by the experience that he submitted a formal written question to Blair at Prime Minister's Questions on this date in June.

40. Johan Dietsch, 'The Holocaust in Ukrainian Historical Culture', *How the Holocaust Looks Now*, 113.

41. 'Background', *Holocaust Memorial Day: Remembering Genocides Lessons for the Future Commemorative Programme*, Inaugural National Commemoration, Westminster Central Hall, 27 January 2001 (London, 2001).

42. Titus Ensink, 'Creating Acceptable Meanings of the Present: Some Discourse Analytic Reflections on Verbal Commemorative Practices', unpublished paper delivered at the symposium *Breaking Silence or Making a Clean Break – Sites and Modes of Commemoration*, Bruno Kreisky Forum for International Dialogue, Vienna, 27 June 2008.

43. *Government Proposal for a Holocaust Remembrance Day* (London, 1999), 4; Sharon Macdonald, 'Commemorating the Holocaust: Reconfiguring National Identity in the Twenty-First Century', in Jo Littler and Roshi Naidoo (eds), *The Politics of Heritage: The Legacies of 'Race'* (London, 2005) 61.

44. Jack Straw, *Holocaust Memorial Day: Remembering Genocides Lessons for the Future Commemorative Programme* (London, 2001).

45. *Holocaust Memorial Day – Remembering Genocides Lessons for the Future Education Pack* (London, 2000).

46. David Cesarani, 'Does the Singularity of the Holocaust Make it Incomparable and Inoperative for Commemorating, Studying and Preventing Genocide? Britain's Holocaust Memorial Day as a Case Study', *The Journal of Holocaust Education*, 10 (2) (Autumn 2001), 40.

47. *Hansard*, 30 June 1999, Columns 362–364.

48. For a sample, see Nicolas Kinloch, 'Parallel Catastrophe? Uniqueness, Redemption and the Shoah', *Teaching History*, 104, 13; Idem, Review Essay: 'Learning about the Holocaust: Moral or Historical Question?', *Teaching History*, 93, 44; Donald Schwartz, 'Who Will Tell Them after We're Gone?' Reflections on Teaching the Holocaust', *The History Teacher*, 23 (2), February 1990, 100; Ronnie Landau, 'No Nazi War in British History?', *The Jewish Chronicle*, 25 August 1989, 20.

49. Stephen Smith, 'The Future of the Past', *Perspectives: A Journal of the Holocaust Centre, Beth Shalom*, (Summer, 2001), 3; Peter Gray and Kendrick Oliver, 'The Memory of Catastrophe', *History Today* (2001), 13.

50. Macdonald, 'Commemorating the Holocaust', 62–63.

51. Alvin Rosenfeld, cited in Tony Kushner, ' "I Want to go on Living after my Death"; The Memory of Anne Frank', in Martin Evans and Ken Lunn (eds), *War and Memory in the Twentieth Century* (Oxford, 1997), 3.

52. Gaby Koppel, 'To Stage a Nation's Remembrance', *Perspectives: A Journal of the Holocaust Centre, Beth Shalom* (2001), 8. McKellen was chosen for this task 'to give drama and credibility to the story of gay persecution'.

53. *Holocaust Memorial Day Remembering Genocides Lessons for the Future Commemorative Programme*; Koppel has described the 'ironic' situation where members of the Rwandan artist Cecile Kayirebwe's band were initially unable to enter the United Kingdom because they did not have EC passports. With the possibility of 'the Home Office ... being unable to get artistes into the country for their own event' the situation was eventually resolved, but the 'irony' of managing to overcome this hurdle in the context of historical parallels with British responses to Jewish refugees of the 1930s was neither included in the ceremony nor made widespread public knowledge – Koppel, 'To Stage a Nation's Remembrance', 8.

54. Macdonald, 'Commemorating the Holocaust', 63.

55. This universalism is best demonstrated by how 'Jews', 'Jewry' or 'Judaism' is not to be found in *any* of the seven statements. Instead 'anti-Semitism' is mentioned but once, and even then in the context of other forms of prejudice and 'evils' which must be fought.

56. For discussion see Paul Connerton, *How Societies Remember* (Cambridge, 1989), 41–71.

57. Tony Blair, 'Speech Delivered at Holocaust Memorial Day Inaugural Ceremony', *Perspectives: A Journal of the Holocaust Centre, Beth Shalom*, (Summer, 2001), 4.

58. Cristian Tileaga, 'What Is a "Revolution"? National Commemoration, Collective Memory and Managing Authenticity in the Representation of a Political Event', *Discourse and Society*, 19 (3) (2008), 363.

59. Tony Blair, 'Reflections on Holocaust Memorial Day', *Perspectives: A Journal of the Holocaust Centre, Beth Shalom* (Summer, 2001), 5.

60. Macdonald, 'Commemorating the Holocaust', 64.

61. *Holocaust Memorial Day Remembering Genocides Lessons for the Future Commemorative Programme.*
62. Macdonald, 'Commemorating the Holocaust', 64–65.
63. Connerton, *How Societies Remember*, 72–73, 88.
64. Isabel Wollaston, 'Negotiating the Marketplace: The Role(s) of Holocaust Museums Today', *Journal of Modern Jewish Studies*, 4 (1) (2005), 74.
65. Donald Bloxham, 'Britain's Holocaust Memorial Days: Reshaping the Past in the Service of the Present', in Sue Vice (ed.), *Representing the Holocaust* (London, 2003), 47.
66. Tony Kushner, 'Too Little, Too Late? Reflections on Britain's Holocaust Memorial Day', *Journal of Israeli History*, 23 (1) (2004), 124; Novick, *The Holocaust and Collective Memory*, 245.
67. James Young, 'Towards a Received History of the Holocaust', *History & Theory*, 36 (4) (1997), 21–43.
68. Koppel, 'To Stage a Nation's Remembrance', 6–7.
69. Saul Friedländer, *Reflections of Nazism: An Essay on Kitsch and Death* (London, 1984).
70. Bloxham, 'Britain's Holocaust Memorial Days', 49; this in fact relates to the basic question 'what do people "do" with their memories' – Alon Confino and Peter Fritzsche, 'Introduction: Noises of the Past', in Alon Confino and Peter Fritzsche (eds), *The Work of Memory: New Directions in the Study of German Society and Culture*, (Urbana/Chicago, 2002), 5.
71. Wollaston, 'Negotiating the Holocaust', 74.
72. Smith, 'Who Wants a Holocaust Memorial Day?', 3; Laurence Rees, 'When it Comes to Mass Murder, Stalin has the Edge Over Hitler', *The Independent*, 26 October 1999, 4.
73. Richard Ned Lebow, 'The Memory of Politics in Postwar Europe', in Richard Ned Lebow, Wulf Kansteiner and Claudio Fogu (eds), *The Politics of Memory in Postwar Europe* (Durham and London, 2006) 15; Kushner, 'Too Little, Too Late?', 118; Bloxham, 'Britain's Holocaust Memorial Days', 42; Dan Stone, 'Britannia Waives the Rules: British Imperialism and Holocaust Memory', in *History, Memory and Mass Atrocity: Essays on the Holocaust and Genocide* (London, 2006), 174–190.

12
From Stockholm to Stockton: The Holocaust and/as Heritage in Britain

Dan Stone

Reviewing the musical *Imagine This* for *The Guardian*, Michael Billington wrote: 'they said it couldn't be done: a musical about the Warsaw ghetto. And now that I've seen it, I know that they were right'.[1] A few weeks later in the same newspaper, Anne Karpf suggested that one could be forgiven for thinking that every day was Holocaust Memorial Day (HMD) in the United Kingdom. The plethora of Holocaust-related films and other 'cultural' events (I use the term loosely, to include the musical of the Warsaw Ghetto and other such ill-considered phenomena) indicated to Karpf that there is an excess of attention being paid to the Holocaust and that, especially at a time when Israel was pounding the life out of the Gaza Strip, such attention is unjustified. Karpf, unintentionally recapitulating a standard trope of British responses, writes that we have 'now become saturated with images and accounts of the Holocaust'.[2]

In comparison with other countries in Europe, the United States and Israel, Britain came relatively late to Holocaust consciousness. As a result of this belatedness, Holocaust 'memory' in Britain has gone straight from 'event' to the stage of 'heritage', bypassing a period of reflective or contested *Vergangenheitsbewältigung*, or coming to terms with the past, whatever that might mean in the British context. The obvious comparison – though in a very different setting – is with West Germany, where initial obstruction and obfuscation was followed by several decades of research and debate about the meaning of Nazism and the Holocaust, culminating in today's Federal Republic's ready – perhaps too ready – incorporation into European memory politics, symbolised by Berlin's Monument to the Murdered Jews of Europe and (following Richard von Weizsäcker) Gerhard Schröder's designation of 8 May 1945 as a 'day of liberation' (*Tag der Befreiung*) for Germany as much as for the rest of Europe. Andy Pearce notes that 'the development of Holocaust remembrance in Britain has followed a somewhat "twisted path" over the course of the past generation, and in certain respects has the appearance of being a highly condensed and intensified form of developments seen elsewhere'.[3] This telescoped memorialisation process means that any attempt to mobilise the Holocaust to reconceptualise British national identity or to provide a historically informed explanation of the events of the Holocaust has been largely sidelined in favour of the desiderata of, on the one hand, the heritage industry (by which I do not, be it noted, mean Finkelstein's 'Holocaust industry') and, on the other hand, the feel-good politics of 'cosmopolitan', European memory. In less than a decade, we have travelled from Stockholm in the year 2000, when the EU – largely at the United Kingdom's behest – decided to commemorate the Holocaust on 27 January each year and to include the Holocaust in school curricula, to Stockton and a hundred other towns and cities across the United Kingdom, in which schoolchildren and local dignitaries take part in earnest ceremonies to condemn the evils of Nazism in particular and genocide in general (those who protest against 'Holocaust Memorial Day' appear not to have noticed that in reality it already is, de facto, a 'Genocide Memorial Day'). Suddenly, and unexpectedly, over the course of the last decade, the Holocaust has become part of British heritage.

This is a trajectory that requires critical attention; what does the 'heritagisation' of the Holocaust teach schoolchildren or the general public about the events themselves? And, more tellingly, what does this move to incorporate the Holocaust into British memory politics reveal about contemporary Britain? What or whose purposes does it serve? Although I do not want to be curmudgeonly and offer only criticisms, one can with good reason follow Wulf Kansteiner's recommendation and display some 'impatience with the dishonest and self-serving nature of a lot of contemporary Holocaust culture' in this context.[4] It seems to be worth asking whether the current focus on the Holocaust – ostensibly with the laudable aim of teaching children to be better human beings – can actually live up to expectations. How do we know, for example, whether teaching children about the Holocaust, or having a culture suffused with atrocity images doesn't result in the belief, as Hannah Arendt suggested to Karl Jaspers in the light of the British decision to hold Jewish survivors trying to get into Palestine in camps in Cyprus, that 'Jews are regarded a priori, so to speak, as potential inhabitants of concentration camps'?[5] Recall Primo Levi's encounter with an Italian fifth-grader who, after listening to his account of Auschwitz, offered Levi a 'sure-fire' way of escaping should he find himself in the same situation again. In response, Lévi wrote:

> Within its limits, it seems to me that this episode illustrates quite well the gap that exists and grows wider every year between things as they were down there and things as they are represented by the current imagination fed by approximate books, films and myths. It slides fatally toward simplification and stereotype; I would like here to erect a dike against this trend.... It is the task of the historian to bridge this gap, which widens as we get further away from events under examination.[6]

However, before proceeding I must admit that as a university professor I also feel torn for several reasons, pragmatic and moral: the topic of the Holocaust (and comparative genocide) fills my classes and the Holocaust itself demands a range of responses that cannot be reduced to HMD-style genuflections. The attention that the Holocaust receives in the public sphere no doubt contributes to the fact that my undergraduate courses on the Holocaust and on comparative genocide – along with others who teach the subject – are heavily over-subscribed. I can hear the voices of certain colleagues telling me: You complained for years that no one took any notice of the Holocaust, and now you complain that everyone is talking about it. I readily acknowledge this apparent paradox, but hope to show that, in my defence, the ways in which the Holocaust is talked about and represented are not always in the best interests of British society in general or Holocaust educators and scholars in particular, not to mention the victims and the historical record. I acknowledge too the many positive aspects of this focus on the Holocaust, not least the important national commissions that have been produced in most countries of Europe into the history of their countries under Nazi occupation, most of which take an unflinching look at issues such as collaboration, looting and anti-Semitism, or the many remarkable monuments that have been built, such as that recently opened on the site of the former death camp at Belżec[7]; or, in this country, the impressive exhibitions at the Imperial War Museum, not just the Holocaust exhibition, but the genocide exhibition and associated temporary activities such as the superb 'Unspeakable' exhibition on art and the Holocaust, shown in 2009.

Yet apart from the pragmatic perspective of filling classrooms, and acknowledging the positive strides that have been made in the sphere of transnational Holocaust awareness, I am also uneasy about being critical because the current cultural 'over-production' is not just a reflection of the 'Holocaust industry' (a revolting concept really, with its implication that all of us involved with the topic are somehow dupes or patsies[8]) but of the fact that the event itself is so challenging to the mind and demands varied responses in order to try and understand it. One can readily understand why there are so many different, varied responses to the Holocaust, whether scholarly or popular. Finally, I feel torn because even if some part of me agrees with Karpf, I want scholarly work to be excluded from her criticism. In other words, I suggest that although one day the current popular fascination with the Holocaust will diminish (along with other facets of our 'memory culture' such as the cult of celebrity, confessional autobiographies and commemorative ceremonies), the Holocaust will remain an intellectual problem that scholars will address. The current infantilisation of Holocaust memory – infantile both because it is directed towards children of all ages and because it is so didactic and prescriptive – is driven by well-meaning attempts to make children (and adults) pay heed to the Holocaust. This is a worrying trend (after all, beating children over the head with instructions is likely to have the opposite effect to the one intended), but will not preclude meaningful reflections about or research on the Holocaust in the future. The heritage industry will itself become a historical phenomenon one day, but it would be mistaken to assume that as a result all interest in the Holocaust will disappear. Nor should it – my plea is for a greater sensitivity and awareness of what one is talking about: perhaps one of the problems of making the Holocaust accessible for children and lay-people is that it inevitably tends towards a belittling of the Holocaust and a removal from the discussion or at least a downplaying of the horror that demanded our interest in the first place. At worst, as in *The Boy in the Striped Pyjamas*, the victim–perpetrator universe is inverted and the reader/viewer ends by feeling sorry for the only really-fleshed out and fully-characterised 'victim', the German son of the camp commandant, who dies in what David Cesarani rightly calls a 'bizarre health and safety incident'.[9] This is what Eric Santner calls 'narrative fetishism', that is to say, 'the construction and deployment of a narrative consciously or unconsciously designed to expunge the traces of the trauma or loss that called that narrative into being in the first place'.[10] By making the Holocaust constitutive of national or European identity or by making it a pedagogical tool in inculcating anti-racism or 'citizenship', many of the challenges of the Holocaust – to the idea of progress, to education, to the state, to national identity – are leached out of the story.

My comments here have been inspired partly by Tony Judt's review of Pierre Nora's *Les Lieux de mémoire* (*Realms of Memory*), the landmark seven-volume study of French collective memory published between 1984 and 1992. Judt predictably (and correctly) notes that Nora's massive collection has itself become a kind of monument to the France it was originally conceived as a critical commentary on. He then goes on to argue that this change in status of the book reflects the emergence of the age of commemoration, in which France – and the rest of Europe – now lives. What Judt finds troubling is not the proliferation of museums and monuments as such, nor that 'the forms of public memory thus proposed are fake, or kitsch, or selective and even parodic', for '[t]hat is just how heritage and commemoration are'. Rather, he is concerned at the 'neglect of history', which he regards as new to the modern era. 'Every memorial, every museum', he writes, 'every shorthand commemorative allusion to something from the past that should arouse in us the appropriate sentiments of respect, or regret, or sadness, or pride, is parasitic upon the presumption of historical knowledge: not shared memory, but a shared memory of history as we learned it.' The rise to prominence of heritage and commemoration has led, in Judt's opinion, to the point at which, given

> the virtual disappearance of narrative history from the curriculum in school systems ... the time may soon come when, for many citizens, large parts of their common past will constitute something more akin to *lieux de l'oubli*, realms of forgetting – or, rather, realms of ignorance, since there will have been little to forget. Teaching children, as we now do, to be critical of received versions of the past serves little purpose once there no longer *is* a received version.[11]

Judt's comments ostensibly concern France, but it is clear that he also has the United States and Britain in his sights, as his coruscating attack on Tony Blair as the 'gnome in the garden' of heritage Britain makes all too clear.

According to the doyen of heritage historians, David Lowenthal, the past represented by heritage is

> a jumbled, malleable amalgam ever reshaped by this or that partisan interest. Flying in the face of known fact, it is opaque or perverse to those who do not share its faith. Those who do share it, though, find heritage far more serviceable than the stubborn and unpredictable

past revealed by history. Such an unrevised past is too remote to comprehend, too strange to be exemplary, too regrettable to admire, or too dreadful to recall. It may also be too dead to care much about. Hence heritage radically restructures historical domains.[12]

By heritage I mean something more than the attempt to make scholarly history more accessible to a popular audience of non-scholars – it is not the same as 'public history'. The term is usually used to designate the deliberate attempt to manipulate the past to make it fit into predetermined stories and patterns which reproduce myths that people want to hear about themselves and which can be nicely packaged and sold. The *marketing* element here is crucial. Shops such as Past Times are great examples of this phenomenon: a jumble of random artefacts thrown together in a shop with no regard for their unity other than the fact that they all somehow represent the 'nicer' side of British history – pleasing Celtic patterns, Anglo-Saxon games, eighteenth-century prints, Victorian recipes and garden furniture, and recordings of Churchill's speeches. All of these things do indeed come from the past, and this is where heritage becomes more interesting and complex than it looks. Since all history-writing is selective and biased (few historians speak the language of 'objectivity' any more) the impression can be given that heritage is no more or less than a valid version of history. Heritage then seems to be about the 'plundering' of the past to find the things one wants to hear, to appeal to them for whatever reason, to sell them, and to fit them together to present a coherent view of the past. In the context of the Holocaust, this is especially evident in HMD, where what Mark Levene calls a 'wish-fulfillment' narrative is clearly in evidence. This is based around Robin Cook's statement at Stockholm that 'Our aim in the twenty-first century must be to work towards a tolerant and diverse society which is based upon the notions of universal dignity and equal rights and responsibilities for all citizens. The Holocaust Memorial Day is a symbol of this.' 'The Holocaust' – a sanitised version without any detail as to the actual course of events or who was involved other than a starkly drawn perpetrator–victim image – could be appealed to by government as the archetypal atrocity, with Britain and the United States as the 'liberators'.[13]

This phenomenon – of simplifying the past, making it safe for commemoration – is what Andreas Huyssen talks about in terms of a 'loss of the past', a 'waning of historical consciousness', and as a perception of 'the simultaneity of all times and spaces readily accessible in the present' (i.e. via electronic means).[14] In other words, the contemporary obsession with the past is a sign of a loss of a historical sense rather than a more developed one. Listen to the words of Sir Roy Strong, a staunch defender of British heritage, in 1978:

> It is in times of danger, either from without or from within, that we become deeply conscious of our heritage ... within this world there mingle varied and passionate streams of ancient pride and patriotism, of a heroism in times past, of a nostalgia too for what we think of as a happier world which we have lost. In the 1940s we felt all this deeply because of the danger from without. In the 1970s we sense it because of the dangers from within. We are all aware of problems and troubles, of changes within the structure of society, of the dissolution of old values and standards. For the lucky few this may be exhilarating, even exciting, but for the majority it is confusing, threatening, and dispiriting. The heritage represents some form of security, a refuge perhaps, something visible and tangible which, within a topsy and turvy world, seems stable and unchanged. Our environmental heritage ... is therefore a deeply satisfying and unifying element within our society.[15]

What all these explanations add up to is that the birth of the heritage industry in the late 1970s not only fulfilled the most basic tenets of Thatcherism – everything is for sale, including our past – but it also reinforced a reactionary middle-class cultural policy in which Prince Charles's visions of kitschy villages such as Poundbury in Dorset are typical (and the most striking thing about Poundbury is how closely it resembles Himmler's blueprint for authentic Germanic villages in occupied Eastern Europe). This cultural policy was one which pretended that everybody lived in a 'community' in the rural south of England where everyone knew each other and cared about one another, that everyone was white, married with kids and went to the pretty village church on a Sunday. And the irony is that neoliberal economic policies since the 1980s have helped to deepen the social deprivation that their cultural policy was trying to ignore.

If the process of heritage promotion is more self-aware, it can be a form of heritage which actively resists the heritage being promoted by ruling elites. This is exactly what Raphael Samuel claims in his book *Theatres of Memory*: the heritage industry is not just the cynical tool of elites, but a way for ordinary people to express themselves and their pleasure in the things that are around them, from photographs to buildings.[16] It can also lead to what John Tunbridge calls 'heritage reconciliation', for example, Franco-German friendship, a shared narrative of Verdun, for example – or, indeed, of shared European Holocaust memory being promoted since Stockholm.[17]

Nevertheless, irrespective of what line one takes, it seems undeniable that, as John Tunbridge puts it, 'heritage, as a political instrument and economic resource, both reflects and perpetuates the divisions within European society and culture'.[18] This is clearly true of British Holocaust memory, which stresses the positive role of Britain and maintains awkward silences over, for example, British refugee policy in the 1930s and 1940s or the transposition of the narrative of appeasement, intervention and liberation into the twenty-first century. Heritage is therefore deliberately used by all who engage with it, whether the state, tourists or purveyors. In the contest between history and heritage, history, as Tony Kushner points out, has been the loser.[19]

It is true that the commemoration of war and atrocity always tends to downplay the horror in favour of a softer, less abrasive narrative; this is what George Mosse called 'the process of trivialisation' or 'inappropriate memories' in his discussion of the commemoration of World War I: 'With the passage of time the sacred was ever more difficult to protect from the encroachment of the trivial.'[20] The difference with the Holocaust is that the rise of 'Holocaust consciousness' occurred in the period that saw the emergence of the heritage industry in Britain. There was really no 'passage of time' whereby the Holocaust memory went from 'sacred' to 'trivial'; instead Mosse's first stage was bypassed altogether. One can argue quite plausibly that the real rise of Holocaust consciousness occurred in the 1990s and is attributable to a variety of factors: the Yugoslav wars and European guilt at failure to prevent them or to intervene soon or forcibly enough; to German unification and fear of what it might mean for European stability; to the Rwandan genocide as a reminder of the absurdity of 'never again'; to the end of the Cold War and the search for a new 'other' to replace communism before the 'war on terror'; to a cosmopolitan discourse of human rights; or to the emergence of genocide studies as a field of study that takes the Holocaust as a methodological and ethical yardstick. All of these factors are relevant and do indeed account to a large extent for the interest in the Holocaust that mushroomed most noticeably in the few years between the release of *Schindler's List* (1993) and the 50th anniversary of the liberation of Auschwitz and the end of the war (1995) when, as Judith Petersen reminds us, British television 'inserted the Holocaust into Britain's war memory'.[21] But the forms taken by this independently-emerging consciousness of the Holocaust undoubtedly replicated the nature of the public commemoration of the past being shaped by the heritage industry. The Holocaust went from 'event' to 'heritage' in Britain because it got swept up in the culture of commemoration that came to dominate British dealings with the past in general in the 1980s and 1990s.

Consider, for example, celebrity culture. It is a curious phenomenon that those who produce such events feel it necessary to win celebrity backing for commemoration ceremonies. For example, Rachel Stevens, singer and star of TV show *Strictly Come Dancing*, gave her backing to HMD 2009. She is reported as having said:

> The Holocaust and the terrible hate-motivated atrocities that took place, are something that we can now look back and learn from. When I was asked to support HMD 2009 it was my privilege to get involved. If by helping to build awareness, people are encouraged to react differently today and that helps to build a better future, then that can only be a positive step forward.[22]

That is quite a big if, as Holocaust educators have pointed out. This problem therefore presents quite a challenge to a strongly 'lessons-centric' model of education.[23] Similarly, consider confessional autobiographies: the way to literary success in the last decade or so has been to publish an account of one's awful childhood – the more gruelling and miserable the better. Not only has this search for the ultimate negative identity encouraged the publication of false testimonies – as Sue Vice and others have suggested, what better victim identity than the Holocaust survivor?[24] – it has even encouraged genuine survivors to embellish their accounts in the hope of making them conform better to cultural expectations of romance and redemption, as in the sad case of Herman Rosenblat and his distorted memoir *An Angel at the Fence*. Finally, we must bear in mind marketing: one does not need to engage in a Finkelstein-style argument about 'the Jews' cynically marketing their suffering in order to note that there is indeed now a very large appetite for Holocaust artefacts, from comics to films with British stars (Daniel Craig, Kate Winslet) to 'dark tourism'.

But phenomena such as the cult of celebrity or confessional literature are hardly unique to Britain, even if it can sometimes seem that they are more highly developed here, where thousands of people can turn out to line the streets for a funeral of a woman famous for nothing except being foul-mouthed on television but where protestors against global capitalism are condemned by the popular press, than in the rest of Europe. Therefore, although the development of Holocaust consciousness in Britain in recent years has a domestic basis, it also needs to be situated in the context of European Holocaust politics.

As is well known, and as Andy Pearce explains in detail, current Holocaust politics in Europe developed in several stages.[25] The question of the restitution of Holocaust-era assets was the factor that led to the International Meeting on Nazi Gold in London in 1997; this in turn meant that in 1998 the UK was invited to become a founder member of the International Task Force (ITF), a Swedish initiative that itself grew out of the government-sponsored *Levande Historia* (Living History) project, best exemplified by the book *Tell Ye Your Children* by Paul Levine and Stéphane Bruchfeld, several hundred thousand copies of which were distributed free to Swedish homes.[26] The ITF's first major appearance was at the Washington Conference on Holocaust-Era Assets in December 1998, when the British delegate put forward a 'Proposal for International Commemoration of the Holocaust'.[27] This was taken up in earnest at the Stockholm conference in 2000 and subsequently in the UN resolution of 2005.[28]

Of course, in the British context, promoting Holocaust memory has its own domestic trajectory, with notable institutions involved being the Holocaust Educational Trust, the Anne Frank Foundation, the Imperial War Museum, the Holocaust Centre (Beth Shalom), the Aegis Trust and the Home Office in its capacity as organiser of HMD (subsequently taken over by the HMD Trust). These developments need not be explained with reference to the work of the ITF, but it seems likely that the shape they have taken – particularly HMD – since 2000 has been influenced by the memory politics of the ITF (though one should not overlook the significant impact of the Claims Conference either, especially for scholarly and educational work).[29] The ITF, as Jens Kroh notes, 'is both the expression and the motor of the political trans-nationalisation of Holocaust memory'. Its wide funding of Holocaust-related initiatives and projects leads to 'the partial synchronisation of national memory cultures' which in turn runs the risk of overlooking other Nazi victim groups and of relativising the specific German responsibility for the Holocaust.[30] As Levy and Sznaider correctly note,

> By the late 1990s, the Holocaust had been reconfigured as a decontextualised event. It is now a concept that has been dislocated from

space and time precisely because it can be used to dramatize any act of injustice. This is particularly salient in the context of what can be addressed as a kind of Western European civil religion.[31]

Although this 'civil religion' has by no means been accepted by all Europeans – there remains a distinct difference between Eastern and Western Europe on this score[32] – it provides the framework for analysing contemporary Holocaust memory politics in Britain. For as Tony Judt suggests, 'Holocaust recognition is our contemporary European entry ticket.'[33]

Does all this wider contextualisation mean that Holocaust heritage in Britain can meaningfully be described in Strong's terms as constituting a defence of 'unity' and 'belonging'? That would be perhaps an over-statement, but Holocaust memory does provide a meaningful narrative, albeit a negative one, for understanding modern British identity. Otherwise, how to account for the popularity of a narrative that has become a cornerstone of EU memory politics in a country that is still the most anti-European of all member states? The ITF undoubtedly funds some worthwhile projects, especially in the former communist countries of Central and Eastern Europe, but the specific trajectories of European 'cosmopolitan' memory and, within that, British memory, lead in a different direction: kitsch and amnesia.

For example, the HMD website now invites people 'to light a virtual candle'. Here is commemoration for the Twitter generation, a click and a tweet and one has done one's duty. On a non-official basis, one can see kitsch aplenty in the ways in which the Holocaust is represented. For example, the Chapman Brothers' *Hell* installation of 1999–2000, destroyed by fire in 2004. The installation-sculpture consisted of four 'wings', forming a swastika, in which various depictions of murder and torture are minutely created, complete with death pits, gruesome medical experiments, mutant figures and the slogan 'Kunst macht frei'. Robert Eaglestone argues that 'Nothing here is new; it is simply recycled "horror" and, cast through the festishised toy soldiers, hardly shocking.' He concludes that

> Apart from peeking at the details of the figures, there is no mental work that the audience has to do: it is simply a picture of bad Nazis being tortured, and this – despite the 'Kunst Macht Frei' – leaves the audience un-implicated and uninvolved in the events. The Nazi regalia no longer have any connection to the Nazi state of 1933–45, but only to a kitsch version of evil.[34]

One does not need to subscribe to the rigid definition of kitsch proposed by Clement Greenberg to know that what we have here is inauthentic in the sense that its engagement with the Holocaust is all surface and no depth. Greenberg argued in his famous 1939 essay 'Avant-Garde and Kitsch' that one could divorce high art from low not only on the basis of formalist criteria, but on social and political criteria too. Popular culture, as it emerged in the industrial ages of the masses (also Benjamin's age of mechanical reproducibility) was parasitic on high culture and succeeded in the market because it was easily accessible and gave the appearance of imitating high art.[35] Kundera defined it in *The Unbearable Lightness of Being* as 'the absolute denial of shit', that is, the writing out of anything uncomfortable or unpleasant. 'All' that has happened with Holocaust kitsch is that the unpleasant and uncomfortable has been turned into the very thing with which we comfort ourselves: the fusion of kitsch and death characterised by 'a rationalization that normalizes, smoothes, and neutralizes our vision of the past', as Saul Friedländer put it in the 1980s.[36]

Of course, it would be reasonable to ask whether this instrumentalisation of the Holocaust as the basis of a post-Cold War European identity is such a bad thing. After all, it is better than simply not discussing it at all, or remaining mute in the face of rising far-right activity, another post-Cold War phenomenon that resulted from the breakdown of the post-war anti-fascist consensus in both East and West.[37] But apart from kitsch – which, as we have already noted, is only to be expected in commemorative events and practices – something more unpalatable is going on. That is precisely what Judt calls the 'neglect of history'.

This neglect is neatly described by Eaglestone as the 'lazy cultural matrix of British collective memory of the Holocaust and the Second World War' in which 'complexities disappear'. Referring to the Chapman Brothers, he expands on the claim thus:

> Despite being 'about history' it is strangely ahistorical: the war and the death camps have become floating signifiers simply for evil. They are far from artists who throw 'into question' assumed ideas about 'the artist as a witness to history'.[38] Instead they produce kitsch 'horror' art growing out of unquestioned cultural cliché, confirming comforting ideas about the British and the Holocaust.[39]

What comforting ideas? Will Hutton suggested at the time of the first HMD that HMD would do no more than pay lip-service to anti-racism and leave intact that sense of superiority that characterised British identity as a result of winning World War II.[40] A similar suggestion has been put forward by other critics of HMD, including Nira Yuval-Davis and Max Silverman, Donald Bloxham, Tony Kushner and Mark Levene. A fuller answer is provided by Tom Lawson:

> In the late 1980s, conservative Europeans in Britain argued against the introduction of legislation which would allow the recommencement of the trial of alleged Nazi war criminals in British courts. Opponents of such legislation repeated the arguments that had been voiced forty years previously against the trial of Erich von Manstein – arguing that Europe had to move on, essentially that the civil war had been won and that there was no need to rake up the past. But the end of the Cold War meant that the European dream now needed a new antithesis – and the Nazis filled that void. Thanks to political pressure and the power of Hollywood, the murder of Europe's Jews became the moral touchstone within western politics and the post-conservative liberal new order of the 1990s cemented Hitler as the ultimate bogeyman. By 1999, British conservative Europeans won their campaign for Britain's HMD. This day, for all its apparent educational worth, seems to be chiefly directed at demonstrating the gap between contemporary Europe and the Nazi nightmare and is as much an attempt to separate extremism from the history of liberal Europe as the conservative European Civil War narratives that preceded it. To use Lawrence Langer's phrase, modern Europe has not 'admitted the Holocaust' but has found a new way of confining it – through the narrative of European progress – as something apart from a European culture.[41]

Thus, contra critics such as Sharon Macdonald, I suggest that Holocaust commemoration has contributed little to the reconfiguration of British national identity; where, for example, does one see a reckoning with Britain's imperial past taking place in the public sphere, other than in a few select instances such as slavery – and then, once again in heritage-friendly ways that present nice stories about good triumphing over evil? Rather, Holocaust commemoration reinforces an existing British identity.[42] It confirms what Ezrahi identifies as the dream of retrospectively recovering strength:

> If the primary experience of the Jews under Nazi occupation was the total loss of control over the shape of their lives and fate, the retrospective projection of the power to define and create reality, by

arrogating in the present the sole authority to authenticate the past, becomes a morally and psychologically urgent impulse to defy former powerlessness by means of present potencies.[43]

Finally, one should note that what I have called an infantilisation of memory is regarded by some critics as very dangerous indeed. In a fine article on modernity and Nazism, Paul Betts discusses what he calls the moment of 'cultural danger' in contemporary responses to Nazism:

> what underlies this cultural sea change is the evident collapse of the once-formidable anti-fascist consensus on both sides of the former Wall. In the end, this may be one of 1989's most potent legacies. How it will all turn out is of course impossible to predict. But one thing is sure: the stakes are still very high, even if (or perhaps precisely because) the one-time passionate debate about Nazi modernity has faded considerably. The cultural fall-out of the "fascist revolution" – as George Mosse indefatigably reminded us through numerous books and essays – may be with us more than we like to admit. In this sense, the "postmodernization" of Nazi culture has simply reproduced one of fascist modernism's most distinguishing features – the untethering of knowledge and liberation, enlightenment and progress.[44]

At the moment we seem incapable of even considering Judt's line of thought:

> Maybe all our museums and memorials and obligatory school trips today are not a sign that we are ready to *remember* but an indication that we feel we have done our penance and can now begin to let go and *forget*, leaving the stones to remember for us. I don't know: the last time I visited Berlin's Memorial to the Murdered Jews of Europe, bored schoolchildren on an obligatory outing were playing hide-and-seek among the stones. What I *do* know is that if history is to do its proper job, preserving forever the evidence of past crimes and every-thing else, it is best left alone. When we ransack the past for political profit – selecting the bits that can serve our purposes and recruiting history to teach opportunistic moral lessons – we get bad morality and *bad* history.[45]

This is in some ways quite a strange argument; after all, what does it mean to leave history to itself? There is no history other than that con-structed by human beings, and thus it is impossible to exclude politics from our handling of the past. But still, Judt has a point: doesn't this permanent focus on the Holocaust lead to banalisation, incorporating the Holocaust into the inanities of celebrity culture? The process of making us feel good for a few moments for not being Nazis ends by anaesthetising us against the horror of the Holocaust, so that, especially for those who are children today and who no longer relate to the events in the self-evident way that their parents and grandparents did, we no longer see it, we just perform the rites and mouth the platitudes. At the time that Holocaust consciousness was just beginning to be all-pervasive, Andreas Huyssen wrote that 'No matter how fractured by media, by geography, and by subject position representations of the Holocaust are, ultimately it all comes down to this core: unimaginable, unspeakable, and unrepresentable horror.'[46] Let us recall Ruth Klüger's words: 'Auschwitz was no instructional institution, like the University of Göttingen... You learned nothing there, and least of all humanity and tolerance. Absolutely nothing good came out of the concentration camps.'[47] In our rush to use the Holocaust to teach people how to be nice to each other, we need to reflect on whether we have forgotten British history, the history of the Holocaust and, first and foremost, the dead.

Notes

*This chapter was originally delivered as the 2009 Aubrey Newman Annual Lecture at the University of Leicester. The informal tone is retained.

1. *The Guardian*, 20 November 2008.
2. Anne Karpf, 'The Week in Books', *The Guardian*, 24 January 2009. Cf. Tanya Gold on 'Hitler porn', *The Guardian*, 23 April 2009.
3. Andy Pearce, 'Britain's Holocaust Memorial Day: Inculcating "British" or "European" Consciousness?' (unpublished manuscript), 16.
4. Wulf Kansteiner, in a review of this author's *History, Memory and Mass Atrocity*, *Central European History*, 41 (4) (2008), 717–720.
5. Arendt to Jaspers 17 August 1946, in Lotte Kohler and Hans Saner (eds), *Hannah Arendt/Karl Jaspers Correspondence 1926–1969* (San Diego, 1992), 54.
6. Primo Levi, *The Drowned and the Saved* (London, 1989), 128.
7. Barbara Buntman, 'Tourism and Tragedy: The Memorial at Belzec, Poland', *International Journal of Heritage Studies*, 14 (5) (2008), 422–448.
8. Judith E. Berman, *Holocaust Agendas, Conspiracies and Industries? Issues and Debates in Holocaust Memorialization* (London, 2006).
9. David Cesarani, 'Review of John Boyne, The Boy in the Striped Pyjamas', *Literary Review*, October 2008.
10. Eric L. Santner, 'History Beyond the Pleasure Principle: Some Thoughts on the Representation of Trauma', in Saul Friedländer (ed.), *Probing the Limits of Representation: Nazism and the 'Final Solution'* (Cambridge, MA, 1992), 144.

11. Tony Judt, *Reappraisals: Reflections on the Forgotten Twentieth Century* (London, 2009), 215–216.
12. David Lowenthal, *The Heritage Crusade and the Spoils of History* (Cambridge, 1998), 147.
13. Mark Levene, 'Britain's Holocaust Memorial Day: A Case of Post-Cold War Wish-Fulfillment, or Brazen Hypocrisy?', *Human Rights Review*, 7 (3) (2006), 26–59. See also Tony Kushner, 'Belsen for Beginners: The Holocaust in British Heritage', in Monica Riera and Gavin Schaffer (eds), *The Lasting War: Society and Identity in Britain, France and Germany after 1945* (Basingstoke, 2008), 226–247.
14. Andreas Huyssen, 'Monument and Memory in a Postmodern Age', *Yale Journal of Criticism*, 6 (2) (1993), 253.
15. Roy Strong, 'Introduction' to Patrick Cormack, *Heritage in Danger*, 2nd ed. (London, 1978), 10, cited in Robert Hewison, 'The Climate of Decline', in David Boswell and Jessica Evans (eds), *Representing the Nation: A Reader. Histories, Heritage and Museums* (London, 1999), 160.
16. Raphael Samuel, *Theatres of Memory, Vol. 1: Past and Present in Contemporary Culture* (London, 1994). For strong criticism of Samuel's claims see Donald Bloxham and Tony Kushner, 'Exhibiting Racism: Cultural Imperialism, Genocide and Representation', *Rethinking History*, 2 (3) (1998), 352.
17. John E. Tunbridge, 'The Question of Heritage in European Cultural Conflict', in Brian Graham (ed.), *Modern Europe: Place, Culture, Identity* (London, 1998), 258.
18. Ibid., 236.
19. Kushner, 'Belsen for Beginners', 244.
20. George L. Mosse, *Fallen Soldiers: Reshaping the Memory of the World Wars* (New York, 1990), Chapter 7; quotation 155.
21. Judith Petersen, 'How British Television Inserted the Holocaust into Britain's War Memory in 1995', *Historical Journal of Film, Radio and Television*, 21 (3) (2001), 255–272, esp. 270: 'the use of Holocaust memory at certain junctures in the televisual landscape of 1995 functioned to underline the moral integrity and the monolithic character of Britain's official war memory'.
22. *Darlington and Stockton Times*, 25 January 2009, online at: www.darlington andstocktontimes.co.uk/uk_national_news/4074411.print/ (accessed 3 April 2009).
23. For example, Terry Haydn, 'Teaching the Holocaust through History', in Ian Davies (ed.), *Teaching the Holocaust: Educational Dimensions, Principles and Practices* (London, 2000), 135–149; and, especially, Paul Salmons' excellent article, 'Universal Meaning or Historical Understanding: The Holocaust in History and History in the Classroom', *Teaching History*, 141 (2010), 57–63.
24. Sue Vice, 'False Testimony', in Richard Crownshaw, Jane Kilby and Antony Rowland (eds), *The Future of Memory* (Oxford, 2010), 155–163.
25. Andy Pearce, 'The Development of Holocaust Consciousness in Contemporary Britain, 1979–2001', *Holocaust Studies: A Journal of Culture and History*, 14 (2) (2008), 71–94.
26. Stéphane Bruchfeld and Paul A. Levine, *Tell Ye Your Children . . . A Book about the Holocaust in Europe 1933–1945* (Stockholm, 1998).
27. Stephen Smith, 'Proposal for International Commemoration of the Holocaust', in J.D. Bindenagel (ed.), *Proceedings of the Washington Conference on*

Holocaust-Era Assets (Washington, 1999), 998. My thanks to Andy Pearce for this reference.

28. For more detail see Jens Kroh, 'Erinnerungskultureller Akteur und geschicht-spolitisches Netzwerk: Die "Task Force for International Cooperation on Holocaust Education, Remembrance and Research"'; Harald Schmid, 'Europäisierung des Auschwitzgedenkens? Zum Aufstieg des 27. Januar 1945 als "Holocaustgedenktag" in Europa', both in Jan Eckel and Claudia Moisel (eds), *Universalisierung des Holocaust? Erinnerungskultur und Geschichtspolitik in internationaler Perspektive* (Göttingen, 2008), 156–173 and 174–202; Klas-Göran Karlsson, 'Public Uses of History in Contemporary Europe', in Harriet Jones, Kjell Östberg and Nico Randeraad (eds), *Contemporary History on Trial: Europe since 1989 and the Role of the Expert Historian* (Manchester, 2007), 27–45.

29. Kroh, 'Erinnerungskultureller Akteur und geschichtspolitisches Netzwerk', 172.

30. Ibid.,173. See also Norbert Frei, 'Geschichtswissenschaft', in Volkhard Knigge and Norbert Frei (eds), *Verbrechen erinnern: Die Auseinandersetzung mit Holocaust und Völkermord* (Munich, 2002), 375: 'The question arises, at least from a historiographical perspective, whether and how a trend towards "globalisation" can succeed in avoiding a decontextualisation of the historical events.'

31. Daniel Levy and Natan Sznaider, 'Memories of Europe: Cosmopolitanism and Its Others', in Chris Rumford (ed.), *Cosmopolitanism and Europe* (Liverpool, 2007), 167. See also Gerard Delanty, 'The Idea of a Cosmopolitan Europe: On the Cultural Significance of Europeanization', *International Review of Sociology*, 15 (3) (2005), 405–421; Lothar Probst, 'Der Holocaust – eine neue Zivilreligion für Europa?', in Wolfgang Bergem (ed.), *Die NS-Diktatur im deutschen Erinnerungsdiskurs* (Opladen, 2003), 227–238; Lothar Probst, 'Founding Myths in Europe and the Role of the Holocaust', *New German Critique*, 90 (2003), 45–58; Jeffrey C. Alexander, 'On the Social Construction of Moral Universals: The "Holocaust" from War Crime to Trauma Drama', *European Journal of Social Theory*, 5 (1) (2002), 5–85.

32. See Adam Krzeminski, 'As Many Wars as Nations: The Myths and Truths of World War II', *Sign and Sight*, 6 April 2005, online at: www.signandsight.com/features/96.html (accessed 2 April 2009), originally published in Polish in *Polityka*, 23 March 2005.

33. Tony Judt, *Postwar: A History of Europe since 1945* (London, 2005), 803. For a positive assessment of this phenomenon, see Uffe Østergård, 'The Holocaust and European Values', *Eurotopics* (6 May 2008), online at: http://www.eurotopics.net/en/magazin/geschichte-verteilerseite-neu/europaeische_nationalgeschichten_2008_05/apuz_ostergard_holocaust/ (accessed 2 April 2009).

34. Robert Eaglestone, 'New Holocaust Kitsch' (unpublished manuscript).

35. Greenberg, 'Avant-Garde and Kitsch', *Essays on Art* (Boston, 1961), originally published in *Partisan Review* in 1939.

36. Saul Friedländer, *Reflections of Nazism: An Essay on Kitsch and Death* (New York, 1986), 59. For an interesting consideration of the use of Friedländer's analysis for contemporary Holocaust representations – today based more on humour than melodrama or tragicomedy – see Gavriel

D. Rosenfeld, 'The Normalization of Memory: Saul Friedländer's *Reflections of Nazism* Twenty Years Later', in Dagmar Herzog (ed.), *Lessons and Legacies, Vol. 7: The Holocaust in International Perspective* (Evanston, 2006), 400–410.

37. See Tony Judt, 'From the House of the Dead: On Modern European Memory', *New York Review of Books*, 6 October 2005, 12–16;Vladimir Tismaneanu, *Fantasies of Salvation: Democracy, Nationalism and Myth in Post-Communist Europe* (Princeton, 1998); and my 'Memory Wars in the "New Europe"' in Dan Stone (ed.), *The Oxford Handbook to Postwar European History* (Oxford, 2012), 714–731.

38. Mark Holborn, Jake and Dinos Chapman, *Hell* (London, 2003), 1.

39. Eaglestone, 'New Holocaust Kitsch'.

40. Hutton cited in Sharon Macdonald, 'Commemorating the Holocaust', in Jo Littler and Roshi Naidoo (eds), *The Politics of Heritage: The Legacies of 'Race'* (London, 2005), 57–58. See also Malcolm Smith, *Britain and 1940: History, Myth and Popular Memory* (London, 2000). For an interesting comparison, see Robert S.C. Gordon, 'The Holocaust in Italian Collective Memory: *Il giorno della memoria*, 27 January 2001', *Modern Italy*, 11 (2) (2006), 167–188.

41. Tom Lawson, 'The Myth of the European Civil War', in Richard Littlejohns and Sara Soncini (eds), *Myths of Europe* (Amsterdam, 2007), 287.

42. Macdonald, 'Commemorating the Holocaust'. See my essay 'Britannia Waives the Rules: British Imperialism and Holocaust Memory', in *History, Memory and Mass Atrocity: Essays on the Holocaust and Genocide* (London, 2006), 174–195.

43. Sidra DeKoven Ezrahi, 'Representing Auschwitz', *History & Memory*, 7 (2) (1996), 141.

44. Paul Betts, 'The New Fascination with Fascism: The Case of Nazi Modernism', *Journal of Contemporary History*, 37 (4) (2002), 557–558.

45. Tony Judt, 'The "Problem of Evil" in Postwar Europe', *New York Review of Books*, 55 (2), 14 February 2008, online at: www.nybooks.com/articles/21031?email (accessed 25 February 2008).

46. Huyssen, 'Monument and Memory', 259. See also Huyssen, 'Present Pasts: Media, Politics, Amnesia', *Public Culture*, 12 (1) (2000), 21–38.

47. Ruth Kluger, *Landscapes of Memory: A Holocaust Girlhood Remembered* (London, 2003), 70.

Bibliography

Suzanne Bardgett, 'The Depiction of the Holocaust at the Imperial War Museum since 1961', *Journal of Israeli History*, 23 (1) (2004), 146–156.

Donald Bloxham, 'Britain's Holocaust Memorial Days: Reshaping the Past in the Service of the Present', *Immigrants and Minorities*, 21 (1–2) (2002), 54–55.

Donald Bloxham, *Genocide on Trial: War Crimes Trials and the formation of Holocaust History and Memory* (Oxford, 2001).

David Cesarani, 'Seizing the Day: Why Britain will Benefit from Holocaust Memorial Day', *Patterns of Prejudice*, 34 (4) (2000), 61–66.

David Cesarani (ed.), *After Eichmann: Collective Memory and the Holocaust since 1961* (Abington, 2005).

David Cesarani and Eric J. Sundquist (eds), *After the Holocaust: Challenging the Myth of Silence* (New York, 2012).

Hannah Ewence and Tony Kushner (eds), *Whatever Happened to British Jewish Studies?* (London, 2012).

Toby Haggith and Joanna Newman (eds), *Holocaust and the Moving Image: Representations in Film and Television Since 1933* (London and New York, 2005).

Tony Kushner, *The Holocaust and the Liberal Imagination: A Social and Cultural History* (Oxford, 1994).

Tony Kushner, 'Too Little, Too Late? Reflections on Britain's Holocaust Memorial Day', *Journal of Israeli History*, 23 (1) (2004), 116–129.

Tony Kushner, 'From "This Belsen Business" to "Shoah Business": History, Memory and Heritage, 1945–2005', *Holocaust Studies*, 12 (1–2) (2006), 189–216.

Tom Lawson, 'Ideology in a Museum of Memory: A Review of the Holocaust Exhibition at the Imperial War Museum', *Totalitarian Movements and Political Religions*, 4 (2) (2003), 173–183.

David B. MacDonald, *Identity Politics in the Age of Genocide: The Holocaust and Historical Representation* (Abingdon, 2008).

Andy Pearce, 'The Development of Holocaust Consciousness in Contemporary Britain, 1979-2001', *Holocaust Studies: A Journal of Culture and History*, 14 (2) (2008), 71–94.

Judith Petersen, 'How British Television Inserted the Holocaust into Britain's War Memory in 1995', *Historical Journal of Film, Radio and Television*, 21 (3) (2001), 255–272.

Joanne Reilly, *Belsen: The Liberation of a Concentration Camp* (London, 1998).

Joanne Reilly, David Cesarani, Tony Kushner and Colin Richmond (eds) *Belsen in History and Memory* (London, 1997).

Dan Stone, 'The Domestication of Violence: Forging a Collective Memory of the Holocaust in Britain, 1945–46', *Patterns of Prejudice*, 3 (2) (1999), 13–29.

Sue Vice (ed.), *Representing the Holocaust* (London, 2003).

Joseph Robert White, ' "Even in Auschwitz... Humanity Could Prevail": British POWs and Jewish Concentration-Camp Inmates at IG Auschwitz, 1943–1945', *Holocaust and Genocide Studies*, 15 (2) (2001), 266–295.

Isabel Wollaston, 'Negotiating the Marketplace: The Role(s) of Holocaust Museums Today', *Journal of Modern Jewish Studies*, 4 (1) (2005), 63–80.

Index

Printed and bound in Great Britain by
CPI Group (UK) Ltd, Croydon, CR0 4YY